AF353019

NOW and NEW

Frank Mattes

Frank Mattes

NOW and NEW

How Companies Can Use Their Capabilities For
Scaling Innovation and Generating New Growth

© 2024 Frank Mattes

First Edition, June 2024

Independently published
ISBN: 978-3-9823154-3-0

Thank You, Co-Creators!

Over 100 corporate practitioners and academic experts provided invaluable support for this initiative. They participated in workshops to design the framework's structure, assisted in its design, collaborated in Learning Labs to explore the modules in greater depth, provided feedback and suggestions on draft chapters, and shared examples and insights.

Pontus All

Gerardo Alvarez-Franyutti

Tania Aydenian

Suzanne Balima

Hans Balmaekers

Becca Barnett

John Beaton

Jan Beger

GH Berghuis

Adam Berk

Dr. Stefan Biel

Andrew Constable

Steve Cook

Andreea Cretu

Sven Damm

Shital Das

Fredy Daza

Maria Duero

Eslam Elshatoury

Martin Feuz

Massimiliano Franco

Rolan Marco Garcia

Johan Gente

David Gilmour

Edward Goodchild

Caroline Gorski

Bob Gravestijn

Peter Guse

Ofer HaCohen

Tommy Hansson Strand

Markus Heinen

Paul Heller

Svan Houcke

Susana Jurado Apruzzese

Valon Kaba

Ekaterina Karpuzova

Arto Kauppila

Kerem Kadayifcioglu

Dominick Kennerson

Tesja Kersten

JT Ko

Maarten Korz

Wieteke Kolner

Steve Kopp

Anuj Kulkarni

Timo Landener

Sören Lauinger

Jessica Linneweber

Marco Locatelli

Brian Lucero

William Malek

Michele Di Marino

Ricardo Mazzolo

Andrew McCoy

Marion Mesnage

David Milner

Nicolas Miravalls

Hitesh Mittal

Renaud De Montaignac

Rob Munro

Trine Nielsen

Jesse Nieminen

Paul O'Connor

Prof. Dr. Georg Oenbrink

Sertaç Oral

Marc Ors

Dana Parsons

Yuliya Pasichnyk

Matthias Patz

Engelbert Pelster

Camilla Penrice

Sandra Perez

Marco De Polo

Pierre Pomper

Paul Quinlan

Arantxa Quitana

Bharat Rachupalli

Jon Rains

Michael Roberts

Claus von Riegen

Robin Rohrmann

Stefan Rötzel

Richard Russell

Tanya Rystwej

Lisa Sacco

Stefan Schmatz

Bernhard Schmidt

Tassilo von Schonberg

Henning Seeschaaf

Esther Seidl-Nussbaumer

Jeannine Siviy

Carina Snijder

Aymard de Scorbiac

Andreas Sprock

Bruno Stefani

Lukas Strniste

Prashanthi Sudhakar

Achim Tappe

Jiaying Tee

Nina Teng

Mikkel Toft-Olsen

Bas van Ulzen

Madalina Uscatu

Jeroen Vandenbosch

Alexander Vencken

Christoph Volbers

Fabian Wabbel

Karst Westra

Owen Williams

Denise Williams

For Tina.

Still the ONE.

/ Table of Contents

Corporate leaders struggle to find the right balance between "perform" and "transform," between "scale/efficiency" and "speed/agility," between running a highly efficient core business while innovating new digital propositions. Compelling ideas can be developed into new minimally viable propositions but translating "viable" into "scalable" is challenging, as systems and cultures clash between the core and the new.

Frank Mattes brings his extensive experience in corporate innovation to this pragmatic guide to dramatically increasing return on investment in digital innovation.

Jeroen Tas,
former Chief Innovation & Strategy Officer, Royal Philips

Frank Mattes has decades of valuable experience in innovation and business-building. This has helped him draw together the key themes, challenges, and solutions for companies needing to transform their businesses through creating value through innovation. He has distilled the key practices that companies need to embrace.

In this time, with the challenges of disruption, the rapid evolution of business models, and the need to redefine the ways business works, the Lean Scaleup provides a route map.

Senior leaders searching for new approaches to drive value in their business, to be better placed to deliver success for themselves, their company, employees, and shareholders can benefit. The Lean Scaleup is an approach built through practice in the field and results from real work supporting companies facing challenges that the market has brought forward.

David Gilmour,
co-founder bp Launchpad, bp

From the many conversations within our global community of innovation leaders, it has become clear this is one of the most important yet most challenging problems: closing the gap between a validated idea and a solid business line with a substantial impact on the top and bottom line.

Frank has been able to address this issue in many organizations success-fully. I am excited for his approach to be "codified" finally.

Hans Balmaekers,
CEO, innov8rs

Corporates usually fail to scale and grow new business ventures outside their existing portfolio successfully. The Lean Scaleup gives them a viable and powerful tool to identify, develop and scale breakthrough innovations very successfully and sustainably for the first time. This book is a must-read for all managers from corporate innovation or strategic innovation.

Prof. Dr. Georg Oenbrink,
former Head of Innovation Networks,
Evonik Industries

The most challenging phase in new-business creation is the Scaling-Up phase. This book provides an excellent framework to address this challenge and is based on the real-life learning journey of +20 corporates, including Philips. A must-read for corporate entrepreneurs and their leaders!

Carina Snijder,
VP, Strategic Business Development Lead,
Precision Diagnosis, Royal Philips

The full value of innovation is reached when it achieves scale. Getting there is one of the greatest challenges. This book provides a practical frame-work and methodology for going beyond the MVP into scale. Frank brings his insightful expertise and leverages the experience of corporate innovation leaders, creating a must-read for corporate innovators and leaders.

Ofer HaCohen,
former Head of Innovation Center Israel, AT&T

Before You Start

Dear Valued Reader,

Thank you very much for your interest in this book. I hope you find this information valuable and that it helps you create new growth via based on scaling out-of-the-box innovations and new-business building.

To maximize the value of this book, I recommend taking a look at the workbook I have prepared. It provides a summary of the key topics covered in the 12 modules of the Lean Scaleup framework.

The workbook is designed to serve as a checklist for identifying areas for improvement. As outlined in Chapter 20, these insights can be used as a starting point to upgrade your company's current setup. You find it at:

https://www.leanscaleup.com/now-and-new-workbook

This web page provides the option to send me a direct message. Alternatively, you may send an email to frank.mattes@leanscaleup.com.

I am looking forward to hearing your thoughts and to engaging in fruitful discussions.

Sincerely,

Frank Mattes
Wiesbaden / Germany, June 2024

Chapter 1: Introduction

Chapter 1
Introduction

One of the world's largest companies had engaged me to assist with understanding their unique challenges in launching new businesses. It was one of more than 20 companies I had gathered in a think tank to work on what appeared to be a widespread problem: well-run intrapreneurship programs, great innovation ideas, and promising corporate startups never became large and profitable businesses. They never reached the scale required for success.

I was the first person in the conference room and had prepared a presentation for the project's steering committee. As the LCD projector came on, I reflected on my work. Building new businesses is a multi-disciplinary and multi-level undertaking. Therefore, I had interviewed about 20 senior managers, spoke with leaders of corporate startups and greenfield startups in which the company had invested. Additionally, I met with functional stakeholders and regional leaders who were supposed to support them.

The room filled as I flipped through the quotes and numbers that supported the points I wanted to make. I nodded to the senior vice president of corporate R&D who had just entered the room. When we spoke, he had said: "When it comes to commercializing great technology, it takes us forever to take even small steps. We must transform the company, but we will not succeed if we continue at this pace."

He had shown me a list of innovation initiatives and explained: "This could generate more than USD 100m in annual revenues. That one could revolutionize an entire industry. We cannot afford to let them sit. If we do not build the new-business building capability, our company will have only the M&A option for corporate transformation, which is costly and risky."

While reviewing my notes, I came across a meeting with the head of a corporate startup. He had said: "I spend a quarter of my time securing funding and dealing with corporate politics. Corporate bureaucracy slows us down and we cannot move at the pace of a greenfield startup. Every decision must be discussed with our governance board. We only meet with them once a month for two hours. But the discussion rarely focuses on our pressing issues. Most of the time we discuss "the plan." We fight in the market, and we fight with bureaucracy; we are fighting a two-front war."

I went through a list I had compiled to understand the size of my client's new-business building problem. The list displayed the company's (non-incremental) innovation initiatives from five years ago, as well as the corresponding investments. These initiatives should be generating revenues by now, given that it typically takes about five years for such initiatives to make an impact. However, my analysis showed that the company was not making money from building new businesses; instead, it was burning money.

As the conference room filled up, I took one last look at the notes from the meeting with the CEO of a corporate scaleup. She had said: "Corporate functions treat us like we are part of the running business. They want us to comply with corporate bureaucracy. They always find reasons why they cannot work with us in an agile way. And we are always at the bottom of their priority list."

Once everyone was settled, I made eye contact and greeted my audience. "Good morning, everyone. As you know, I spent the last weeks analyzing your new-business-building setup. I have some news, both bad and good. The bad news is that for every dollar you spend on new-business building, you only earn 7 cents. That means you burn a lot of money, and your transformation ambitions are at risk. If things do not change, you will have two options for corporate transformation: acquiring startups or buying transformational companies. Both options are expensive and risky."

After a brief pause, I continued: "Fortunately, there is good news as well. I have identified several symptoms that all stem from one root cause: your company has not yet found out how to balance running the existing business with creating new businesses. When we address that single root cause in a way that customers win, we avoid hurting today's cash flows, and we accelerate the growth of emerging business opportunities, your company can unleash a new wave of growth and transformation."

I paused again to ensure that I had the attention of my audience before explaining what I had found and suggesting what to do next.

What Is This Book About?

This book addresses a key challenge in corporate innovation. Most companies are reasonably good at NOW, at running their existing businesses and at incremental innovations. However, they struggle to create NEW. If a company does not solve this challenge, it fails in:

- Creating new growth from innovation.

- Succeeding in corporate transformation.

- Future-proofing the company.

- Attracting and retaining top talent.

Most companies are stuck with their past success stories and cannot create new ones. This explains why Kodak did not create Instagram, AT&T did not create WhatsApp, Ford not launching Uber, and Hilton not creating Airbnb. It is also why Universal Music Group did not launch Spotify, MasterCard did not create Stripe, and JBS—a USD 50bn meat producer—did not create the market for plant-based meat alternatives[1].

Innovation and Out-of-the-Box Innovation

The term innovation is frequently used in business, perhaps even overused. For example, in the first quarter of 2024, close to 300 new books with the term innovation in their titles were released on amazon.com.

---

[1] CAGR 2023-30 20.14 percent to USD 18.5bn in 2030, see https://bit.ly/3uzs2Li.

Nevertheless, despite this awareness, there is no commonly accepted definition of this term. I define innovation as follows.

Innovation:
Capturing the value from meaningful insights via new offerings.

Innovation is about capturing value. It is not simply about inventing something. The innovation process starts with finding new value pools. It starts with insights, not ideas. Insights provide guidance on where the company must be to capture new value. And finally, there are various options for offerings that allow for capturing that value: a new product, a new service, or a new business model.

There are two main categories of innovation. First, there is inside-the-box innovation, which is often referred to as incremental innovation. The term "box" in this context refers to the existing business, operational, and mental models of the company and the management system around these elements. I will call this "NOW."

Second, there is **"out-of-the-box" or non-incremental innovation**. One type of out-of-the-box innovation is business model innovation. To innovate in that space, a company must conceptualize, validate, and scale a new business model. As explained in chapters 2 and 3, the different categories require different approaches.

Many say that out-of-the-box innovation and new-business building
do not work because they do not scale.
But it is the other way around.
They do not scale because NOW is not prepared for them to scale.

To many people, out-of-the-box innovation and new-business building seems to be a skill that only a few companies and people possess, such as Amazon and its founder Jeff Bezos. This creates a myth of an entrepreneurial genius at work that seems out of reach for most companies.

However, having worked with some of the best change-makers in the world, such as Airbus, Amadeus, bp, ING, Philips, Robert Bosch, and Scania, I know that this is not the case.

Out-of-the-box innovation comprises adjacent and new capabilities / business models. New business models are of particular importance.

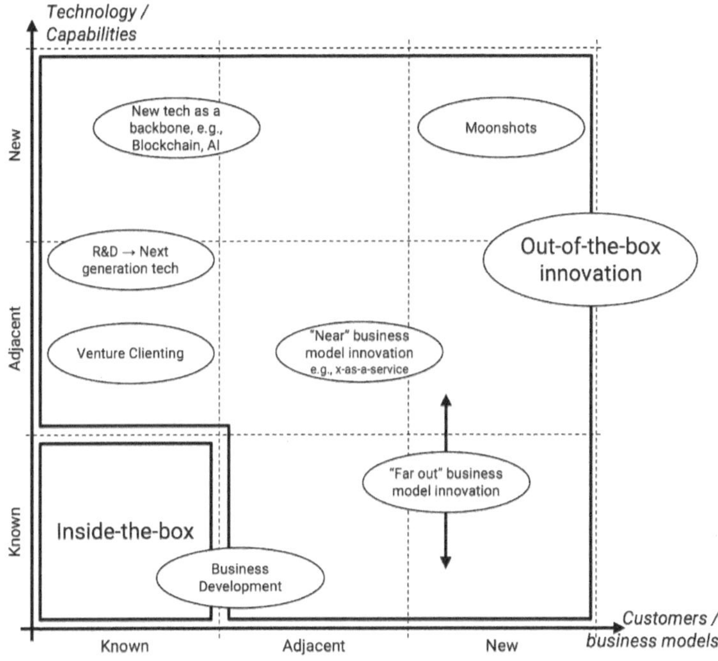

Exhibit 1–1: Out-of-the-box innovation, including new-business building.

The core message of this book is simple. Success in out-of-the-box innovation and new-business building is not about an entrepreneurial genius. Companies can create new growth by building a bridge between NOW and NEW and by acquiring four learnable skills.

To prepare NOW for the scaling of emerging business opportunities, a system problem must be solved. Two incompatible systems, NOW and NEW, must be made to work together.

Who Should Read This Book and Why?

This comprehensive system solution to the NOW/NEW system problem is the result of a seven-year collaboration with hundreds of corporate practitioners and dozens of academic experts in the fields of corporate innovation and corporate entrepreneurship.

Most people of the former group fall into one of the three categories mentioned below. The book is written for these individuals at the largest 10,000 companies in the world[2].

First, senior managers who want to find an effective way to create new growth while the company's "Performance Engine" runs at full speed. Typically, these individuals are aware of the NOW/NEW challenge, but they lack a solid model and a practical language to guide internal discussions. The book provides them with the necessary guidance.

Second, leaders of corporate startups and scaleups. I call these people, in the most appreciative way, corporate mavericks. They burn for their idea that should create new growth and a piece of the corporate transformation agenda.

They go the extra mile, get tarred and feathered on Friday by people who want to preserve the status quo but return even more motivated on Monday to push their ideas and the company forward.

The book offers this group of people a transparent business graduation scheme and the playbooks they need to take their ambition from one stage to the next. Furthermore, it provides them with a concise language to effectively discuss with the people from the first category.

---

[2] Companies with more than USD 500m in revenues (Source: Forbes and ChatGPT).

Third, heads of innovation centers, digital labs, and business model incubators/accelerators who manage a portfolio of emerging business opportunities. These people often find that their stakeholders want to apply NOW's management approach to create NEW. The book offers these individuals an upgrade to their existing approach that accelerates corporate startups and facilitates an effective discussion with their stakeholders.

Three Success Stories, but Most Companies Struggle

Coburg is a picturesque town in Bavaria, Germany. It is home to many stunning examples of historic architecture, including a castle that was built 900 years ago and offers panoramic views of the countryside and the town with its 40,000 inhabitants. Coburg is also the headquarter of Kaeser Kompressoren, a USD 1bn specialist in compressed air, founded in 1919.

Pressurized air is a key element in industrial production. It is also very energy-intensive: Germany's industry uses some 64,000 compressors which consume roughly 5 percent of the country's industry energy consumption. Energy costs make up 75 percent of a compressor's total lifecycle costs.

About ten years ago, Kaeser began to build a new service business by leveraging corporate assets such as its customer base and by building new capabilities in the so-called internet of things context. The company's compressed-air-as-a-service offering provides customers with the compressed air they need, with 100 percent availability, 30 percent lower operating costs, and no upfront investment.

To deliver on this value proposition, Kaeser continually monitors the compressors used by its customers. When the algorithms predict potential problems, field service teams perform preventive maintenance. 20 percent of the company's customers have already switched to this business model, and Kaeser has been able to win many new customers as well.

Another success story is Infosys from India. About 40 years ago, six student friends founded the company with an initial capital of USD 250. Today, Infosys has more than 330,000 employees and annual revenues of USD 16bn. About a decade ago, Infosys embarked on a mission to augment its existing service offerings with a new product business which leveraged the company's engineering capabilities and customer base. This newly created business is now USD 800m in size and a key asset for the company to connect with an ecosystem of complementary platforms.

Moving on to a third success story, this time from Japan. In the early 2000s, Kodak and Fujifilm were in a close race for the top spot in the global silver-based photo film market. Both companies were in the same industry, comparable in size, and faced with the same challenge of digital imaging disrupting their established businesses. While Kodak went bankrupt, Fujifilm thrived[3]. The company identified its excellence in surface chemistry as a key corporate capability and leveraged it to develop new businesses such as cosmetics, pharmaceutical coatings, and coatings for electronic parts.

The stories above offer three key takeaways:
- Established companies can successfully create NEW.

- Creating NEW is about leveraging corporate assets and capabilities.

- It is not necessary to be headquartered in Silicon Valley to succeed in creating NEW.

However, as the statistics in chapter 2 demonstrate, the number of failures in out-of-the-box innovation greatly outnumbers the number of success stories. While companies typically have a 35-65 percent success rate in inside-the-box innovation[4], the chances of building a new USD 50m

---

[3] See the case study in chapter 4.
[4] See https://mck.co/3SwTMrh.

business are only 3 percent[5]. This NEW that senior managers and corporate new-business builders aim for must possess three qualities:

The emerging business opportunity should solve big customer problems, leverage corporate assets and create a business that the corporate investor can invest in.

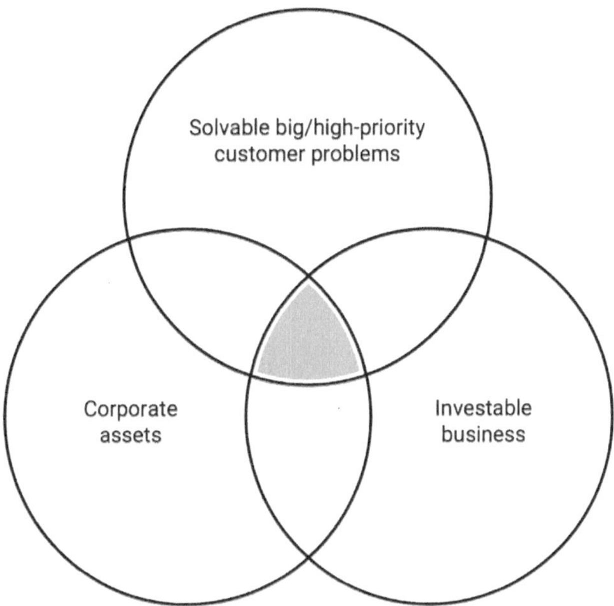

Exhibit 1–2: The sweet spot of out-of-the-box innovation.

- There is a solvable, high-value/high-priority customer problem. Customers are willing to pay for a solution and take the efforts and risks to switch from existing practices to the innovation.

- The envisioned new business around that solution is by its size, margins, and strategic nature suitable for the corporate investor.

- That envisioned new business fits with corporate assets and capabilities to de-risk and accelerate the journey.

---

[5] See chapter 2.

Lean Startup Is Not Sufficient

Companies are designed to optimize the operations of an existing business; they are **Performance Engines**. They are not structured for building NEW; they are not **Transformation Engines**. In most cases, senior management has a bias towards the Performance Engine, for four reasons:

- They built their careers in this environment.

- The metrics used to measure their performance relate to the Performance Engine and not to the Transformation Engine.

- They understand how the Performance Engine works and they know which levers to pull to optimize it.

- They do not fully understand the Transformation Engine.

However, senior managers in large companies are neither myopic nor blind to the future. They care about what the future holds beyond the annual goals and three-year strategic horizon, and they want to build a valuable and defensible position for their company in that future.

To achieve this goal, many senior managers believed that the Lean Startup approach, which gained widespread adoption in the 2000s, was the most effective way forward. They established units that should create NEW where teams could work like greenfield startups and perhaps even infuse the company with the startup spirit. 82 percent of large companies use the Lean Startup for their ambition to create NEW[6].

But despite the best efforts to succeed in out-of-the-box innovation, the results are disappointing. The current approach to building new businesses is simply not working[7]. Something is missing from the equation.

---

[6] See https://bit.ly/3YaP2ZP.
[7] See the statistics in chapter 2.

Enter the Lean Scaleup

The missing piece is a system solution to a system problem because the challenge to create and scale NEW alongside NOW is fundamentally a system problem. **Every company has two value-creation systems: NOW, the "Performance Engine," which generates margins in the present and NEW, the "Transformation Engine," which explores new value pools and a business model that captures that value and creates new growth.**

The Lean Scaleup: a bridge connecting NOW and NEW and four learnable skills to succeed in out-of-the-box innovation and new-business building.

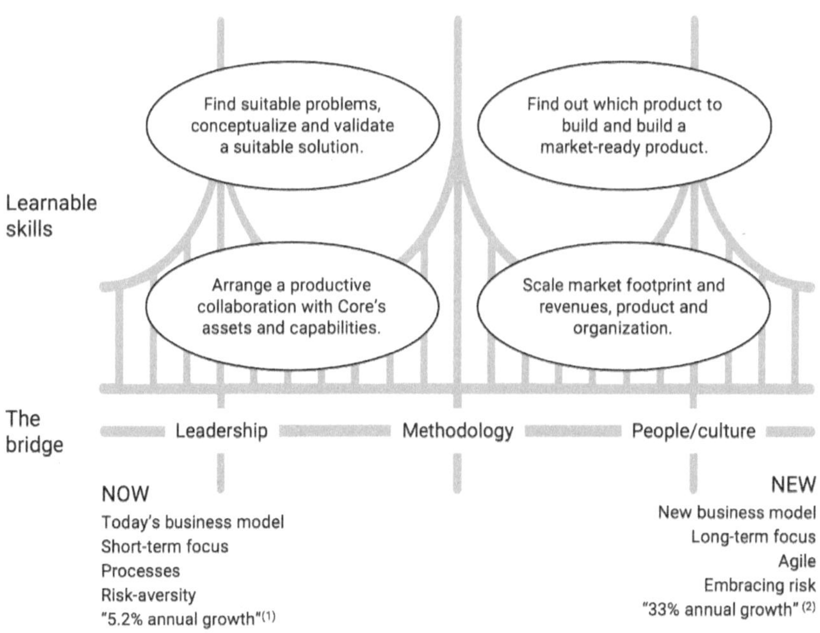

Exhibit 1–3: The bridge and the skills required for out–of–the–box innovation.

However, these two systems are incompatible[8]. Therefore, to make these two incompatible systems work together, a system solution to this system problem must be found. This solution must not harm the existing business, while at the same time it must allow driving new business opportunities through the utilization of the company's assets and capabilities.

Enter the Lean Scaleup, a system solution originally developed by more than 20 companies and two leading business schools. It describes the bridge between NOW and NEW and the skills required to create new businesses with that bridge in place.

Lean Scaleup and Lean Startup

You may be wondering how the Lean Scaleup relates to the Lean Startup. They both contain the word "lean." This term comes from the manufacturing industry. Its core principle is to create value by minimizing waste. What sets the Lean Startup and the Lean Scaleup apart is that they have different target audiences. **The Lean Startup is designed for greenfield startups, while the Lean Scaleup is designed for corporates.**

Around 20 years ago, UC Berkeley's Steve Blank introduced the customer development method, which acknowledged that greenfield startups are not small versions of large companies, and they need their own set of approaches to find customers for their offerings. Ten years later, Eric Ries, a student of Steve Blank, added customer-centricity to the development of products. These two concepts, customer development and customer-centric product development, are the foundations of the Lean Startup.

But as the statistics in chapter 2 show, applying the Lean Startup does not solve the corporate new-business-building problem. The main reason is that, as Steve Blank puts it: "The Lean Startup is not a methodology for

---

[8] As discussed in chapters 2 and 3.

large companies; it is a methodology for [greenfield] startups, which are very different beasts[9]."

Since the Lean Startup is not sufficient for corporate new-business building, a new framework is needed. This should be "a framework for effectively scaling promising concepts by taking the best ideas from the venture capital and Lean Startup worlds and adapting them to a corporate context," as David Eyton, former member of bp's executive team, said about the Lean Scaleup.

The Lean Scaleup in a Nutshell

To make the framework actionable, the Lean Scaleup organizes the critical factors for success in out-of-the-box and new-business building into 12 modules. Each of the pillars of the bridge between NOW and NEW— leadership, methodology, and people/culture—has four modules.

These 12 modules comprise the corporate infrastructure. Each role in out-of-the-box innovation and new-business building needs only a subset of these modules. This design ensures that each role can work effectively and efficiently on a consistent framework for the entire company. Chapter 5 provides an overview of the framework, while chapters 6-17 offer detailed information on the individual modules.

---

[9] See https://s.hbr.org/3SDZKH7.

The Lean Scaleup framework comprises 12 modules, with 4 modules allocated to each of the Methodology, Leadership, and People/Culture dimensions.

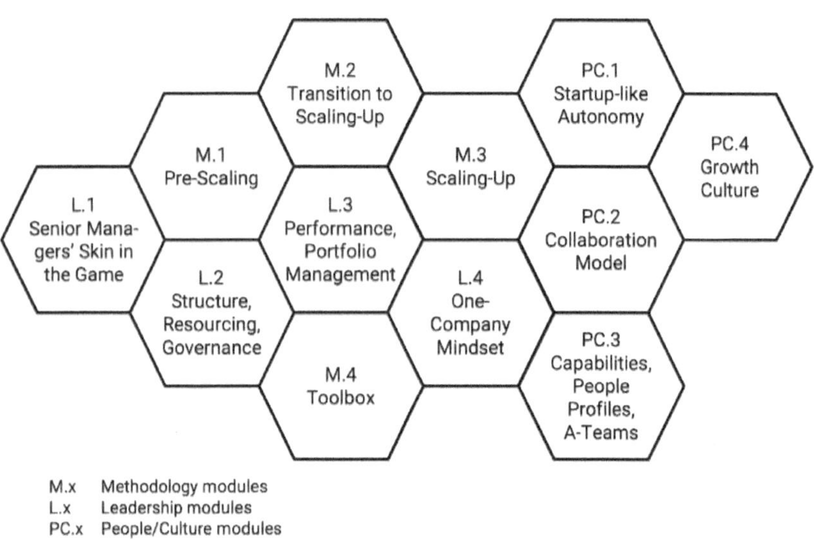

Exhibit 1–4: The Lean Scaleup framework.

How Is This Book Organized?

The book is divided into six logical parts:

- Chapters 2 and 3 present the symptoms and the root causes of the challenge to build NEW alongside of NOW and an effective language for discussing the challenge.

- Chapter 4 provides case studies and insights into the thinking and the actions of successful out-of-the-box innovators.

- Chapters 5-17 present the Lean Scaleup and its 12 modules.

–   Chapter 18 highlights the specifics in building new businesses via collaborating with greenfield startups.

–   Chapter 19 provides guidance to out-of-the-box innovators on how they could steer clear of frequently made mistakes.

–   Chapter 20 illustrates how your company can benefit from the content of this book, in particular from the Lean Scaleup framework.

How Can You Apply What Is Inside?

Companies can benefit from the Lean Scaleup framework in three levels, described in more detail in chapter 20:

–   **Level 1: Cherry-picking.** A company might take a few bits and pieces from the Lean Scaleup, e.g., the validation of customers' barriers to innovation adoption, and leave the rest of their approach untouched.

–   **Level 2: Use corporate startups/scaleups as change catalysts.** A company assigns a dual mission to one corporate startup/scaleup: first, to create a new business and second, to identify areas for improvement in out-of-the-box innovation. These will then be addressed with senior management support, using guidance from the Lean Scaleup.

–   **Level 3: Upgrade the system using the "theory of constraints."** The company identifies the module of the Lean Scaleup that is impeding performance the most and resolves it before moving on to the next critical constraint.

Dictionary: Naming Conventions for Easier Reading

"Core" comprises corporate, functional and regional units that run the day-to-day activities, for example, marketing, sales, supply chain management, procurement, manufacturing, customer care, IT, finance, controlling, and HR. Although innovation is a part of Core, (and there is also innovation work in the mentioned units), it helps in thinking through to separate Core and innovation.

"NOW" encompasses both Core and the management system built around it. If a specific part of the text is more on the corporate assets and capabilities, I use the term Core. When the focus is more on managerial aspects or on the entire current corporate setup, I use the term NOW. NOW transcends Core by adding, for example:

- The corporate identity.

- Strategy, planning and budgeting processes.

- The operating model and key business processes, including their performance indicators, controls, and the corresponding rewards and incentives schemes.

- Governance schemes, including cross-silo decision-making processes and the corresponding committees.

- Target people profiles for recruiting purposes.

- Corporate culture and its manifestation in norms, values, attitudes, and collaboration.

When a company aims to build a new outside-of-Core business, it must design an appropriate **"NEW"** that comprises the future functional and regional units and a corresponding management system.

"Out-of-the-box innovation" refers to innovations that transcend NOW[10], i.e., they play out in beyond the company's base of technologies/capabilities and customers/business model. Out-of-the-box could mean a new-to-the-company technology that should create a new business line[11] or become the new backbone of a business process[12]. It could also mean winning new customer groups or introducing a new business model into the market, which is of particular interest to many companies. I refer to these ambitions as **"new-business building."** In the text, I use the former term for more general statements; when the focus is more on the new-business building aspect, I use that term.

A **"corporate startup"** is a team launched by companies to explore and validate new value pools and a business model that captures that value. It can originate from various sources, including explorative innovation units, corporate intrapreneurship programs, or determined initiatives taken by individual staff members[13]. The team is racing against time to provide this validation before it runs out of corporate funding and support.

Corporate startups can be seen as brownfield startups since they operate within an existing corporate setup. This implies that they must consider the corporate context and coexist with what is already in place. Besides this aspect and the different funding sources, corporate startups differ from **"greenfield startups"** in two other ways:

- Since they should contribute to the corporate transformation agenda, they have limited flexibility to alter their course of action.

- In theory, they have access to tangible and intangible corporate assets and capabilities.

When a corporate startup discovers a viable business model and receives investment from stakeholders to scale up, it becomes a **"corporate scaleup."**

---

[10] See also exhibit 1–1.

[11] Well beyond a mere product line extension.

[12] For instance, via blockchain or AI.

[13] In the last century, 70 percent of the most significant innovations were developed by corporate staff, see https://bit.ly/3Khil8f.

If a certain aspect of the text relates to both corporate startups and corporate scaleups, I use the term **"corporate startup/scaleup."** A company may also choose to invest in a VC-backed greenfield startup and help it scale. I refer to this as a **"corporate venture."**

"Scaling-Up" is the phase of the innovation journey in which a validated business concept with an initial product version and some customers is developed into a sizeable business. Companies have different criteria for what constitutes a "sizeable business." For example:

– A beverage company considers the Scaling-Up phase to have ended when the innovation is launched into three densely populated markets.

– A retailer defines it as "availability at all stores."

– A German global engineering company sets the bar at annual revenues of USD 10m.

– A global energy company requires USD 50m in annual revenues.

"Product" stands for the outcome of an innovation, which might be a physical product, a service bundle or a bundle of products and services. The term **"market"** is used to describe the group of **"customers"** who will want, use, adopt, or somehow engage with the innovation—not necessarily, but in most cases, people with wallets.

"Discovery," "Business Foundation," "Business Strategy," and **"Business Design"** are the first stages of the Lean Scaleup's business graduation scheme. Together, these stages comprise the **"Pre-Scaling"** phase. When validation in the Business Foundation and the Business Strategy stages has found proof points that it makes sense to scale a business model innovation concept, it is deemed **"scale-worthy."**

This concept is **"scale-ready"** when an operating model has been designed that can scale from the get-go, a first version of the product has found market resonance, key processes are at least repeatable and provisions for Scaling-Up have been made.

What This Book Does Not Cover

This book's objective is to illustrate the bridge between NOW and NEW that companies must build and the four learnable skills that they must master to increase their chances of succeeding in out-of-the-box innovation. As the author, I had to make cuts to keep the content manageable. I intentionally omitted deep-dives into individual topics or some aspects that touch on the bridge and the skills, such as:

– Advancing the corporate culture to be more innovative.

– Foresight, i.e., sensing weak signals in the business environment.

– Open approaches to innovation with universities and suppliers.

– Intellectual Property strategy and management.

– Design Thinking.

– Defining and running experiments.

– Working with innovation ecosystems.

– Greenfield startup scouting and investing.

– Platform business models.

Intellectual Property

Lean Scaleup™ is a registered trademark. All trademark regulations apply. To improve readability, I omitted the trademark symbol.

I would like to invite and encourage you to help spread the word about the Lean Scaleup how it helps in creating new businesses. I hope that, if you find the content valuable, you share it with your colleagues, business friends and your professional networks on LinkedIn, and so on.

Although I want the content to reach a wide audience, I also need to safeguard my Intellectual Property. To accomplish this, the guidelines below will help you distinguish between what is proprietary and what is not.

* *

The creative works in this book and the overall framework and organization of the content, are protected by copyright laws. The NOW / NEW bridge with its three elements along with the four learnable skills, the corresponding 12 modules of the Lean Scaleup and the related exhibits are original content and therefore copyrighted, unless noted otherwise.

The Lean Scaleup methodology is made up of two main components: third-party tools that are publicly available under a Creative Commons license—like, for example, the Business Model Canvas, (CC) strategyzer. com—and Lean-Scaleup-proprietary tools like the 4x4 pre-Scaling matrix described in chapter 6.

The latter are publicly available under a Creative Commons (CC) license. You are free to share (copy and redistribute the material in any medium or format for any purpose), adapt (remix, transform, and build upon the material) under the following terms:

- Attribution. You must give credit to leanscaleup.com and indicate if changes were made. You may do so in any reasonable manner, but not in any way that suggests the licensor endorses you or your use.

- ShareAlike. If you remix, transform, or build upon the material, you must distribute your contributions under the same license.

- No additional restrictions. You may not apply legal terms or technological measures that legally restrict others from doing anything the license permits.

For-profit companies and not-for-profit organizations may use the content and creative work for internal purposes. If these are to be used externally, explicit permission must be obtained.

To make it more actionable, here are some Dos and Don'ts regarding Intellectual Property.

Do:

- Talk about the Lean Scaleup. Although Lean Scaleup is a registered trademark, please use that term when you refer to the concept and how it helps companies to succeed in out-of-the-box innovation and new-business building.

- Share insights. I encourage every corporate practitioner to share the big ideas, the key concepts, and the tools of the Lean Scaleup.

- Link to my content. If I have made something publicly available, feel free to share or publish the link.

Don't:

- Distribute our materials without permission. I worked hard and invested considerable resources to develop them. Please do not upload, publish, or share copies without asking me first.

- Plagiarize my work. I do not claim to own all ideas underlying the Lean Scaleup. But the way that those ideas are organized, augmented, and communicated is my original creative expression, protected by copyright. You cannot just take my content, change a word here or pixel there, and claim it as your own.

- Call your product "Lean Scaleup." Apart from copyright considerations, how would anyone be able to distinguish us?

- Say or imply you are affiliated with Lean Scaleup if you are not. Even if your product or service is called something totally different, you should not use our trademarks in a way that might suggest Lean Scaleup gave its approval or was otherwise somehow involved.

About the Author

I think it is remarkable that an expert from Germany has been chosen by companies such as a Fortune 10 company, a global leader in aerospace, a leading Swiss financial services company, and a mid-sized global niche market leader to help them improve their new-business building. I believe this is due to my broad expertise in innovation and my multi-year focus on the topic at hand.

When I began my career in the 1990s, the term innovation was not yet mainstream. For the majority of companies, this was synonymous with new product development. I helped them bring new products to market through waterfall-style project management approaches. In the late 1990s, I joined one of the world's leading consulting firms. We helped our clients implement phase/gate processes for incremental innovation, install innovation portfolio management, and implement business model innovations.

In the early 2010s, I specialized in open innovation. Around 2017, I realized that for many companies, the real problem was not in the early stages of innovation. Companies have more ideas than they could ever execute. The real problem was creating business impact from ideas, measured in revenues or in business transformation. Since then, I have worked full-time in the new-business building space.

This is my third book in that area. The previous two were "Scaling Up Corporate Startups" (co-written with Dr. Ralph-Christian Ohr) and "Lean Scaleup."

Last, but certainly not least, I would be very much interested in your feedback. If you find the content valuable, please leave a review on Amazon.

If you want to get in touch, please send me a message at

frank.mattes@leanscaleup.com
https://www.linkedin.com/in/frankmattes/

Chapter 2:
The Problem

Chapter 2
The Problem

Key Points in This Chapter

1. The majority of companies operate in a volatile, uncertain, complex, and ambiguous (VUCA) world, where change is occurring at an increasing rate. To protect themselves from disruption and to seize the opportunities, they must become more adept at out-of-the-box innovation and new business building.

2. There is no issue with awareness. Two out of three CEOs believe that new competitors represent a significant threat. However, there is a translation problem: 29 out of 30 attempts to create a new USD 50m business fail.

3. The root cause is that to succeed, the NOW/NEW system problem must be resolved. Separating NOW and NEW is necessary, but it is not sufficient.

4. There are compelling reasons to solve the system problem: (1) unleashing new growth; (2) playing offense and defense in the face of disruption; (3) achieving a Return-On-Innovation; (4) improving the Employer Value Proposition to win top talent.

5. In theory, corporate startups/scaleups have an "unfair advantage" since they can leverage corporate assets and capabilities. However, in practice, the theoretical advantage does not materialize due to how access to these is organized.

6. The frameworks that most companies use for out-of-the-box innovation and new-business building lack one critical dimension: the corporate context, the so-called Contextuality.

** **

Gone are the days when companies could enjoy defensible market positions for decades. In the past, a company's size and position were often the result of consistent day-to-day business performance and its ability to succeed in incremental innovation that kept its products relevant. The business environment was rather predictable, and the drivers of change were known.

Today's business environment is different. **The rate of change has increased by 183 percent in the four years between 2019 and 2023,** and 88 percent of senior managers expect an even higher rate of change in 2024[14]. To ensure continued success in the next decade and beyond, companies must be able to identify changes in their business environment, mitigate associated risks, and seize opportunities as they arise.

VUCA and Squandered Ideas

The defining characteristic of today's business landscape is unpredictability. After the end of the Cold War, the US Army War College identified four distinct dimensions that characterize this unpredictability[15]. They coined the acronym **VUCA, which stands for volatile, uncertain, complex, and ambiguous.**

Some companies are better equipped than others to handle their VUCA business environments. Conversely, companies that struggle to handle it face a heightened risk of decline: more companies lose top-three positions in their industries than in the past, and a growing number of companies fall out of the top ten within just five years[16].

Every VUCA disruption is a threat, but also an opportunity. Big ideas can become the seed of a multi-billion-dollar business. But all too often, big companies squander their big ideas. Two well-known examples are:

---

[14] See https://accntu.re/3PYB5N3.
[15] See https://bit.ly/3xgq4gw.
[16] See https://on.bcg.com/3XntPv2.

- In the 1970s, Xerox's Palo Alto Research Center (PARC) developed the world's first personal computer with a graphical user interface and a mouse. Microsoft's Bill Gates and Apple's Steve Jobs turned this big idea into multi-billion-dollar businesses. Xerox barely survived and later donated PARC to a non-profit scientific research institute.

- In 1975, Kodak's Steven Sasson built the world's first digital camera. Unlike Fujifilm, its biggest competitor, Kodak was unable to adapt to technological disruption[17].

In order to mitigate the risks and to seize the opportunities, a company must strive for excellence in innovating beyond the box of its historic business, operating and mental model. In particular, they must master building new businesses that create new growth and drive corporate transformation. However, this is incredibly hard. 29 out of 30 attempts to develop a new USD 50m-business end in failure, as the statistics below show. To paraphrase Albert Einstein, if you had one hour to future-proof your company, you should spend 55 minutes on defining the problem.

This chapter focuses on precisely that. It reveals the key challenge companies face when trying to establish new growth alongside their existing ones. Specifically, this chapter will address the following questions:

- What are the major driving forces of change?

- Why do companies need to strive for excellence in out-of-the-box innovation and new-business building?

- What are the reasons why companies struggle?

- How can a company quickly determine the level of urgency to act?

---

[17] See the case study in chapter 4.

The Driving Forces of Change

Companies around the world are feeling the pressure of their VUCA business environments. They see that:

- A relentless stream of new competitors, including greenfield startups and incumbents from other industries, transform historic industries into new competitive arenas.

- Customers are no longer satisfied with buying products. They now demand seamlessly integrated solutions and services.

- External stakeholders demand that companies address net-zero and sustainability-related concerns in order to remain relevant.

- Digital technologies such as Generative AI or blockchain enable out-of-the-box innovations and new business models.

In this dynamic landscape, companies must stay ahead of the curve and proactively shape their own destiny. By becoming excellent in out-of-the-box innovation, companies can build a resilient and successful future. When working with my clients on future-proofing their company, we typically focus on five VUCA drivers.

Driver 1: Dissolving Industry Boundaries

Most established large companies were founded and grew their business lines to deliver on one value proposition for one type of client and expanded later in their corporate history. Take Intel, a key player in the IT revolution, as an example. The company was founded in 1968 and entered the memory chip market a year later, selling these chips to established computer manufacturers. With the success of the IBM PC, Intel extended its market and sold its microprocessors to all companies making IBM-compatible PCs. The famous "Intel Inside" marketing campaign established the company as a household name.

5 strategic drivers created an unprecedented level of unpredictability and an extraordinarily high "pulse of change."

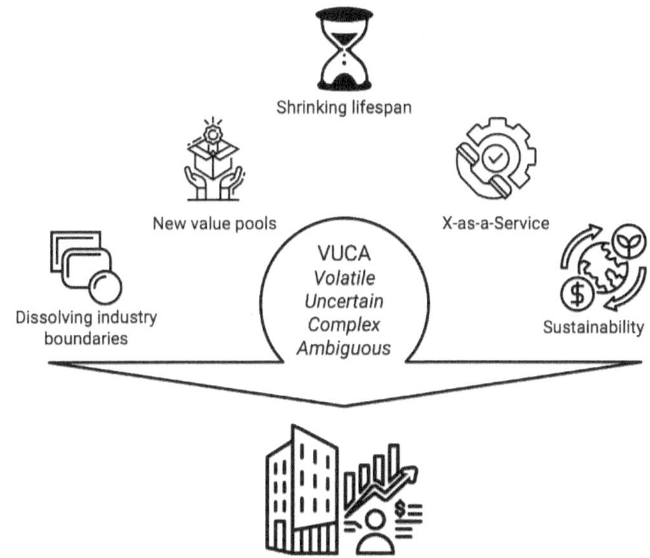

Exhibit 2–1: Five strategic drivers that increase the "pulse of change."

However, after the turn of the century, growth in demand for high-end microprocessors slowed and Intel's competitors gained market share. They initially targeted low-end market segments and subsequently outperformed Intel across its entire product range, leading to a decline in Intel's dominant position.

To offset the losses, Intel attempted to innovate out of the box and create new businesses that ranged from solar cells to video conferencing systems. However, these attempts had only a small impact. Today, the company's revenue comes mainly from two areas that are closely related to its original core business: PC processors and components for server platforms. These two accounted for about 90 percent of Intel's revenue in 2020.

In the past, Intel and almost any other company ran and optimized their business with a linear view. They used linear value chains to visualize a value stream that connects certified suppliers, the company, and its customers. This linear view is also reflected in a popular thinking tool, the Business Model Canvas[18]. In this tool, the left side represents value creation, the middle part shows the company's value proposition, and the right side represents value delivery.

However, such a linear view is no longer sufficient in a VUCA world in which historic industry boundaries are dissolving:

- A manufacturer of computers and consumer electronics establishes a foothold in the global payment system and outsells the entire Swiss watch industry (Apple Pay and Apple Watch).

- Retailers become global leaders in IT infrastructure (Amazon).

- Retailers become leading Logistics players (Amazon, having surpassed UPS and FedEx in parcel volumes).

- Logistics players become manufacturers (UPS' network of 3D printing factories[19]).

- PC graphic cards manufacturers become key players in automotive hardware and software (NVIDIA).

- Manufacturers become service providers (using service-centric business models, as described below).

Dissolving industry boundaries do not reshape industries; they un-shape them. Incumbents lose their positions and new winners emerge. These new winners serve the incumbents' customer base with new value propositions, which are created and delivered in new value chains and ecosystems.

In most cases, digital technologies are the primary drivers behind dissolving industry boundaries, but not in all cases. For example, one of my clients, a dairy company, started to innovate in the functional food space to respond to healthcare and specialty chemical companies entering this market which is adjacent to its core business.

---

[18] See https://bit.ly/40TmrdO.
[19] See https://bit.ly/43Rx3dE.

Driver 2: New Value Pools Emerge

Game-changing out-of-the-box innovations and new businesses can create new value pools. They fulfill a job-to-be-done much better as before, solve an unsolved problem or serve an unaddressed customer base. Five examples may illustrate this point.

Improve the job-to-be-done: Procter & Gamble Swiffer. Procter & Gamble's Swiffer line of cleaning products introduced a new and improved way to clean the home. The initial product was an electrostatic dust remover, which represented a significant advance over conventional cleaning techniques.

The brand uses the so-called razor-and-blades business model, where consumers buy the handle at a low price and rather expensive refills. Since its launch in 1997, Swiffer has been one of Procter & Gamble's most successful products, generating global sales of at least USD 500m.

Solve an unsolved problem: Nestlé Nespresso. Nestlé solved an unsolved problem for coffee drinkers. Before Nespresso's capsule-based espresso system, consumers had to choose between top-quality coffee away from home or less tasty coffee at home. Nestlé created a new category by combining convenience at home with great taste.

The company invented a new technical system and a new business model. The technical system includes a coffee machine that creates immense pressure to extract more flavor from coffee capsules. These capsules came only from Nestlé[20], which bypasses traditional retail by relying on its own points of sale and a direct-to-consumer business model. Nespresso generates more than USD 10 bn annually from its business model innovation.

Solve an unsolved problem: Apple iPod and iTunes. In 2001, Apple's founder Steve Jobs realized that existing solutions for enjoying digital music

---

[20] This was the original concept. Since 2012, when patents expired, other companies have been able to sell compatible capsules.

were too complicated for the average consumers. To solve this problem, Apple introduced iTunes, a software that offered a convenient way to manage their music. In the next two years, Apple released the iPod, a hardware companion to iTunes, and the iTunes Music Store, which allowed consumers to purchase digital music with embedded digital rights management.

By offering consumers software, hardware, and an online store, Apple established itself as a new intermediary in the digital music value chain. Ten years after the launch of the iTunes Store, the company had sold over 35 billion songs, generating approximately USD 10 billion in revenues.

Serve an unaddressed customer base: Amazon Web Services. Amazon Web Services (AWS) is a cloud computing platform that provides on-demand computing on a pay-as-you-go basis.

AWS was originally designed as a platform for its own retail computing infrastructure. However, Amazon soon realized that by letting customers access its infrastructure, AWS could become a large, profitable, and highly scalable business. In 2004, Amazon launched the first public AWS service. By 2015, AWS had become profitable, with annual revenues of USD 7.8bn. As of early 2024, AWS has an annualized revenue run rate of USD 100bn and generates three quarters of Amazon's profit.

Serve an unaddressed customer base: Netflix. Over the course of its 25-year history, Netflix, an American media services and production company, has undergone several significant transformations. Founded in 1997, it started out as a mail-order movie rental service: customers ordered movie DVDs online, received them in the mail, and returned them after watching.

In 1999, Netflix introduced a subscription-based business model. Ten years later, the company built a video streaming business and four years later, a content creation business. Today, Netflix has more than 200 million paid subscribers worldwide.

Improve the job-to-be-done: Hilti Fleet Management. Hilti is a machine supplier to the construction industry. In addition to its product business, the company has established a successful service business. Hilti's

Fleet Management offers a one-stop solution in which a monthly fee covers all expenses related to financing, service, maintenance, and repair of tools.

A decade after its launch, Hilti had more than 1.2 million tools under Fleet Management, representing a contract value of more than USD 1.4bn. Hilti's CTO said: "Hilti has developed many innovative products over the years. However, they pale in comparison to Fleet Management, which has been the most important innovation in Hilti's history."

Driver 3: Lifespan of Business Models Shrink

Of the innovations mentioned above, only Procter & Gamble's Swiffer is inside the box of the company's existing business model. All other innovations were out of the box and introduced new business models that reduced the lifespan of their competitors' business models.

Every business model has a lifecycle. In the early stages, when a few innovators are developing a breakthrough product in a garage or in a corporate innovation lab, the value of the business model is small. As the business model gains traction, the value grows rapidly. But when the underlying technology becomes outdated or customer preferences change, the value begins to decline.

To future-proof the company, new business models must be created and scaled before the current one loses relevance.

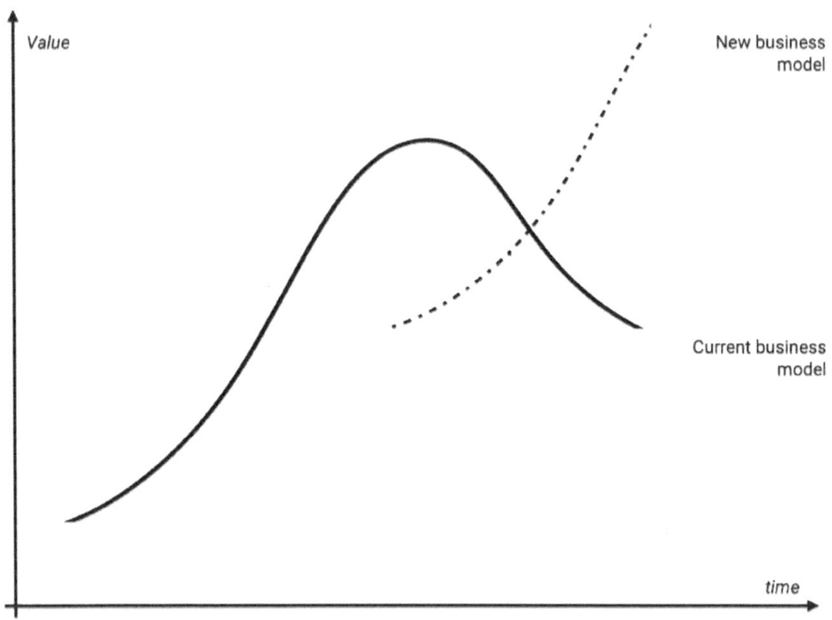

Exhibit 2–2: Life cycle of a business model.

The challenge is that in a VUCA business environment, a company may have only a few years to sense the comet that will hit its business model and to develop **the capabilities to thrive in an altered business landscape.**

There are three reasons for this. **First, disruption can come from many angles.** Kodak, Blockbuster, Encyclopedia Britannica, and Skype are examples of companies that failed to adapt to technological disruption. But disruption can also come from changes in customer preferences. For instance, meat producers must adapt to rapidly changing consumer preferences.

Second, many companies are capability-oriented and not customer-oriented. Amazon's founder Jeff Bezos noted that when companies think about out-of-the-box innovation, they usually ponder if the company has capabilities in that area. He then writes: "That puts a finite lifetime on a company. Because the world changes, and what used to be cutting-edge capabilities has turned into something your customers may not need anymore.[21]"

Third, the average lifespan of business models is decreasing. In the last five decades, it fell from about 15 years to less than five years[22]. If companies do not find new, sustainable business models in due time, they risk becoming another data point in the statistics on shrinking corporate lifespans[23]:

- The average company in the 1965 S&P 500 stayed in the index for 33 years. By 1990, this average was 20 years, and it is forecasted to shrink to 14 years by 2026.

- At the current churn rate, half of today's S&P 500 firms will be replaced in the next ten years.

For these three reasons, forward-thinking senior managers understand that simply exploiting existing assets and capabilities is not sufficient for ensuring long-term survival. They prioritize the ongoing search for new and profitable business models to future-proof their companies. They explore and scale new businesses well before the existing one declines.

This proactive approach can make the difference in today's fast-paced business environment. And it delivers superior shareholder returns[24]:

- Companies that regularly rejuvenate their business model portfolio generate more shareholder returns than those who fixate on their historic business model.

- Six of the world's ten largest companies are serial business builders, having launched at least five new, significant businesses during the past 20 years.

---

[21] See https://bloom.bg/3PYG1l3.
[22] See https://on.bcg.com/3YJ5PUh.
[23] See https://www.aei.org/.
[24] See McKinsey Quarterly, July 2020: Why you've got to put your portfolio on the move.

Driver 4: Service-Centric Business Models

A specific type of business model has gained significant traction in recent years. In so-called service-centric business models, companies shift from selling products to offering customers a convenient service that provides a one-stop solution. Typically, services are charged via monthly subscriptions or metered usage. Two examples for these business models are Kaeser Kompressoren (see chapter 1) and Hilti (see above).

Service-centric business models have a financial and a strategic rationale. The financial motivation is to provide a steady income stream for ongoing contracts, improve resilience to macroeconomic challenges and extend product life cycles. The strategic rationale is to increase customer retention: if customers are satisfied with the company's service, switching barriers are high. Hence, service-centric business models help to protect the company's competitive advantage.

Driver 5: Sustainability

From a purely profit-maximizing management approach, when the daily pressures of generating cash flow guide every boardroom decision, it might be understandable that senior managers see environmental and societal sustainability as a secondary priority.

But the role of business in society has evolved. Investors, customers, employees, public authorities, and the public are demanding more. Today, business is not about just making profits and creating jobs anymore; it is also about environmental sustainability and ethical business practices. In other words, stakeholders expect companies to have a meaningful purpose beyond financial results.

An increasing number of investors are incorporating Environmental, Social and Governance (ESG) metrics into their evaluation of companies. These metrics include factors such as a company's carbon footprint, water usage, community development efforts, board diversity, and staff diversity, equity, and inclusion.

The financial benefit is that companies with high ESG ratings have a lower cost of debt[25]. If companies seize opportunities in that space, they can create growth opportunities. Additionally, aligning with stakeholder expectations on sustainability and ethics can enhance their reputation and brand image—which can be crucial in attracting and retaining top talent as well.

Here Comes the Problem

When a company wants to protect itself against disruptions from one of the above trajectories or wants to seize the opportunities that come with it, it has three possible strategies to shape its future—provided that the remaining shelf life of its business model allows it (in other words, that it is not a "burning platform[26]").

First, the startup route. The company could collaborate with greenfield startups or acquire their technology and talent. This strategy is challenging. Only 1 in 12 companies consider their relationships with startups to be very satisfactory[27]. Talent retention is also not easy: 50 percent of acquired talent leaves the company within two years[28].

Second, the M&A route. The company could acquire innovative, larger businesses. This approach is expensive and risky. M&A failure rates are between 70-90 percent[29], and over the long-term, organic growth generates more value than acquisitions[30].

---

[25] Devalle, A. et al.: The Linkage between ESG Performance and Credit Ratings. International Journal of Business and Management. 12. 53. 10.5539/ijbm.v12n9p53.

[26] See https://bit.ly/3R6ZBw3.

[27] See https://on.bcg.com/3VMIlPM.

[28] See https://bit.ly/3yw6ccV.

[29] See https://hbr.org/2011/03/the-big-idea-the-new-ma-playbook.

[30] See https://mck.co/4bQ8cLr.

Third, build the capability for out-of-the-box-innovation and new-business building. Statistically, this is the best of organic growth options[31] and organic growth creates more value than M&A[32]. I have witnessed hat new USD 100m businesses can be built in just three years. But as the statistics below show, this is the rare exception.

In Theory, There Is an Unfair Advantage

Established companies with limited portfolios and budgets often find themselves competing against VC-backed greenfield startups and aggressive attackers from other industries. So, how can they win? An answer that looks good on paper is to act fast, to act smart, and to leverage the company's assets and capabilities to create a competitive advantage.

Almost every established company has a vast array of assets and capabilities, both tangible and intangible, that a greenfield startups can only dream of. Some of these, listed below, should be present in every out-of-the-box innovation. If none of these are used, the company is effectively building a venture in the wild, and there is no reason to believe that it will outperform VC-backed greenfield startups.

Operational and functional capabilities provide deep functional expertise in areas such as sales, supply chain management, sourcing and procurement, production and quality management, logistics, financial controlling, IT, legal, R&D, recruiting, HR, M&A, management of external partners, contract management, market and technology foresight, market research, contact and customer management, service level management, order fulfillment, product and service delivery, risk management, portfolio management, tax optimization, settlements and payments, and regulatory affairs.

---

[31] ibidem
[32] ibidem

Quite literally the multi-million-dollar question: how can companies generate new growth with the "power of both?"

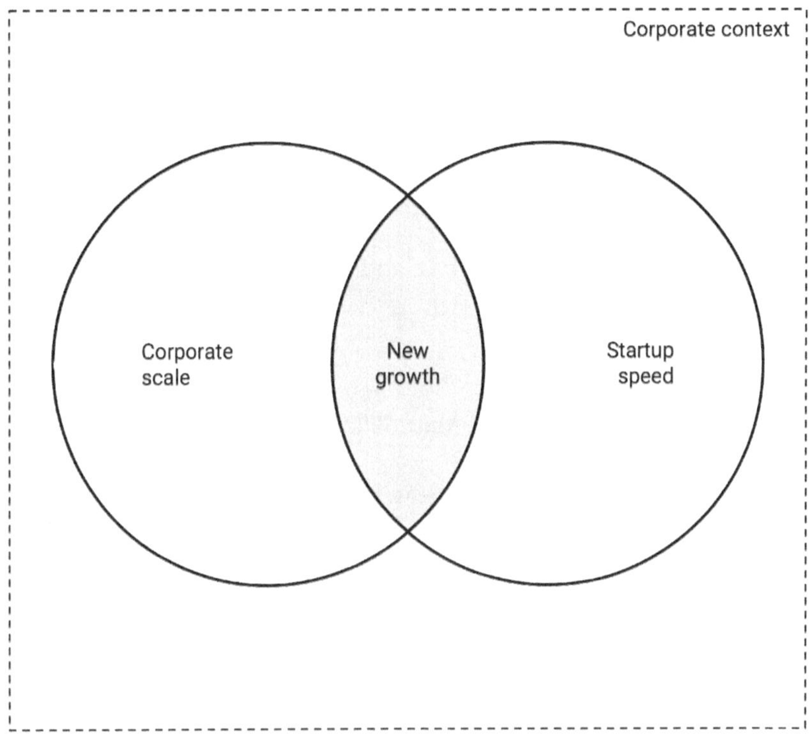

Exhibit 2–3: How corporates can beat greenfield startups at their own game.

Advanced expertise and know-how enable cutting-edge digital solutions. Examples are market insights, models for risk and fraud detection, AI and Machine Learning models, advanced analytics for supply chain risk management, cybersecurity, and regulatory compliance.

Growth-enabling capabilities accelerate the Scaling-Up journey. These include, for example, large contracts for the efficient sourcing of licenses, resources, raw materials, components, and interim staff. They also include online and offline marketing expertise and access to influencers, opinion leaders and regulators.

Privileged assets provide differentiation options and accelerate the journey. Examples are brand and reputation, access to customers and channel partners, presence in ecosystems, patents, and trade secrets.

Technology and IT reduce investments, time-to-market, and unit costs during Scaling-Up. This category comprises items such as individual technologies, technology platforms, technology toolkits (e.g., e-vehicle platforms in the automotive industry), back-end systems for transactional purposes, safety and security systems, and AI / Machine Learning platforms.

Transactional data enables fast and effective statistical analysis and training of Large Language Models in the AI context.

But Companies Do Not Materialize the Unfair Advantage

Few areas of business show a greater gap between ambition and results than innovation, especially when it comes to out-of-the-box innovation and creating new businesses:

- Two out of three CEOs believe that new competitors with new business models are a major threat to their company's core business and that in the next five years, their main competitor will be different from today's[33].

- Only 20 percent of Chief Strategy Officers see their company prepared for disruption[34].

- 84 percent of senior managers say that innovation is critical for their business, but only 6 percent are satisfied with the results[35].

- 54 percent of senior managers believe that getting ideas to market quickly and at scale is the number one innovation problem[36].

---

[33] See https://bit.ly/40MojFg.
[34] See https://bit.ly/3QYE34G.
[35] See https://mck.co/3yC33bK.
[36] See https://bit.ly/3yvNzWO.

- As a matter of fact, only 1 of 8 corporate startups make it to market launch[37] and only 19 percent of the ones who do create a business with more than USD 50m in annual revenues[38].

- Multiplying these two data points show that the chance of an average corporate startup to create an USD 50m business is 3 percent.

These data points spell doom for many companies. When they cannot become better in out-of-the-box innovation, they will fall prey to the five forces shown at the beginning of this chapter. They will be another company that did not make it.

SMEs Are Not Doing Better than Large Companies

Conventional wisdom suggests that smaller firms are better at innovation than large corporates because they:

- Are faster and more agile in their decision-making.

- Have an organization that is less bureaucratic.

- Are closer to the customer.

- Are less tied to existing technology and infrastructure.

- Have a longer time horizon since they are more often privately owned and do not have to eye the quarterly analyst calls.

However, company size is not a differentiator[39]: smaller companies are not significantly better at building new businesses than large corporates.

---

[37] See https://bit.ly/3KgMCEo.
[38] See https://bit.ly/3DZapWu.
[39] See https://on.bcg.com/4bUtCHE.

The Root Cause of the Problem

Some 25 years ago, Michael Tuschman and Charles O'Reilly discovered that when a company separates operations and innovation, it could achieve better business results[40]. They called this approach ambidexterity, which means doing two different things at the same time: running and optimizing the current business while conducting out-of-the-box innovation.

Many companies have taken up the research and set up separate facilities to conduct out-of-the-box innovation and create new businesses. Frequently, these units are called innovation centers, incubators, accelerators, project houses, or digital labs. When you step inside these facilities, you will notice a stark contrast to the traditional corporate office. Vintage furniture, sticky notes on the walls, an Italian espresso machine, table football and beanie bags create a vibrant and creative atmosphere that is a far cry from the conventional and often monotonous office environment. However, this observation only touches the surface of a deeper issue.

The issue is that every company has two different value creation systems under one roof: NOW and NEW (also known as "Exploit" or "Perform" and "Explore" or "Transform"). These two systems are inherently incompatible. The key challenge is to find a productive and win-win way to achieve these two goals. This is where most companies struggle.

One Company, Two Systems

The NOW system encompasses the day-to-day operations, incremental innovations that ensure the relevance of today's products and services, and the management system around these activities. This system, in which 99 percent of staff works, is designed to exploit a proven business model. Its context has a lot of knowns: the company knows the products that customers want to buy, the best distribution channels, the most effective revenue

---

[40] See https://journals.sagepub.com/doi/10.2307/41165852.

model, the best pricing strategy, how to create and deliver value, how to collaborate with certified suppliers, and so on.

Other market players understand the logic of the company's business model as well—and so NOW competes in a "Red Ocean[41]" with intense competition.

NOW puts productivity and predictability at the center. Predictability refers to outcomes (for example, revenues and margins) and to the processes that ensure those outcomes. These processes have been fine-tuned over decades to handle individual transactions with high productivity, high reliability, and high predictability. In NOW, risk is a bad thing. It must be carefully examined and mitigated.

Although it may seem ironic, focusing on daily operations and avoiding risks in the present can actually lead to even greater risks in the future. For instance, a leading European bank's core banking system was designed and implemented in the 1980s, which poses a clear issue of obsolescence in the future. However, replacing this system is extremely risky, complex, and requires a significant investment. Consequently, senior and middle managers shy away from taking personal risks and instead keep the system running, leaving the problem for the next Chief Information Officer.

The other system is **the NEW system**. This system is about exploring new value pools with little competition and the right business model to enable a scalable and profitable business with relatively low competitive intensity—a "Blue Ocean" business. If this exploration finds a suitable value pool and the right business model, it has found the germ cell of a new large and profitable business.

Since NEW is new, there are many unknowns in this exploration. For example, it may not be clear at the outset who the paying customer will be, what the problem is that needs to be solved, what would customers

---

[41] The terms "Red Ocean" and "Blue Ocean" refer to a strategy framework developed by W. Chan Kim and Renée Mauborgne.

keep away from adopting the innovation, how the value proposition should be created and delivered, what the right revenue models are, what the biggest cost blocks will be, and so on.

The Cynefin framework[42] states that the optimal strategy in such an environment is an agile build-test-measure-learn approach. **Exploration is therefore not a process, but a flow of diligent entrepreneurship**. Exploration teams need to operate under an agility paradigm that systematically reduces inherent uncertainties in order to succeed.

NOW's productivity/predictability paradigm and NEW's agility paradigm are inherently incompatible. **If a company assumes that its new-business building activities should create NEW while using NOW's productivity/predictability paradigm, it will fail.** Bolting these two systems together will not work either. The inherent incompatibility of NOW and NEW will manifest in so-called areas of tension[43] that will prevent productive collaboration.

The Journey through the "White Space"

When a new value pool and the right business model has been found, it must be scaled up. Without success in Scaling-Up, all previous activities are just a costly hobby. During Scaling-Up, a corporate scaleup grows the business model concept, a "Minimum Marketable Product[44]," and a few initial customers, into a multi-million-dollar business.

When NOW operates at full speed, focusing on the old business model, and NEW is busy creating new ideas, there is no conflict. Both systems can coexist peacefully within their respective organizational homes. Conflicts arise when the new business concept is scaled, and the two systems are

---

[42] See https://en.wikipedia.org/wiki/Cynefin_framework.

[43] See chapter 3.

[44] See chapter 6. Think of it as a feature-poor product version 1.0.

required to collaborate, for example when the corporate scaleup wants to get access to Core's functional experts or the existing customer base.

Scaling-Up often plays out in a "white space" with no organizational home, no suitable governance and no playbook that outlines how to collaborate.

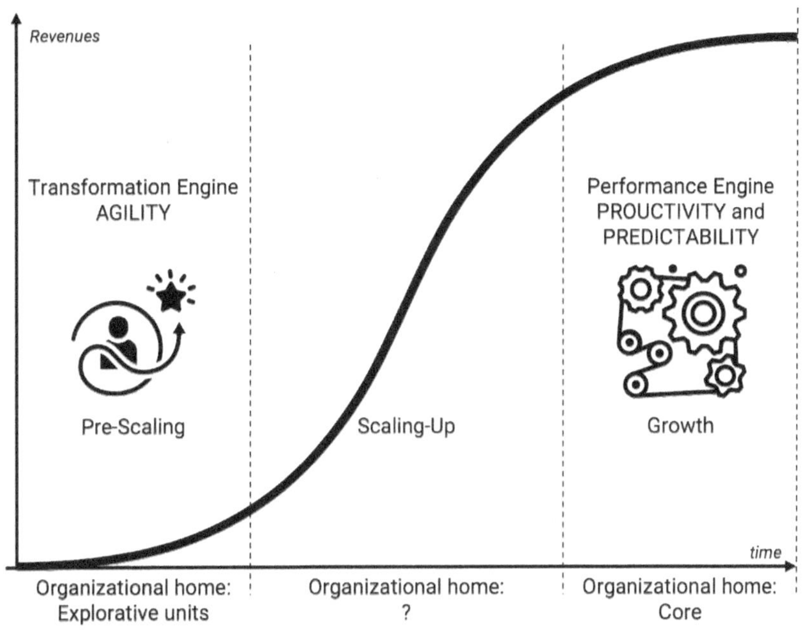

Exhibit 2–4: Scaling-Up is often a journey through a "white space."

If there is no new-business building infrastructure[45], Scaling-Up takes place in an ill-defined "white space" where there is no organizational home, no suitable governance and no playbook that outlines how to collaborate.

Conflicts in such environments escalate quickly, leading to a scenario where there is no win/win and only one system emerges as the dominant winner. **NOW will always win since it provides the margins.** Consequently,

---

[45] The 12 modules of the Lean Scaleup framework, see chapter 5.

the corporate scaleup will flame out along the way and there will be no new growth and no new revenue streams.

Limited Access to Corporate Assets and the Two-Front War

Earlier, I mentioned that in theory corporate startups have an advantage over greenfield startups: they could use the company's assets and capabilities to create an "unfair advantage." However, the fact that only one out of thirty corporate creates a USD 50m business suggests that in most companies there is a significant problem with leveraging these assets and capabilities.

The problem lies in the way they are managed: they are optimized to support NOW. **Access is controlled by functional managers whose KPIs are aligned with NOW and not with out-of-the-box innovation.** As a result, corporate scaleups seeking functional support are often deprioritized and relegated to the long tail of activities.

To illustrate this point, let us consider two examples. First, one of the company's assets is access to customers, which is controlled by sales functions. I have found that salespersons are very rational people. They ruthlessly prioritize their activities to meet their sales goals. Consequently, Core's salespersons are more likely to sell products that they are familiar with, rather than spending precious time promoting innovative products which need extensive explanation and add friction to the sales process.

Second, when inhouse experts from units such as legal, marketing, procurement and HR are faced with out-of-the-box innovations, they need time to think through unfamiliar issues like, for example, a legal framework for a new business model, the best way to advertise a new value proposition, or how to hire individuals with unique skill sets. However, these experts are often fully booked with day-to-day tasks and are required to adhere to corporate rules designed for the existing business.

So, in practice, a corporate scaleup may not have access to the sources of a potential "unfair advantage." Or it may have access but is hamstrung by corporate bureaucracy. For example, Bayer's CEO stated that its internal rules for employees span 1,362 pages[46]. In either case, **the corporate scaleup may find itself in a two-front war.** The first front is in the market, where it must retain existing customers and win new ones. The second front is within the company, where the corporate scaleup loses time in navigating areas of tension and corporate bureaucracy.

Apart from being slowed down by corporate bureaucracy, corporate startups/scaleups face three more significant disadvantages. Greenfield startups:

– Can raise funds in the market. Corporate startups/scaleups can typically only access company-internal funds.

– Get the grace of time from their investors before they need to be cash-positive. Corporate startups/scaleups are often marked from the get-go against the company's revenue-generating units in a corporate context that has a short-term focus.

– Can attract the best talent in the market to achieve their goals. Corporate startups/scaleups may have to share resources or team members, making it harder to shape their team to meet objectives.

Incompatible Governance

Governance is a system that aligns goals, allocates resources, and structures decision-making. In new-business building, governance includes both process and content. However, even the best corporate explorers with a professional process and a world-class agile, build-test-measure-learn approach may not be able to provide proof points for all aspects of an out-of-the-box innovation initiative. In this case, the corporate investor must be convinced to take an entrepreneurial leap-of-faith-decision to proceed.

Core's governance is fundamentally different. It is designed to ensure efficient execution of a well-known business model and tight control of processes and business risks. Leaps of faith are not part of Core's governance

---

[46] See https://bit.ly/3JeeLLJ.

since NOW is not designed to handle uncertainty. When it comes to innovation, it can only accept incremental improvements with calculable risks.

A Different Time Horizon, a Different Pace

The clock of a corporate startup/scaleup operates differently than Core's in two significant ways: it has a longer time horizon, yet it runs faster when executing individual activities.

Building a new business requires a long-term perspective. The time-to-impact between finding a meaningful idea and the first tangible revenues is typically at least three to five years for businesses that are adjacent to Core. It may even be longer if the innovation relies on new technologies or requires customers to change their behavior. This means that **out-of-the-box innovation operates on a timeline that transcends Core's strategic horizon and the typical tenure of senior managers**.

Additionally, re-integrating a scaled-up business into an operational unit is a time-consuming process. It is not a one-time event but rather a gradual process. The receiving unit must prepare; it must have time to build the necessary skills and to consolidate operative systems and departments—but often, they do not have the capacities for that.

Six Issues That Amplify the Problem

The previous section explained why most companies struggle in creating NEW while at the same time winning NOW: they have not yet discovered how to make their two value creation systems work together productively. Six other issues amplify this problem.

Issue 1 – Ineffective Frameworks

The Cambridge Dictionary defines a framework as "a supporting structure around which something can be built."The frameworks to manage out-of-the-box innovation and new-business building that I encounter in my advisory work share a lot of similarities. Typically, they structure the journey from idea to a scaled-up business in stages such as:

- Problem/solution-fit. Corporate explorers talk to potential customers to find a significant pain point and to envision a solution that fits with the company's base of assets and capabilities.

- Minimum Viable Product. An early prototype of the product is built, and customer acceptance is tested.

- Product/market-fit. Corporate startups develop a product version that can satisfy an interesting market. They see that first customers are getting value out of the product, word of mouth is spreading, press reviews are raving, and that the length of the sales cycle is shrinking.

- Scale. In this stage, the team doubles down on what works with respect to go-to-market and product. Furthermore, the corporate scaleup is supposed to grow the organization that supports a rapid revenue growth.

What is wrong with this picture? In my view, such frameworks have six shortcomings.

First, they fall short on the corporate context in which out-of-the-box innovation and new-business building takes place. In general, out-of-the-box innovations face uncertainties in four dimensions: customer/market, technical, financial, and organizational. However, these frameworks only address the first three uncertainties; they undervalue the organizational uncertainty.

To succeed in new-business building, the mandatory dimensions desirability ("will customers buy what we intend to create?"), feasibility ("can we master technical challenges and industrialization?"), and viability ("can we create a profitable business?") must be augmented by a fourth dimension that reflects the organizational context. I call it "Contextuality."

Most corporate new-business building frameworks focus only on Desirability, Viability and Feasibility. They miss the corporate context.

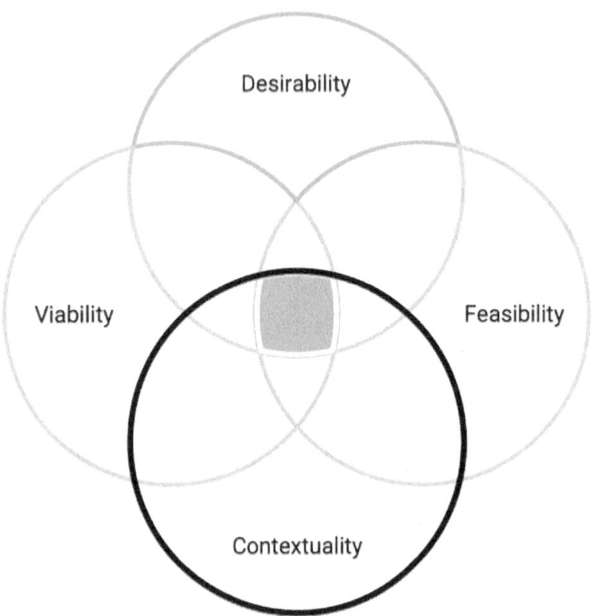

Exhibit 2–5: Four validation dimensions, including Contextuality, are needed.

Chapters 5 and 6 show that Contextuality is a pervasive factor throughout the entire innovation journey. For instance, in:

– Defining the meaningful search fields in which corporate explorers search for new value pools.

– Selecting meaningful ideas from many ideas in these search fields.

– Validating scale-worthiness with respect to leveraging or building corporate capabilities.

– Validating scale-readiness with respect to the availability of corporate support in the docking points with the corporate scaleup.

– Achieving tactical alignment in how to scale up by, for example, integrating Scaling-Up milestones into the goals of Core's functions.

- Collaboration in Scaling-Up to de-risk and to accelerate the journey.

- Re-integration into Core, if relevant.

Second, they focus on building products, not businesses. As a result, many teams find out too late that key ingredients for success are missing, such as the readiness of the wider ecosystem, the customers' preparedness to adopt the innovation, or the access to corporate functions.

Third, they have a narrow view on the process. Of course, all these frameworks have a checkbox labelled "strategy fit." But the corporate strategy is often too fuzzy to provide guidance to corporate explorers, and the fit with Core's functional strategies is often lacking. When Contextuality is not an integral part of out-of-the-box innovation, corporate startups/scaleups emerge unexpectedly for Core's managers. No wonder they have trouble embracing NEW—and corporate startups/scaleups then pay the price for the freedom they enjoyed initially.

Fourth, they lack clear and transparent progress monitoring. Inevitably, a focus on building products rather than businesses, coupled with a narrow view of the process, makes it difficult to track progress. But without a robust progress monitoring, it is difficult to effectively manage a portfolio of emerging business opportunities and to nail down the leaps of faith that require an entrepreneurial decision.

Fifth, they use innovation jargon. Core's senior and middle managers have a distinct language to describe business objects and business processes. However, terms like problem/solution-fit or product/market-fit are usually not in their vocabulary.

Sixth, they do not address the dual mission of the first phase of Scaling-Up. As explained in chapters 8 and 19, one mission is to increase the number of customers and revenues by an order of magnitude. The other—equally important—mission is to make the emerging business digestible for Core's functions with which the corporate scaleup should collaborate.

Issue 2 – Inability to Sense IT-Disruption in Due Time

In the introduction to this chapter, five strategic drivers that can disrupt a company's business model were introduced. When competing incumbents or greenfield startups are better at exploiting cutting-edge IT, they can also disrupt a company.

In the IT area, disruptions tend to occur approximately every 14 years. For instance, in 1966, the ARPANET (the precursor to the Internet) and memory chips were invented. In 1977 and 1981, Apple and IBM respectively introduced the Personal Computer. In 1994, the first web browser was made publicly available. In 2007 and 2008, Apple introduced the iPhone and the mobile internet, and the concept of the Blockchain was published. In 2022, Generative AI, such as ChatGPT, became mainstream.

If a company fails to sense these weak signals of IT disruption or is unable to translate them into effective innovation activities, it may find itself caught off guard—and it may be too late to catch up.

Issue 3 – Incomplete Understanding of Innovation

Roughly 99 percent of a company's workforce is dedicated to day-to-day operations and incremental innovations. NOW relies on processes that ensure repeatability, predictability, and productivity. This operating model is fundamentally at odds with out-of-the-box innovation, which intentionally departs from NOW and creates something entirely new. NEW has no precedent and hence it is initially unpredictable and unrepeatable.

NOW's senior managers often try to apply the Performance Engine's mental and operating models to out-of-the-box innovation, which amplifies the new-business building problem. This is a common challenge, which manifests in three issues.

First, the relationship between investment and learning. NOW's paradigm is "invest before learning." In NOW, investments are planned, payback projected, and return on investment estimated before optimizing the investment by continuous improvement starts. In contrast, to succeed in NEW, a staged process with an agile approach to reduce uncertainty is needed. NEW follows the paradigm of "learn before investing."

Second, how to place bets. In NOW, the optimal solution for a business challenge is selected from a basket of choices, carefully planned, and executed. NEW requires a different approach. Due to the inherent uncertainty, nobody can predict which meaningful idea will become a sizeable business. Therefore, concentrating funds on one or two ideas only carries significant risks. A VC-like portfolio approach is the optimal strategy.

Third, the right distance between NOW and NEW. Distance encompasses factors such as physical locations, financial autonomy, and management processes. If the distance is too large, NEW becomes disconnected from corporate decision-making processes regarding goals, strategies, budgets, and initiatives.

Conversely, having too little distance is also not ideal. When exposed to Core's immediate priorities, big ambitions often experience "death by a thousand cuts:" they are chopped down to fit the mindset of the operative units, but the outcomes are far too small to address the disruptive forces.

Issue 4 – The Gravitational Pull of past Success

An ancient proverb states: "Whom the gods want to destroy, they send forty years of success." It appears that senior managers find it easier to repeat past successes than to create new ones. They establish clear responsibility structures, run and optimize processes, implement sophisticated IT systems, and recruit people who align with the company's culture.

However, this has a drawback. It creates **organizational and cultural inertia**. The company's operating and mental models can become entrenched, like a river carved into the bedrock of a massive canyon, which cannot break out of the canyon it carved. Organizational and cultural inertia manifest in cultural traits such as:

- Strong and unquestioned beliefs about the business environment.

- Overreliance on what has worked in the past.

- Unproductive habits and company norms.

- Stubbornness and a passionate but unreflective reliance on past processes, habits, and values.

- Strong vested interests and politicking.

- Managerial overconfidence or even arrogance.

- Contentment and complacency.

- Passive and uncritical thinking.

- Confirmation bias: quick dismissal of information that conflicts with current view.

- Bias towards fitting in: the belief that individuals must adhere to NOW's written and unwritten rules.

- Bias towards expertise: the belief that an individual's status is defined by the level of expertise in running NOW's operations.

Issue 5 – The Corporate Identity

Another reason why companies are hesitant to strive for excellence in out-of-the-box innovation and new-business building is understandable, albeit misguided. They define themselves by their products, markets, or business model. Building new businesses then creates an identity crisis. Let me illustrate this with an example from a mid-sized German company.

The company views itself as a top-notch, high-end machinery manufacturer. Its customers are top companies in the aerospace and automotive industries. To deliver its value proposition, the company works exclusively with a small circle of carefully selected partners. High-end technology, high margins, low volumes, and a strong brand image are crucial to the company's corporate identity.

When we began working together, the company was already under pressure to enter new markets. Asian competitors had moved from the low-end into the high-end market segment where the company operated. To unleash new growth, the company's corporate explorers had already identified several target markets. They discovered that potential customers demanded a service-centric business model[47] since high upfront investments was a switching barrier for these customers.

To succeed in these target markets, the company must embark on a long journey. This journey involves hiring people with new skills, developing new capabilities, exploring opportunities for acquiring new technologies through licensing and acquisitions, adapting existing back-office systems, revising financial projections, and adjusting shareholder communication, among other things. If the company can overcome these challenges and create new businesses, it will have a new identity.

However, senior managers often find it difficult to let go of the long-established corporate identity[48] and to dismantle the structures they have meticulously put in place without any certainty that the endeavor will be successful.

Issue 6 – Scaling-Up Requires Different People

Scaling a validated business concept requires people with a specific profile that are in short supply. These individuals are action-oriented, entrepreneurial, passionate about the new business' mission and highly motivated to build it, as explained in more detail in chapter 16.

How High Is Your Need to Act?

When I begin working with new clients, some of them have specific inquiries regarding their approach to out-of-the-box innovation or regarding

---

[47] See above.

[48] This is the deeper reason why one of the 12 Lean Scaleup modules is the so-called one-company mindset.

individual activities. For example, they seek advice on how to adapt corporate metrics to support new-business building or an outside-in view of their corporate startup's scale-readiness.

Others prefer a more open-ended approach. They are interested in learning more about the principles and success factors of new-business building. With these clients, I typically begin by discussing three "litmus tests." This often results in a meaningful and in-depth conversation, which additionally provides a deeper insight into the level of urgency to act.

Test 1: What Is the Financial Impact of past Activities?

The first test provides insight into the financial scale of the company's out-of-the-box challenge. It examines a 3-5-year timeframe, as this is the typical time-to-impact. The test consists of three questions:

- Which out-of-the-box innovation initiatives did the company pursue three to five years ago?

- How much money was spent on these activities?

- How much revenues do these initiatives generate today?

After conducting this analysis, clients are often surprised by the results. For instance, the company mentioned in the first chapter found that it generated only 7 cents of revenue for every dollar spent five years ago. Another client discovered that they were earning a mere 1.5 cents on every dollar.

In both cases, the companies were not generating profits from their innovation efforts—they were experiencing significant financial losses. Once they saw the results, both companies took prompt action to address their respective challenges.

Test 2: How High Is Core's Management Attention?

The second test aims to illustrate the amount of management attention that out-of-the-box innovation receives. I ask senior managers to note how much time they spent on related activities.

Senior managers typically devote only a small fraction of their time to NEW, with most of their activities revolving around participation in governance boards. They focus on NOW's Key Performance Indicators because they are evaluated on these dimensions. Consequently, while NEW may be a top-three priority for the company, senior managers in practice often prioritize NOW.

As a result, building new business inevitably becomes a low priority for senior managers, which then trickles down to the managers reporting to them. Senior managers are often aware that corporate startups/scaleups require a lot of care and attention. However, it can be almost too much to do two fundamentally different things—running and optimizing the existing business and nurturing a future business—at the same time.

Test 3: How Deep Is the Valley of Death?

A third test aims to figuring out how many corporate startups progressed beyond the "Minimum Viable Product" (MVP)[49] stage. This point marks the end of the purely conceptual work and should be the beginning of the collaboration between NOW and NEW. Judging by the statistics mentioned earlier, only a few companies have a new-business building infrastructure that catapults corporate startups through this phase.

Every company has an "Innovation Valley of Death" after the MVP stage, but the depth of this valley varies. Interestingly, the Valley of Death phenomenon also applies to the scaling of digital technologies within a company. For example, the World Economic Forum studied smart factories and their related technologies[50] and identified the lack of resources and of knowledge about Scaling-Up as the biggest barriers after the MVP stage.

---

[49] Think of it as a semi-engineered yet still unfinished early-stage prototype that hints towards the product, see chapters 6 and 19.

[50] See https://bit.ly/4aK6PhQ.

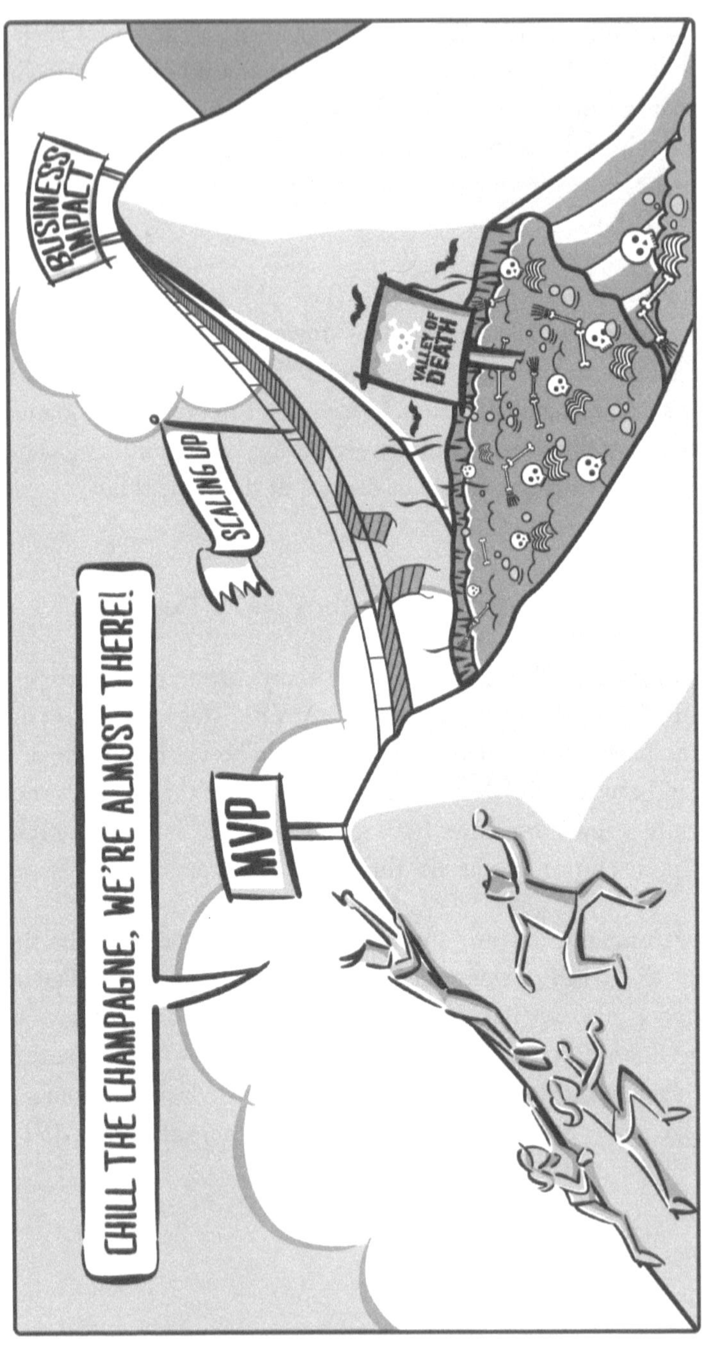

Exhibit 2–6: "Valley of Death" after the MVP stage.

Summary: Why You Must Embrace Out-of-the-Box Innovation

This chapter showed three things. First, there are good reasons to embrace out-of-the-box innovation and new-business building. Second, this is a unique discipline. Third, existing approaches do not produce results, as the statistics clearly show.

A new and effective approach is needed. This approach must **incorporate and transcend two significant ideas: it must effectively integrate Lean Startup and ambidexterity within a corporate context.**

Before turning towards the solution, let me nail down the four reasons why any company must strive for excellence in out-of-the-box innovation and new-business building.

First, to create new growth. 8 out of 10 CEOs[51] see new-business building as a top-five priority, even in times of economic volatility. They find that every dollar of revenue from NEW creates twice as much shareholder value as a dollar earned in NOW.

Second, to future-proof the business and ensure corporate transformation. If a company does not have the capability to build new businesses, it may be disrupted. In addition, every corporate startup delivers a piece of the company's transformation agenda. Without excellence in new-business building, this part of corporate transformation will not happen.

Third, to achieve "Return On Innovation." Here is the math. Depending on the industry, companies spend between 4 and 25 percent of their sales on R&D, which we could use as a proxy for innovation spend. Historically, around 30 percent of that has been spent on out-of-the-box innovation. Multiplying these figures suggests that most companies spend between 1.2 and 7.5 percent of their revenues on out-of-the-box innovation.

---

[51] See https://mck.co/3TKdsL0.

However, as statistics in this chapter have shown, the average return on this investment is far too low. By striving for excellence in out-of-the-box innovation, especially new-business building, companies can significantly increase their top line growth.

Fourth, to win top talent. Success in building new businesses improves the "Employer Value Proposition" that supports the recruitment and retention of top talent. Leading scientists, rock star business builders and outstanding experts in digital technologies are in short supply.

Millennials—those born between 1980 and 1996, who already make up 35 percent of the global workforce—are motivated (beyond pay and financial prospects) by factors such as being in the best place to work and creating the best possible products in their field[52]. As a result, millennials are skeptical of companies that fail to build new businesses. But without top talent, the company falls further behind.

For some companies, this aspect is as much a priority as the other three. One of my clients was a senior vice president at bp. I helped him to design and build bp Launchpad, the company's "Scaling-Up factory." He said: "A lot of fantastic people want to come and work in this environment. They are millennials. I want bp to be able to retain those people, to find the space where if they have a brilliant idea, they can take it to scale and be the entrepreneur they want to be and for bp to get the best value from that."

---

[52] See https://bit.ly/48oxrU0.

Chapter 3:
An Effective Language To Solve the Problem

Chapter 3
An Effective Language to Solve the Problem

Key Points in This Chapter

1. NOW and NEW have two fundamentally different missions. The former must exploit a proven business model to deliver margins safely and predictably. The latter must identify new value pools, find an effective way to capture that value and build a new business.

2. To fulfill their respective missions, NOW and NEW operate on fundamentally different paradigms. NOW pursues productivity and predictability, while NEW builds on agility and systematic reduction of uncertainties.

3. A concise language is needed to effectively discuss NOW/NEW issues. There is no need to change language on either side, but there needs to be a shared language in place.

4. "Ambidexterity," i.e., separating NOW and NEW is necessary for succeeding in out-of-the-box innovation but not sufficient. The missing piece is to integrate these two at defined points.

5. One of these points is "Playing Field 2" in which "Reshape Core" takes place. This is the space in which NOW and NEW should collaborate in scaling up corporate startups. The paradigm for this space is a blend of NOW's and NEW's paradigms.

6. In "Reshape Core," corporate scaleups compete with other initiatives such as corporate/digital transformation for key resources.

* *

To enhance communication and decision-making quality, it is crucial that NOW's senior managers share a concise language with corporate startups/scaleups and units that drive out-of-the-box innovation and new-business building. **Language barriers can impede progress and lead to costly misunderstandings.**

However, a shared language is not only about translating technical terms from NOW to NEW or vice versa. The shared language must reflect different mindsets. To illustrate this point, imagine that you are one of Core's functional managers. Your job is to ensure that a particular business process runs smoothly and that you squeeze a little more productivity out of it. Your professional network tells you that a new technology can help you achieve a productivity gain that will take you a step closer to your goals.

You would create a high-confidence plan that outlines activities, estimate the budgets and timings for each activity, calculate the expected savings, and identify when Return On Investment will be achieved. Additionally, you would use an internal-rate-of-return approach based on reliable cash flow estimates of the investment to make the case for why the company should invest in your proposal and not in other opportunities.

New-business building jargon such as "problem/solution fit," "MVP," "product/market fit," "traction," or "pirate metrics" is completely unfamiliar in this environment. Even one of the foundations of agile approaches, the term "experiment," is unfamiliar in this environment. As one of my clients said: "We are not running experiments here, we are engineering processes."

This chapter aims at providing a concise and effective language. There is no need to change the professional jargon on either side, but it is crucial to have a shared language when people from these systems discuss.

Exploit and Explore

Many of us know IKEA, the Swedish furniture and lifestyle company renowned for its affordable flat-pack furniture. This furniture is sold in large warehouses outside of city centers and assembled by the customer using the Allen wrench provided. While IKEA continues to develop these types of products and to optimize this business model, the company is also involved in activities that go beyond.

For instance, just off Oslo's main shopping street, there is a design studio where customers can design their new kitchen and see almost the entire range of materials for cupboard doors and countertops. Moreover, IKEA has become a significant property investor, acquiring prime real estate in Paris' Rue de Rivoli and London's Hammersmith. The company's objective is not limited to being a landlord; it aims to establish new ways of engaging with consumers by innovative formats.

Furthermore, in response to criticism that the IKEA business model encourages people to buy cheap products and dispose of them quickly, the company is also promoting the reuse of its furniture through second-hand sales or rentals to small businesses or students.

The company's actions demonstrate that it is playing two games at the same time. IKEA is **exploiting its established business model while also exploring new business models and formats**. Both exploitation and exploration are necessary: maximizing margins in today's business environment requires exploitation, while exploration is necessary to build tomorrow's success in a transforming business environment.

Exploit's focus is NOW. Its goal is to safely deliver predictable growth in a known environment in which the company:

- Knows which products and services customers want to buy.

- Figured out the pricing model and the price point that appeal to customers.

- Knows how to create and deliver its value proposition by orchestrating the activities, resources, and partners and controlling the associated processes and costs.

- Has well-defined approaches for small-step product improvements with a good level of certainty concerning the commercial success.

Explore's focus is NEW. NEW thinks outside of the box of NOW's business, operating, and mental models. It is driven by the thought that the electric light did not come from incrementally improving candles[53]. NEW's mission is to:

– Discover new value pools and business models that capture that value.

– Develop a portfolio of new-growth initiatives.

– Build new businesses from scale-worthy and scale-ready initiatives.

– Create a compelling growth story for investors.

Given the nature of this mission, many aspects of the business environment may be initially unknown. For instance, it may not be immediately apparent whether the target customer is a business partner or a consumer.

Corporate explorers and corporate startups cut through the underwood of unknowns by making assumptions about the business environment and running experiments to validate those assumptions. They evaluate the results of these experiments to determine whether it is safe to progress or if they need to restate their assumptions. **When done correctly, the exploration process is scientific in nature, and not based on guesswork.**

Exhibit 3–1 below illustrates the main differences between Exploit and Explore. To operate effectively and efficiently in either domain, a company must ensure coherence across all dimensions.

For instance, it is neither safe nor efficient to run processes in a chemical production plant with employees who possess a generalist skill set and take leaps of faith. Similarly, new value pools cannot be discovered, and new margins cannot be captured with a recipe for success that relates to a different context and a mindset that avoids any risk.

---

[53] Attributed to Oren Harari.

Dimension	Exploit/NOW	Explore/NEW
In a nutshell	Run and optimize the existing business/operating model	Find new value pools and a new business model
Environment	Known and understood	Unknown or partially known
Organizational home	Core (company org chart, except explorative units)	Explorative units (incubators, accelerators, digital labs, etc.)
Business goal	Safely deliver revenues and margins (ESG compliant)	Create new revenues and margins (ESG compliant)
Modus operandi	Process-driven; risk-averse; short-term focus	Reducing uncertainty; learning-driven; long-term focus
Success metric	Meeting or outperforming revenue and margin goals	Validation scale-worthiness and scale-readiness
Market strategy	Known; extrapolated from NOW to next 1-3 years	Emerging; beachhead and bowling alley hypotheses
Structure	Solid; silos; committees; functional excellence	Adaptive; end-to-end; "single-threaded responsibility"
Culture	Risk-averse; process-driven; change = plan + execute	Experimental; leaps of faith; change = learning
People: Profiles	I-shaped people, fit with culture mentioned above	T-shaped people, fit with culture mentioned above
People: Capabilities	Productivity- and quality-driven; functional experts	Learning-driven; Entrepreneurial individuals
People: Motivation	Perfectionism, functional excellence	Create NEW; "make a dent in the universe"
People: Incentives	"Almost sure" bonus; defined career paths	Financial upside, inspiring work; career paths?

Exhibit 3–1: Differences between Exploit/NOW and Explore/NEW.

Areas of Tension

Chapter 2 explains that success in new-business building requires a productive collaboration between NOW and NEW. However, exhibit 3–1 shows that these two systems are inherently incompatible. The incompatibility manifests in "areas of tension" that hinder productive collaboration. Exhibit 3–2 on the following page displays some of these.

Ambidexterity and Ambidextrous Organizations

These tensions cannot be eliminated because they originate from fundamental differences. However, balancing Exploit and Explore is crucial. Over-investing in Exploit delivers short-term success but ultimately undermines the company's long-term viability. Conversely, over-investing in Explore will disappoint short-term-focused shareholders.

One approach for companies to achieve balance is to separate Exploit and Explore. This concept is known as "ambidexterity[54]." To implement this separation, it is common practice to assign each a distinct organizational home. Exploit people operate within Core's units while Explore people operate in dedicated units, such as innovation centers, incubators, and accelerators that are structurally—and most often also physically—separated from Core's units.

---

[54] See https://journals.sagepub.com/doi/10.2307/41165852.

Area of Tension	Exploit/NOW	Explore/NEW
Business model	Existing, known, detailed	Emerging
Ecosystem	Managed pool of certified partners	"Unusual suspects" such as start-ups and universities
Governance	Top-down; committees; hierarchical structures	Flat and lean; autonomous and aligned teams
Organizational complexity	High complexity; matrix organizations	Low; easy-to-understand
Processes, rules	Rigid processes; hundreds of rules; detailed playbooks	Agile processes; few rules; emerging or best practices
Tech stack	Historic; tightly managed	Cutting-edge; managed via agile approaches
Metrics	Comprehensive set of quantitative, lagging metrics	Focus on qualitative and quantitative, leading metrics
Rewards	"Sure" bonuses, typically small percentage of salary	Wide spectrum, up to 7-dgit bonuses for building unicorns
Brand	Needs to be protected and nourished	Might be useful in some cases but unsuitable in others
Culture	(See above, exhibit 3–1)	(See above, exhibit 3–1)
People	(See above, exhibit 3–1)	(See above, exhibit 3–1)
Leader's viewpoint	"Manager" view on things	"Leader/owner" view

Exhibit 3–2: Areas of Tension between Exploit/NOW and Explore/NEW.

But here is the thing that many companies struggle with: separating Exploit/NOW and Explore/NEW is only one side of the coin. It is necessary, but not sufficient to future-proof the company. This is not just a theoretical statement: global investors see prioritizing out-of-the-box innovation to be crucial, but they also see a wide effectiveness gap[55].

The other side of the coin is that the company must integrate the two systems. Only then, the company has the chance to get the best of both worlds: excellence in its existing business and a high-performance growth engine. The integration issue arises whenever corporate assets and capabilities are required for out-of-the-box innovation, when the company is:

– Deploying new-to-the-company technologies as the backbone of a business process.

– Scaling up corporate startups.

Three Playing Fields[56]

A recent study[57] in 1,600 companies from nine industries found that 80 percent of their growth came from their home industries and the remaining 20 percent from adjacent or new industries. The study also showed that there is a significant difference in out-of-the-box growth. Financial services companies generate 34 percent of their growth outside of their traditional home, while healthcare companies only generate 9 percent.

Looking at industries and their corresponding customer groups is a good starting point for creating a success recipe for out-of-the-box innovation. However, this innovation space also requires considering new-to-the

---

[55] See https://pwc.to/3PAOD0t.
[56] This concept was co-created with Dr. Ralph Christian Ohr, a dual innovation expert.
[57] See https://mck.co/3yOLou0.

company technology and new capabilities. If we add this dimension, we can create a portfolio diagram.

To win in new-business building, the company's innovation space must be segmented into Three Playing Fields, each with its own operating model.

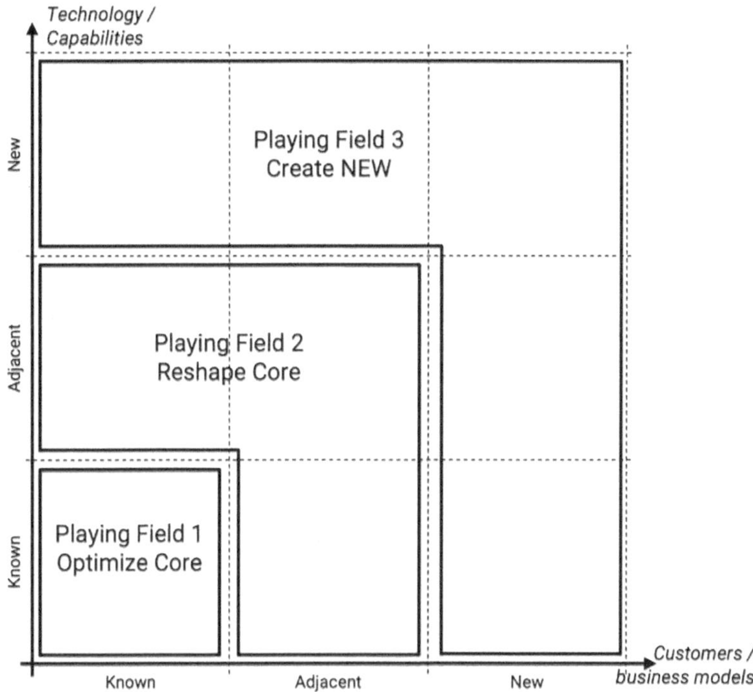

Exhibit 3–3: The Three Playing Fields model.

The portfolio diagram's lower left area represents the day-to-day business and incremental improvements for known customers within a known technology base and an established business model. Beyond this box is the space of out-of-the-box innovation. This space comprises an "adjacent NEW" and a "far-out NEW." The latter involves new, breakthrough technologies and/or new capabilities and distant, new customer groups and/or business models.

Reshape Core, Managing the Transition

Here comes the crucial point. The "adjacent NEW" space is vital for new growth for three reasons. First, corporate explorers may intentionally focus on staying close to the existing technology and customer base. In other words, this area may be the focus for out-of-the-box innovation.

Second, this is the space for "Reshape Core." It involves transforming Core through both "inside-out" initiatives, such as opening new sales channels, and "outside-in" initiatives such as scaling corporate startups that originated in the upper-right sector. Consequently, Scaling-Up of corporate startups competes for Core's functional resources with all initiatives that aim to "Reshape Core."

Third, innovation in the three areas require different approaches to succeed. For the lower-left sector, stringent phase/gate processes with a clearly defined sequence of activities and detailed Return On Investment calculations are required. The upper-right sector requires an agile approach. But in the "adjacent NEW," an effective mix of these is necessary. For these reasons, "Playing Field 2," as I will call the "adjacent NEW" in the next section and the rest of the book, is the most challenging part of out-of-the-box innovation and new-business building.

It is in that space where most out-of-the box innovations fail and corporate scaleups flame out. Success in that space requires additional thinking. As an illustration, exhibit 3–4 below demonstrates how a financial services firm blends the operating models from "Optimize Core" and "Create NEW" in Playing Field 2 when they re-integrate corporate scaleups into one of Core's operative business units.

	Create NEW	→	Playing Field 2	→	Optimize Core
Strategic alignment	Deliver "business in a box" for a Business Unit (BU)	→	Corporate scaleup and receiving BU share some KPIs. At least one KPI is reflected in the quarterly goals of the receiving BU		
Governance	Innovation Board (IB) (until begin of Scaling-Up)	→	IB until sufficient operational readiness. Buy-in from BU mandatory	→	BU Management Board; IB in advisory role until full operational readiness
Budget and funding	Earmarked, ring-fenced Pre-Scaling budget	→	Earmarked and ring-fenced transition budget. Metered funding. Scaling-Up milestones	→	As previous. By absorbing the innovation, BU's OPEX Increase. Needs to be covered!
Technology	Determine non-negotiables and wiggle rooms	→	Assure compliance with BU architecture guidelines and scalability of tech stack. Plan and budget migration to target tech architecture (if relevant)		
Staffing	New-business building team	→	Mixed team, new-business builders + BU	→	BU teams, collaboration with operational mindset
Work style	Lean Scaleup Pre-Scaling (see chapter 6)	→	Lean Scaleup Scaling-Up (see chapter 8)	→	Scaling-Up until BU's business-as-usual KPIs are met

Exhibit 3–4: Example for transitioning Playing Fields 3 → 2 → 1.

Three Playing Fields, Three Managerial Approaches

The previous section makes it clear that if a company wants to win NOW while at the same time creating and scaling NEW, it needs three managerial approaches concurrently:

- Playing Field 1, "Optimize Core:" excellence in business processes and in incremental innovation.

- Playing Field 3, "Create NEW:" agile approaches with a scientific mindset, based on a stringent validation methodology (see chapter 6).

- Playing Field 2, "Reshape Core:" a blend of the above, as for example shown in exhibit 3–4.

Farewell, Three Horizons. Hello, Three Playing Fields

When I introduce the Three Playing Fields model to my clients, they often mention that they already use a "Three Horizon" model. This model divides innovation activities into three buckets[58]:

- Horizon 1, "Now," with a 1-2-year perspective.

- Horizon 2: "Next," with a 3-5-year timebox.

- Horizon 3: "New," with a perspective of more than 5 years.

In my view, **the Three Horizon model is no longer useful in a VUCA business environment**:

- The timeboxes are no longer useful. Technology has advanced to a point where ideas can reach a massive scale much more quickly than in the past. For instance, just two months after its market launch, ChatGPT achieved 100 million users[59].

- The model does not offer guidance on how to operate in near-Core areas. While Horizon 3 might be addressed by augmenting the Lean Startup

---

[58] Three horizons framework – See for example https://mck.co/4aMXNQg
[59] See https://bit.ly/3FARz8V.

(see chapter 2), the model falls short on Playing Field 2. Attempting to build an adjacency with NOW's approach is almost sure to fail because there is more uncertainty than NOW can handle. Similarly, leaving new-business builders without a defined bridge to Core is also a recipe for failure, as described above.

– The Three Horizons model does not address the fact that "Reshape Core" requires a thorough portfolio management, due to the large number of outside-in and inside-out initiatives.

– Since language shapes thinking, the term horizon can lead stakeholders to organize initiatives into static categories, ignoring the transitions, for example when corporate startups are scaled up in Playing Field 2.

For these reasons, I advise my clients to replace their Three Horizons model with a modern Three Playing Fields model. The latter also makes it easier to adapt the innovation portfolio to the macroeconomic business environment. When external conditions are tough, the company may want to focus on Playing Field 2's near adjacencies and when conditions are more positive, the company may want to venture farther away from Core.

Radical Innovation and Disruptive Innovation

A concise language is needed to categorize innovation initiatives with respect to the best organizational setup. I refer to the top-left area of exhibit 3–3 as "radical innovation" and the right edge as "disruptive innovation."

Radical innovation refers to a technology that is always new-to-the-company, and maybe even new-to-the-industry or new-to-the-world. This technology can be a unique selling point of a new product or the backbone of a new business process:

– The touch technology that Apple introduced in its first iPhone in 2007 was a unique selling point for a new product.

– Two examples for the latter are a dairy manufacturer that implements blockchain technology to track and trace milk and other ingredients from its 4,000 farmers, ensuring that its products are organic when the company makes that claim or a farming company that industrializes vertical farming.

Disruptive innovation involves introducing a new business model, which may or may not include radical innovation. For example, when a Med-Tech company wanted to shift from a product-centric to a service-centric business model, the technologies include AI for generating therapy recommendations and low-tech solutions for storing these in the cloud. The AI components of this example are radical innovations, while the low-tech solutions are not.

These distinctions are also beneficial when a company discusses the effective organizational setup. To illustrate, consider an engineering company and refer to exhibit 3–3:

- The left edge of the portfolio diagram can be handled using established engineering processes.

- Moving to the right, for example by adding remote monitoring to products to support a service-centric business model, a significant change in the company's engineering units and development processes are needed.

- Disruptive innovations at the right edge of the portfolio diagram require the company to build the bridge between NOW and NEW and to acquire four learnable skills mentioned in chapters 1 and 5.

Leveraging Corporate Assets and Capabilities

To accelerate and de-risk out-of-the-box innovation, a company must create an "unfair advantage" by **leveraging corporate assets and capabilities.** These include tangible assets such as production facilities and points-of-sale, as well as intangible assets and capabilities. As shown in chapter 2, there are **six categories of intangible assets that are relevant for innovation:**

- Operational and functional capabilities,

- Advanced expertise and know-how,

- Growth-enabling capabilities,

- Privileged assets,

- Technology and IT, and

- Transactional data.

Scaling-Up Pathways, Pathways to Value

There are four different organizational homes for the corporate scaleup during the Scaling-Up phase. I refer to them as **Scaling-Up pathways**:

- Inside an operative business unit.

- Inside the company, but outside of operative business units (for example, in a "New Business" business unit or in a "Scaling-Up function" that sits between the explorative units and operative business units).

- In a separate legal entity, often referred to as "spin out."

- Outsourced to a third-party "corporate venture builder."

After the Scaling-Up phase, the future growth can play out in four organizational homes, which I call **pathways to value**:

- Inside a business unit, i.e., re-integration of the corporate scaleup into Core; this is often referred to as "spin in."

- Inside the company, but outside of the existing business units (for example in a newly founded "Digital Solutions") unit.

- In a separate legal entity, but still governed by the company.

- Outside the company with limited governance, as part of a joint venture or a "project house" in which several companies collaborate to create new end-to-end value chains.

Chapter 4: New-Business Building Case Studies

Chapter 4
New-Business Building Case Studies

Many companies are aware that they need to create NEW while winning the NOW. However, the statistics in chapter 2 indicate that there is a translation problem: high awareness does not guarantee high success rates. Success is not easy to achieve, but it is possible. This chapter presents four in-depth case studies. These case studies are designed to provide insight into the "how to" of out-of-the-box innovation; they are not intended to showcase the impressive achievements of these companies.

The first one examines **Amazon** at a pivotal point in its corporate history. At the time, the company had established a profitable and substantial online retail business. Nonetheless, there were indications that disruption was imminent. The case study illustrates why Amazon made the strategic decision to disrupt its business model and the steps it took to create a new digital media business.

The second case study places **Kodak and Fujifilm** in the spotlight. At the turn of the century, both companies were in the same industry, at the same size, and faced the same disruption challenge. While Kodak was forced to file for bankruptcy, Fujifilm was able to transform itself by building new businesses.

The next case study shows how **PVH**, a global fashion leader, identified new, digital growth spaces and how it created the first successes. The last one is about **Amadeus**, a globally leading technology company that powers the global travel and tourism industry. It tells the story about why and how its business model incubator **Nexwave** upgraded its existing Pre-Scaling approach to the Lean Scaleup.

The chapter concludes with two vignettes from my advisory work, showcasing crucial aspects of new-business building. The content of the case studies and the vignettes is structured in a way that seamlessly transitions into the next chapter, which introduces the Lean Scaleup framework.

Amazon: Building the Digital Business

Amazon is probably the world champion in out-of-the-box innovation and new-business building. Starting with a B2C online retail business model, it has built new businesses—and keeps on building—in various categories, among them:

- Logistics (for example, Amazon Marketplace and Amazon Global Logistics[60]),

- IT Cloud solutions (Amazon Web Services),

- Digital media (for example, Amazon Kindle, Amazon Prime Video),

- Consumer electronics (for instance, Amazon Kindle devices), and

- Health Care (e.g., Amazon One Medical[61] or Amazon PillPack[62]).

The company has a unique approach to creating new businesses. As the case study shows, the Amazon way of innovating is based on four pillars[63]:

- PR/FAQ: Six-page memos that ensure every senior manager is on the same page and supports a particular out-of-the-box initiative. The document establishes alignment between Amazon's senior management and a corporate startup/scaleup.

- Careful selection of the leader of the corporate startup/scaleup. This individual is responsible for driving the innovation initiative and has the authority to define the necessary steps to achieve success. The individual in question reports to a single senior manager whose KPIs include the success of the corporate startup/scaleup.

---

[60] See https://amzn.to/49PuMmu.

[61] See https://bit.ly/3wW7LR9.

[62] See https://www.amazon.com/pillpack.

[63] The case study is organized according to the Lean Scaleup modules (as detailed in the next chapter), rather than the bullet points provided above.

– Single-threaded teams. These are small teams with an end-to-end responsibility and all necessary capabilities for a particular innovation initiative, staffed with members that work full-time on that initiative.

– Funding will be provided contingent upon the demonstration of satisfactory progress.

The case study is set in 2007. At that time, Amazon had been in business for 13 years and was already a dominant player in the online retail industry, with annual revenues of USD 14.8bn. The company had achieved profitability five years earlier and was growing with an annual rate of 38.5 percent. Amazon appeared to have discovered the formula for online retail success.

That same year, Amazon made the bold move to disrupt itself. It created a digital media business that today includes offerings such as Prime Video (video streaming), Amazon Music (music streaming), Kindle (e-books, consumer devices and digital book publishing), and Audible (audiobooks). The company does not publish figures about the size of that business, but three data points provide an idea[64]:

– In 2022, Amazon Music had more than 82 million subscribers with an annual growth rate of 20.7 percent[65].

– Kindle devices account for 72 percent of the e-reader market.

– More than 200 million Amazon Prime subscribers globally have access to Amazon Prime Video.

Background on Amazon in 2007

In 2007, Amazon had already successfully created two new businesses alongside its online retail business:

– Amazon Marketplace, launched in 2000, allowed third parties to sell their products on the company's worldwide websites. In 2007, this was a USD 630m business.

---

[64] See https://bit.ly/3VfuDVa.
[65] See https://musicalpursuits.com/music-streaming.

– Amazon launched Amazon Web Services (AWS) in 2002, enabling customers to access the company's technology infrastructure. In 2007, this corporate scaleup generated USD 60m in revenues. As of early 2024, AWS is a USD 100bn business.

A VUCA Environment for Amazon

In 2007, the digital media industry was still in its infancy. The market for electronic book readers (e-readers) was just beginning to develop. The first e-readers hit the market in 1999, but they were not user-friendly and lacked a wide selection of e-books. Second-wave e-readers such as the Sony Reader were easier to use and allowed consumers to purchase e-books directly from Sony's e-bookstore or from other online stores and libraries.

Outside the book category, the proliferation of digital music signaled that media transitioned from analog to digital. For example, sales of physical music CDs had peaked in 2005[66]. It appeared to be only a matter of time before physical books were replaced by digital downloads.

Major players in the media ecosystem—retailers (Amazon, Walmart and Barnes & Noble, etc.), media giants (Disney, Universal Music, Warner, Random House, etc.) and tech companies (Microsoft, Apple, Google, Netflix, Samsung, etc.)—saw the disruption coming. A few new digital media companies, such as Google's YouTube and Spotify, already booked initial successes, but most incumbent companies experienced failures.

Senior Managers' Skin in the Game

Amazon was facing a pivotal moment in its history. Its established business was growing and profitable, but early signs of a disruption made it clear

---

[66] International Federation of the Photographic Industry.

that this would not last. Before Amazon's senior management embarked on building a digital media business, they aligned on three strategic questions[67].

Build, buy, or partner? Jeff Bezos, Amazon's founder and CEO, was adamant that the company should not rely on other companies for its value proposition in digital media. In his view, the company's long-term success in that space depended on offering a superior customer experience. He argued that buying a digital media platform or partnering with another company would significantly limit Amazon's degrees of freedom in the future.

If the company followed these routes, it would only be able to choose from a menu of options offered by these companies. Much of the knowledge and know-how would accrue outside. Suppliers or partners might further develop the technology and eventually offer an even better e-reader to other companies, especially Amazon's competitors.

At best, Amazon would be a fast follower of what these companies built; at worst, the company would have to patch an end-to-end customer experience, connecting physical products, its own and third-party websites, order management systems, fulfillment centers, and delivery methods. In Jeff Bezos' view, a superior customer experience cannot be outsourced. Consequently, the senior management team decided to take the "build" route.

First-to-market or fast follower? Amazon decided to pursue a first-to-market strategy. A fast-follower strategy may have been easier. But by the time the company deployed a reasonable reply to a competitor's service, that competitor would have already created something better.

What is the beachhead market? Amazon chose books as its initial category in the digital business for four reasons:
– Books were the largest category at Amazon and were strongly associated with the company.

---

[67] Most of the Amazon-internals are taken from Colin Bryar, Bill Carr, Working Backwards, St. Martin's Press, 2015.

- The e-book business was still small and lacked a good customer experience. Amazon anticipated that customers wanted an e-book experience akin to the iTunes/iPod experience[68]: mobile devices paired with software that offered e-books at a low price, enabling consumers to purchase, download, and start reading in seconds.

- The music market had already moved to digital, but Apple had a significant head start in that space.

- The movie video market had not yet gone digital, but there were several barriers to creating a great video experience. These included getting the distribution rights from studios, a long download time, and uncertainty about how customers would watch video on their TVs.

As a result of these strategic discussions, Amazon's senior management decided to prioritize the digital book space and to focus on e-books and e-readers. Much smaller teams were set up to work on digital music and digital video offerings.

Capabilities, People Profiles, A-Teams

Jeff Bezos[69] states that out-of-the-box innovators must start with crafting a superior customer experience and then work backwards to determine which technologies and processes are needed to create and deliver it. After several iterations of the PR/FAQ, Amazon's senior managers realized that only an e-bookstore deeply integrated with a reading device was able to create a superior customer experience.

Since Amazon at that time did not have hardware capabilities, they had to find a way to acquire them. Jeff Bezos remarked that a typical company would ask: "What can we do next with our capabilities?" While this approach may work in some cases, in his view there is a fundamental problem with it: when a company sticks to its existing capabilities, it will never

---

[68] See chapter 2.
[69] And also Steve Jobs, see https://youtu.be/48j493tfO-o.

be driven to master new skills, develop new competencies, hire new kinds of leaders, or create different types of organizations—all of which are necessary to succeed in a rapidly changing business environment.

Once the decision was made for Amazon to become a device manufacturer, Jeff Bezos appointed Steve Kessel as the leader for the new business. In other words, instead of focusing on what product to build, Amazon focused first on who was the right leader to create the new business. When he recruited his team, Steve Kessel paid careful attention to close capability gaps and staff critical interfaces to the ecosystem properly. He recruited from both inside and outside the company, especially from companies that knew how to create hardware and media streaming applications.

One hire was Bill Carr, the co-author of the above-mentioned book "Working Backwards." Before joining the Kindle team, he served as a director in Amazon's U.S. books, music, and video unit. Bill Carr knew the key people from the partners and managed the relationships with them. If he had not been on the team, Amazon would have two different groups responsible for business relationships with the same partners and suppliers.

Another hire was Gregg Zehr, a Silicon Valley veteran who had been a vice president of hardware engineering at Palm Computing and Apple. He set up a separate office in Silicon Valley to tap into the local hardware capability pool. In parallel, a team of Amazon engineers built the back-end systems that should power the Kindle experience and the e-bookstore.

The "Amazon way of innovating" achieves two goals: it aligns NOW and NEW, and it grants the new-business building team a startup-like autonomy within the corporate context. Additionally, "two-pizza teams" are an effective solution to team challenges in scaling up a validated business model innovation concept.

The objective is to ensure that each internal team is small enough to be fed with two pizzas. This way, communication is streamlined, and there is less bureaucracy and overhead, which allows teams to focus on customers and to experiment and innovate quickly and effectively. Smaller teams also help mitigate the Ringelmann Effect[70], a phenomenon where individual productivity decreases as group size grows. With larger teams, there is less focus on individual effort as team members rely more on others to shoulder the load. Conversely, individual effort increases as team size decreases, allowing for greater ownership and empowerment among team members.

Each of Amazon's two-pizza teams is accountable for one end-to-end process and the corresponding internal or external customers. They have the experts they need to design and implement solutions and to innovate the process. All two-pizza teams report to managers who help them to remove obstacles so that they can move quickly and make high-quality decisions at pace. This is in stark contrast to other companies where corporate bureaucracy establishes bloated approval lines before allowing teams to move forward. The role of these managers is usually to guide the team in situations where the path forward may not be clear.

As the process scales up, Amazon rather splits the original two-pizza team than expanding the team. This maintains a flat organizational structure that preserves agility, autonomy, and ownership.

One-Company Mindset

Bill Carr was initially not happy when Steve Kessel asked him to join Amazon's future digital media business. As the director of a unit that generated 77 percent of Amazon's global revenue, he was confident that his career was on an upward trajectory. In contrast, Amazon's digital media business was relatively small, with a team of five people and annual revenues of a few million dollars.

Furthermore, the idea that Amazon should develop its own hardware was met with considerable opposition within the company. Many managers questioned the decision and considered it to be an extremely expensive and risky path. And finally, at a time when resources were scarce across the

---

[70] See https://en.wikipedia.org/wiki/Ringelmann_effect.

company, other teams were envious of the new digital media unit, which was hiring a 150-person team of engineers and product managers.

These symptoms are typical when a company builds a new. Some people might feel being demoted when asked to move from a stable position in one of Core's functions to an uncertain future in a small team that is surrounded by widespread skepticism about its chances for success. And there might even be some envy in Core about a corporate startup that receives an over-proportional part of funding, human resources, and management attention.

Jeff Bezos solved these tensions by communicating relentlessly that there is only one Amazon, providing customers with a superior experience, regardless of their preferences. He argued: "We see a future in which books are digital, and we want to be at the forefront of that revolution[71]." This one-company mindset was supported by two management provisions. Without these arrangements, it would have been difficult, if not impossible, for Jeff Bezos to run NOW and create NEW at the same time:

- A "top-down meets bottom-up" goal-setting process and the PR/FAQ provided him with a quick and comprehensive overview of all major NOW improvement programs.

- To manage these programs at an operational level, he was able to work efficiently with the leaders of the "two-pizza teams" who were responsible for the end-to-end processes specified in the PR/FAQ document.

Structure, Funding, Governance

In 2007, Amazon did not have billions to spend on out-of-the-box innovations. Thus, the challenge was to devise a smart approach that allowed it to move faster than its competitors. To achieve this, the company established a new, separate structure and made sure that NEW got a seat at the C-suite table by implementing a "single-threaded responsibility."

---

[71] See Jeff Bezos' Kindle Fire announcement, The Verge, September 28, 2011.

Jeff Bezos firmly believed that for a new business model to succeed, it had to be structurally separated from Core. Managing NEW as part of the established business would mean it would never receive the necessary management attention. The established business would always take precedence.

Jeff Bezos appointed Steve Kessel to be a "single-threaded leader," giving him responsibility for developing and growing the new business without distraction from other responsibilities. Steve Kessel reported directly to Jeff Bezos and his KPIs were initially tied to progress and, later to commercial success metrics. One of his first progress milestones was to build a management team, each with a single-threaded responsibility for a specific aspect, such as hardware or e-books.

Putting NEW on par with NOW is a powerful concept that can also be seen at Ford Motor Company (see chapter 11). Before Steve Kessel took over the digital media team, the highest-ranking digital manager was four levels below him. In such an environment, building a new business is doomed to fail because the people in charge will not think big enough to create a new customer experience; it will likely be a hodgepodge of the existing business and some aspects of the new business model.

Funding for the new business was provided through a fund that Jeff Bezos controlled. He made it clear that funding was not an issue if there is progress. For example, when it became evident that the project was taking longer and costing more than initially expected, Jeff Bezos was asked how much more money he was willing to invest into the project. He responded calmly by asking the company's CFO: "How much money do we have?"

Fujifilm: New Life after the End of the Business Model

Eastman Kodak Co. (Kodak) is often cited as an example of a company that failed to adapt to technological disruption. As a pioneer in silver-based film photography, Kodak developed the first digital camera in 1975. However, according to the public narrative, the company miscalculated the scale and pace of the transition from analog to digital photography, ultimately leading to its bankruptcy.

The issue with this version of events is that it is wrong. Kodak's senior managers were well aware of the approaching storm. As early as mid-1997, just as digital photography was taking off, they were constantly tracking the rate at which digital media was replacing silver films. However, several factors made it extremely difficult for Kodak to adapt and to shift gears. Refocusing the company with so many forces at work proved impossible.

There is one more story in this context that is told less often, the story of Fujifilm (Fuji). In 2001, when film photography was being replaced by digital, both companies were at eye level:

- Fuji's and Kodak's global market share were 37 and 36 percent, respectively.

- Both companies had a focus on selling film and cameras, a big retail presence, similar business models, and strong manufacturing skills.

- Both companies faced the same challenge.

However, Kodak had to file for bankruptcy, and Fujifilm is now about 20 times the size of Kodak. This case study is about how Fuji thrived and prospered by creating new, substantial businesses while its closest competitor could not adapt to a changing environment and failed.

Kodak: The Burning Platform

Kodak's first challenge was indeed technology. Over the course of a century, the company had developed and refined manufacturing processes for film photography. Manufacturing color film is a highly intricate process. It involves coating 1.2-meter-wide rolls of plastic base material with up to 24 layers of sophisticated chemicals at precise thicknesses while traveling at a speed of 100 meters per minute. The coated rolls need to be continuously changed over, spliced in real-time, cut and packaged—all while working in the dark. The entry barriers into film manufacturing are high, due to the heavy investments and the number of patents and trade secrets involved.

Digital photography at that time was less complex. To excel in digital photography, a company did not need decades of experience or extremely expensive manufacturing equipment. A skilled engineer could purchase all the necessary components and assemble a camera in just a few weeks.

With the shift from analog to digital photography, Kodak suddenly found itself in a market with much lower barriers to entry. The company lacked a "techy" brand, the capabilities, and the scale to compete in this new environment. Despite investing heavily in semiconductor R&D and producing some notable inventions, Kodak failed to create a truly distinctive product or service.

Kodak's second challenge was that it defined itself via markets and products. The company saw itself in the silver-film market. Kodak was aware that the transition to digital would bring significant changes, such as the substitution of mechanical cameras with digital ones, film rolls with memory cards, film chemicals with inks, and photo labs by digital printers. But it failed to see that consumer behavior would shift as well. Digital photos are predominantly viewed on digital screens. Very few of the more than fifty billion photos on Instagram have ever been printed.

Kodak's third challenge was that its previous scale advantage in production became a liability in the new market. Economies of scale drive company growth by reducing unit costs and improving capital efficiency as volumes increase. However, scaling down is difficult. When production runs decrease in size, there comes a point where there is not enough volume to absorb fixed costs.

And finally, Kodak failed because it did not manage to generate a one-company mindset. Kodak's management has faced criticism for allegedly prioritizing silver film over digital efforts. This criticism is only partially true. In the mid-1990s, the company established a new consumer-centric division to capitalize on the digital opportunity. Unconstrained by legacy assets or practices, the new division was expected to build a leading market position in digital photography.

However, thousands of people in the legacy businesses knew that they did not have the right skills for the new business and only a few of them would make the transition. It was also clear to them that their mission was to extract as much profit from the declining business until the lights were switched out.

At the upper management levels, the NOW/NEW organizational challenge was even more pronounced. NOW managers, who had worked at Kodak for decades, felt entitled to be reassigned to NEW. To ease tensions, Kodak's senior management merged the newly created division with its legacy silver-film divisions in 2003, ultimately hampering its digital efforts.

In a final attempt to compensate failing film sales, Kodak invested hundreds of millions of dollars into a printer ink business. But it lost the battle in this business against Hewlett-Packard and filed for bankruptcy in 2012.

The Digital Storm Hits Fujifilm

Like Kodak, Fujifilm (Fuji) saw the writing on the walls[72]. The company, founded in 1934 and headquartered in Tokyo, noticed that the demand for films peaked in the year 2000. But the actual decline was much more rapid than expected. By 2005, the global film market had fallen to 50 percent of its peak and experts predicted that the complete shift to digital would happen in the next ten years.

At its peak, photographic products generated over half of Fuji's profits. Only five years later, the film business barely broke even. Shortly before, Shigetaka Komori was named Fuji's president and CEO and charged with the task of implementing the first restructuring in the company's history.

---

[72] Most Fuji-internals are taken from Shigetaka Komori, Innovating Out of Crisis, Stone Bridge Press, 2015.

The company let go of 5,000 employees, eliminated facilities, and took a charge of USD 1.4bn against fiscal years 2006 and 2007 earnings. At that time, Fuji's core business had practically vanished. Traditional competitors in the film business had already given up[73]. But Shigetaka Komori was confident that he could build a "second foundation" for the company and win the battle against new competitors like Canon, Sony, and Hewlett-Packard.

Structure, Funding, Governance

Historically, Fuji created new markets in a decentralized, organic fashion from within the business units. Decentralized R&D labs researched new applications of existing technologies, and Fuji's Industrial Products Division acted as an incubator until new divisions were formed. As Shigetaka Komori recognized that the silver-film business model approached the end of its life cycle, he set the company for a more aggressive, yet systematic process for discovering and evaluating new opportunities.

He took three steps to set up the structure, funding, and governance to support the transformational ambition. First, focusing of the R&D resources. Shigetaka Komori established a centralized Advanced Research Laboratories (ARL) and an affiliated centralized marketing group. The setup included a formalized coordination between the ARL and decentral R&D units and an institutionalized buy-in from the heads of each product division.

The ARL and the connected centralized marketing group concentrated their efforts on early-stage and novel technologies and received a quarter of Fuji's overall R&D budget. Furthermore, the budget distribution in the remaining decentralized R&D units was modified. Between 2002 and 2006, the R&D budget for the historic silver film business decreased from 30 to 18 percent. In contrast, new strategic businesses received 76 percent of the company's decentralized R&D budget during this period.

---

[73] Konica had merged with Minolta but exited from the film businesses and Polaroid had filed for bankruptcy in 2001.

Additionally, ARL was challenged to develop a new mindset. In the past, the company had a fast-follower strategy. The company's former head of R&D said: "Exploratory research was not our main theme. We observed carefully what other firms did and adopted it quickly. This attitude was deeply ingrained in our people's mindset. Our technical people were talented and sophisticated—but we did not have an exploratory attitude."

Second, Corporate Venture Capital and M&A. Fuji established a "business development fund" to invest in companies that had synergies with existing businesses or technologies. For instance, between 2004 and 2005, the company invested in approximately 30 companies. This fund also served as a means to fund intrapreneurial initiatives by Fuji employees.

Third, reorganization. Before the transformation, Fuji had been more or less a single-business-unit company with a few peripheral divisions. In 2006, it was a highly decentralized organization with 14 business units.

One-Company Mindset

Since assuming the role of CEO, Shigetaka Komori had been working tirelessly to change the corporate mindset, as he believed that the existing one was at odds with his transformation agenda. For instance, even after the establishment of ARL, Fuji's middle management did not demonstrate a strong sense of urgency in identifying new opportunities.

In 2006, he wrote: "With photosensitive material products as our core business, we have become used to a relatively comfortable climate. This complacent attitude is harming our ability to adapt during fierce competition from companies in other industries. It is essential that we distance ourselves from this self-satisfied mindset and have the courage to take on reforms swiftly and forcefully."

Shigetaka Komori dedicated significant time and effort to instilling a sense of urgency for change, ensuring that staff and middle managers understood the vision and took ownership. He gave numerous speeches and held lunch meetings where he engaged in open-ended discussions with small groups of middle managers, focusing on the vision and reorganization. In this context, each of Fuji's top 1,000 employees was tasked with writing a two-page memo identifying the key factors necessary for the company's growth and any potential obstacles to improvement and growth.

In his book, Shigetaka Komori writes: "My biggest challenge is changing the mindset of the employees. Fuji moves away from its historic core—but it is not yet clear what our new core will be. How can I convince the organization to make such major changes when it is not clear exactly where we are headed? How do I get people to be more entrepreneurial? How do I create a sense of urgency when we are still a profitable company?"

Although digital imaging appeared to be a part of Fuji's future, Shigetaka Komori believed that the company's future was not limited to imaging alone. He asked: "If we are not an imaging company, then what are we?" and believed that this was the key question that needed to be answered.

Senior Managers' Skin in the Game

When it became apparent that Fuji would become a new company on a new foundation, Shigetaka Komori and his senior management team asked themselves how they could leverage corporate assets and capabilities to seize new value pools. To answer this headline question, they broke it down to three sub-questions:

- Which applications for new markets build upon our current capabilities and technologies (this relates to the marker 1 in the exhibit below)?

- What are additional applications for adjacent markets that build upon new capabilities and technologies (marker 2)?

- What are meaningful business ideas for us, building on new applications and new markets (marker 3)?

To provide an example, take the first bullet point. Fuji discovered that three of its core technologies could be applied to Life Sciences markets, in particular to Formulation, Targeting, and Delivery (FTD).

Fujifilm carefully selected new growth arenas in Playing Field 3.

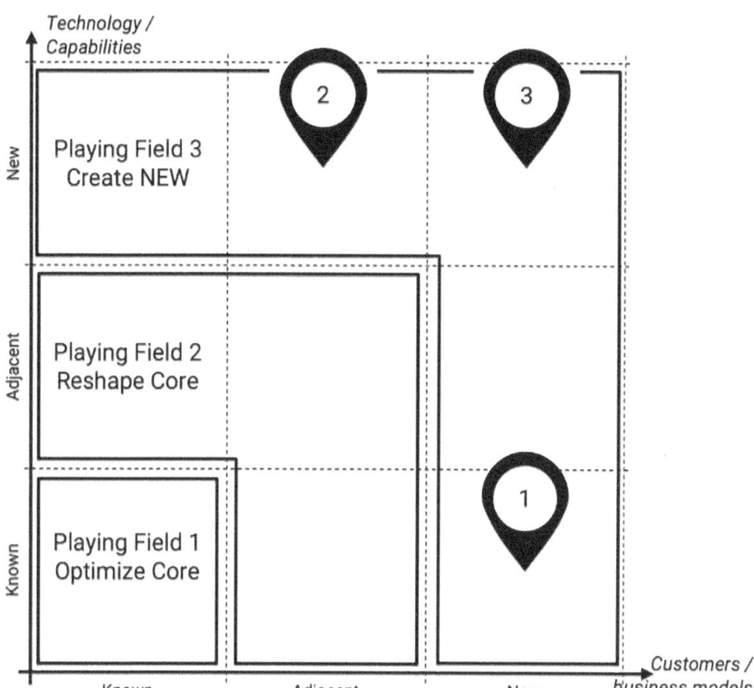

Exhibit 4–1: How Fujifilm defined its search fields for creating new businesses.

The company's expertise in directing chemicals to react in specific locations could be utilized to improve the absorption and penetration of pharmaceutical substances, thereby maximizing the efficacy of functional ingredients. Twenty years after discovering FTD's potential, Fuji's Life Science Solutions business generates roughly USD 800m in annual revenues.

Five years into the corporate transformation, Shigetaka Komori had established the "second foundation" for Fuji. The company was active in four distinct business fields:

– Healthcare (which encompassed medical imaging systems, biologics contract development and manufacturing, and the previously mentioned Life Sciences solutions).

- Materials (which included digital printers, display materials, fine chemicals, and electronic materials).

- Office Solutions, focused on office and production printers.

- Imaging, which encompasses professional and consumer digital photography.

The latter, which was Fuji's core business around the turn of the century, currently generates approximately 13 percent of the company's annual revenues. In other words, 87 percent of Fuji's current business was newly created after the start of the corporate transformation.

Kodak vs. Fujifilm

The success of Fuji and the downfall of Kodak serve as a warning to companies operating in a VUCA environment. In the 1990s, both companies realized that their core business would be disrupted. They invested in the disruptive technology and continued to extract profits from the existing business model. Both companies initially assumed that the decline of the established business model would be a gentle downward slope. So why did Fuji succeed while Kodak failed? In my opinion, there are four important lessons to learn.

First, a company can survive and prosper during disruption by having the courage to cannibalize the existing business, the determination to build a new foundation, the courage to establish the right structure, and a one-company mindset.

Second, there is no easy way from NOW to NEW. Fuji's former CEO commented: "Kodak was so confident about their marketing capability and their brand, that they tried to take the easy way out." He realized that his company needed to develop in-house expertise in the domain of new businesses. In contrast, Kodak believed that with its brand, marketing, and cash flow, it could simply buy its way into new industries. But without the relevant capabilities, Kodak lacked the ability to integrate the companies it had purchased.

Third, a one-company mindset is crucial. Kodak's corporate culture was slow to adapt and lacked a strong, visionary leader to foster a one-company mindset. One of the company's senior managers said[74]: "When product-test magazines considered Fuji's film to be as good as Kodak's, everyone at Kodak agreed it simply was not true. Kodak always believed it had the right to own 100 percent of the market. It never bothered to look over its shoulder at what was coming up from behind."

Fourth, building the capability to create and scale new businesses cannot be outsourced. A company needs expertise in selecting the right growth spaces, domain expertise in these spaces, and expertise in creating and scaling these new businesses, including integration of acquired companies to accelerate transformation.

Xerox: A Closing Remark to the Kodak / Fujifilm Story

In 2018, Fuji acquired a majority stake in Xerox, ending the independence of another iconic American company. Xerox invented game-changing technologies such as laser printing, graphical user interfaces for computers, Ethernet-based computer networks, the computer mouse, and a precursor to PDF, among other things—but it was not able to create new businesses from these out-of-the-box innovations.

PVH

This case study shows how PVH Corp. (PVH), one of the largest global lifestyle companies in the world, fostered a commitment to innovation. It provides insights on how the company accomplished:

---

[74] See https://econ.st/3U0CKVg.

- Establishing governance and aligning NOW and NEW.

- Aligning current and future business strategies.

- Validating an out-of-the-box innovation.

- Cultivating a one team mindset.

- Enhancing internal teams by integrating corporate venture builders.

- Successfully launching new business models.

About PVH

PVH is headquartered in New York City and has a 27,000 staff, generating USD 9.2bn in revenue in 2023. Five key strengths set PVH apart from other apparel companies:

- PVH owns global iconic brands, including Calvin Klein and Tommy Hilfiger. This diverse portfolio allows the company to cater to a wide range of consumers and markets.

- The company is widely recognized for its exceptional ability to create innovative and iconic products. The company consistently delivers innovative materials and products that stay ahead of the latest fashion trends.

- With operations in over 40 countries, PVH has established a global presence. This allows the company to engage with a diverse customer base and capitalize on a broad range of opportunities.

- PVH has a proven track record of delivering consistent revenue and profit growth, establishing itself as a leader in the apparel industry.

- The company is dedicated to driving the fashion industry towards a responsible future, including initiatives to accelerate climate action, advance human rights and champion inclusion and diversity.

About oneUp

PVH partnered with oneUp, an Amsterdam-based business model innovation agency, to accelerate its new-business building goals. oneUp specializes in helping leading companies turn significant disruptions into opportunities, particularly in the tech, culture, and sustainability spaces.

Structure, Funding, Governance

Following the spin-out of two corporate startups (now known as STITCH) in 2021, PVH decided to take its new-business building to the next level. The company wanted to create a steady stream of corporate start-ups that deliver a piece of its growth and diversification strategy, which in turn is aligned with the corporate multi-year strategy[75]:

– Win with product.

– Win with consumer engagement.

– Win in the digitally-led marketplace.

– Develop a demand- and data-driven operating model.

– Drive efficiencies and invest in growth.

PVH's innovation team focuses on exploring consumer-centric opportunities that enhance the desirability of PVH's brands and have the potential to generate new outside-of-Core growth. It sees a systematic, data-driven new-business building process and a startup-like autonomy (see chapter 14) as essential for achieving excellence in new-business building.

Senior management provides financial support to each corporate startup until it has achieved product/market-fit. Once it reaches this stage and the concept is deemed ready for integration or for spin-off, PVH invests further to secure additional resources. This decision is made by senior managers from across the organization, who view themselves more than just gate-keepers. They provide valuable strategic advice and facilitate connections within the organization to support the new-business builders.

---

[75] See https://bit.ly/3wxWVkg.

Senior Managers' Skin in the Game

The company's senior management asked the innovation team to identify promising opportunities through analysis and experiments with the goal to have a few concepts in the Minimum Viable Product stage each year. To align their innovation activities with senior management, the innovation team then conducted an innovation strategy process. This process was organized in five phases and comprised a mixed team of business designers, members of PVH's business development and senior managers.

In the first phase, the team focused on establishing consumer-centric, strategic areas of focus. They looked at the fashion industry, adjacent industries, and technology culture. To identify drivers of change in these areas of focus, the team conducted desk research and consulted with external experts, collecting more than 500 signals of a changing business environment. These signals were grouped into a dozen "drivers of change."

Together with PVH experts, the team then extrapolated the drivers of change five years into the future and created future scenarios that outlined potential innovation areas. Some 20 areas emerged which provided ideas for "where to play." Next, the team assessed the company's "right to win" in each of the potential areas and prioritized the set of innovation areas.

Finally, the team consolidated these results into six value spaces with the highest potential for business model innovations. These included, for example, "the creator economy," "e-commerce experiences," "mixed reality tech," and "digital-first fashion."

The latter was identified as the value space with the highest untapped potential for new business opportunities. The case study below illustrates how the innovation team launched a corporate startup in that space with three key objectives in mind:

– Win a new generation of customers for the brand.

– Create new revenue streams by selling digital products and services.

– Strengthen Core by blending the physical and the virtual world.

Pre-Scaling

PVH's innovation process aims at efficient exploration and validation of innovation theses within the defined value spaces. It builds on the Lean Startup method with additional elements that ensure customer development and Contextuality. It stretches out over five phases:

- Opportunity radar.

- Discovery and ideation.

- Problem/solution-fit.

- Minimum Viable Product.

- Product/market-fit.

Opportunity radar

Within the value space "digital-first-fashion", the team analyzed more than 100 market signals to gain insights into emerging trends and opportunities. Understanding existing and emerging customer needs and preferences had the highest priority in this work.

During the exploration, the team saw the potentials of the "digital twins" concept. In the digital-first-fashion context, the team found indicators that pointed towards a growing interest from consumers in personalized and immersive experiences that seamlessly blend the digital and physical worlds. In particular, consumers asked for solutions that allowed them to have virtual representations of themselves, with fashion being an essential element.

Through the analysis of market trends and active engagement with consumers, the team observed a significant gap between the existing market offerings and the evolving needs and aspirations. This gap presented a compelling innovation opportunity.

The innovation hypothesis was that digital twins had the potential to revolutionize the fashion industry by enabling individual consumers, especially in the gaming space, to have virtual avatars that accurately reflected their unique identities and allowed for creative expression.

Discovery and ideation

In the second stage of the innovation journey, identifying the initial paying consumer is crucial. The team had initially assumed that these could be found in two segments:

- "Fashionistas." Consumers who spend significant money on the latest fashion trends.

- "Sneakerheads." People who have a high interest in collecting sneakers, in particular, limited-edition models.

However, results from validation experiments revealed that these two consumer segments are much more interested in showing their purchases in real life and did not have a high motivation to buy virtual fashion. But during the research, the team identified a segment that was excited about digital twins. For serious online gamers, personalizing their online avatar and connecting it to their real-life self is an innovation opportunity, as these statements show:

- "I look at the style of skin, the color, how things fit with each other. It must be a complete package."

- "There are certain things you can do with accessories."

- "Every time I unlock a new level, I will update my appearance."

The team discovered via proprietary research that 42 percent of online gamers style their avatars with their preferred brands, and 30 percent regularly spend on updating their avatars. Consequently, the Total Addressable Market (see chapter 6) is in the tens of billions of dollars range.

Problem/solution-fit

In the third stage, the team outlines a compelling solution to the needs of the identified customer segment and identifies the right partners to create and deliver the solution. For the former, the team collaborated with selected online gamers and co-created a concept with four cornerstones:

- Drops: Limited-edition branded items.

- Own your style: Wear it in multiple virtual worlds.

- Digital self-expression: Style your avatar with unique items.

- From screen to street: Get matching physical items to own your style also in real life.

To test the blending of the virtual and the physical world, which was a crucial piece of the innovation hypothesis, the team conducted a so-called "smoke test." They placed an online ad using Tommy Hilfiger's social media presence that directed visitors to a landing page where they could sign up for early access.

The goal of this experiment was to test the target audience's appetite for the value proposition of "apparel for parallel worlds:" how interested were they in wearing Tommy Jeans outfits in virtual worlds and in real life? The team established success criteria based on industry benchmarks to assess the customer desirability. The results exceeded expectations:

- The total number of signups was twice as high as expected.

- The cost per lead was three times lower.

- The click-through rate was 22 percent higher than the benchmark.

- 68 percent joined the Tommy Parallel co-creation community, giving the team a valuable audience to engage with.

To find the right partner to create an MVP in the next stage, the team selected a company that offers a platform for creating avatars in virtual and augmented-reality-applications. This platform provides a fast and easy way to integrate avatars into applications without requiring users to create custom avatars for each application. Consequently, the team could reduce development time and costs, drive user engagement and immersion in virtual environments and test the product in a wide range of environments.

Minimum Viable Product

In this stage, it is crucial for the team to have a profound understanding of the features that satisfy the needs of both the customers and the company. This will guide the team in determining what product to build. PVH considers an MVP a learning tool, as discussed in chapters 6 and 19. To support learning, the team developed a consumer website with two primary learning objectives:

- Gather insights into consumer preferences and behaviors.

- Explore the feasibility of back-end integrations with existing systems such as how existing 3D-designs of clothing could be transformed into avatar outfits.

The website allowed consumers to select a virtual Tommy Jeans outfit for their online avatars with matching physical items for the real world. The team tested consumers' willingness-to-pay by displaying different price points and conducted online surveys and interviews to gain qualitative feedback on the customer journey. Again, the experiment results were higher than the defined success criteria:

- The conversion rate of digital outfits was 41 percent.

- The overall conversion rate for physical items was on par.

- 23 percent of the consumers in the co-creation community bought physical garments, and many of these had not bought Tommy Hilfiger apparel before.

In addition to testing the MVP, the team also searched for suitable external partners to add value to the proposition and develop the product-market/fit-pilot. They also began connecting with internal stakeholders to align with Core's functions and processes with the corporate startup to ensure rapid progress in the next phase.

Product/Market-Fit

This next phase presented technical challenges of a much greater magnitude. As the MVP was a prototype without a checkout and payment flow, the team was now tasked with creating an end-to-end solution which should support the entire customer journey. It should be integrated into PVH's back-end platform for processing payments and fulfilling orders for virtual and for physical clothing.

The team designed and developed the back-end in a way that would allow for a rapid adaptation to a potential change in the front-end, depending on the outcome of the product/market-fit pilot launch. Doing so allowed the team to minimize time-to-market for future innovations while still utilizing the existing Tommy Parallel website and community.

To achieve this goal, a higher level of integration with PVH's Core had to be arranged. As a result, the stakeholder group was expanded to include branding, marketing, social media, product design, legal, finance, tax, procurement, 3D product development, and front-end/back-end development. For onboarding and engaging the extended stakeholder group, the team used an internal "innovation sandbox" which was designed to:

- Bypass business-as-usual processes when running experiments.

- Generate the ambition to build NEW at pace and at scale.

- Foster cross-organizational collaboration.

- Establishing a collaborative team spirit.

- Create soft incentives like reputation and being associated with the "Next Big Thing."

- Set up a network of functional tags in Core's functions and processes.

The team who worked on new business ventures successfully launched the Tommy Parallel product-market/fit pilot in mid-2023. It remained live for two months and would later be evaluated to determine its future shape.

One-Company Mindset

All the elements described above are necessary factors for succeeding in creating new businesses:

- Align the innovation search fields with senior management.

- Set up an innovation team in the right distance from Core.

- Empower corporate startups as they create and validate concepts along a well-defined and efficient process.

- Engage the company at the right point in time and in the right way.

However, the story of how PVH builds new business models would not be complete without an element that is deeply rooted in the company's culture: one team, with one vision and one approach that comprises NOW and NEW has allowed the company to position itself as a leader in the innovation space.

To secure further support for bringing new ventures to market, the innovation team has built a network of "special internal and external points of contact" (the "functional tags" mentioned in chapter 14) who support with their functional expertise and keep functional stakeholders in the loop.

The speed at which the team could build these relationships and the willingness of other teams to support is a testament to PVH's entrepreneurial and collaborative company culture. It also provides a prime example for an innovation identity that spans across NOW and NEW and helps to future-proof the company.

About the Co-authors

Valon Kaba serves as Director at PVH Europe, overseeing a team of Business Designers and Venture Builders in the creation of new cutting-edge business models. In this role, he guides PVH in adapting to changes in technology and consumer trends, while he also identifies opportunities that the company should seize with ventures such as Tommy Parallel.

Prior to joining PVH, Valon worked as a strategy consultant. He consulted Fortune 500 companies on launching new products and services in existing and emerging markets and driving transformations. His LinkedIn profile is at https://www.linkedin.com/in/valonkaba/.

Lisa Te Velde serves as the Lead Venture Builder at PVH Europe and is passionate about driving innovation and growth. Lisa has a strong background in entrepreneurship and service design, which she leverages creating and scaling ventures based on research and evidence. Lisa is a strategic thinker, adept at identifying emerging trends and validating innovative business models.

Her leadership skills, coupled with a track record of transforming ideas into thriving businesses played a vital role in the development and launch of Tommy Parallel. You can reach out to her on LinkedIn at https://www.linkedin.com/in/lisa-te-velde-35b720a8/.

Amadeus Nexwave

Amadeus is a technology company that powers the global travel and tourism industry. Headquartered in Madrid and listed on the Spanish stock exchange, the company employs over 18,000 people globally and generates EUR 5.4bn in revenue by serving travel players in more than 190 countries. For instance:

- Amadeus supports over 400 airlines, boarding more than 1.5 billion passengers annually.

- Over 180 airports rely on the company's technology solutions for their operations.

- Amadeus' global distribution system enables travel agencies to access more than 1 million hotel properties and to conduct over 450 million bookings annually.

- In addition, the company offers solutions for tour operators, cruise lines, mobility providers, insurance groups, destination marketing organizations, rail operators, ground handlers, metasearch companies, and corporate travel departments.

Amadeus offers its technology solutions in B2B and B2B2C business models. The company operates in a heavily regulated industry. Consequently, the company's operating model includes working with multiple regulatory stakeholders and the entire travel and tourism ecosystem.

Innovation at Amadeus

Innovation at Amadeus has a variety of organizational homes, depending on the Playing Field (see chapter 3) they relate to.

First, Amadeus' business units drive incremental innovation and adjacencies. Take Air Distribution and the New Distribution Capability as an example. This XML-based data transmission standard helps airlines to tailor their offers more efficiently and to improve their selling activities, while travelers benefit from an enhanced shopping experience.

Startup co-innovation takes place within Amadeus Ventures and Amadeus' Startup Universe. The former is the corporate venture capital program, which invests in early-stage startups with the dual objective of identifying strategic value and generating financial returns. The latter is a platform that connects startups and scaleups with travel industry experts, facilitating collaboration and driving innovation in the industry through field testing.

Third, Amadeus practices open innovation with strategic partnerships, including Microsoft and many other global leader companies in the industry. The Amadeus4Developers program offers developers a self-service portal that provides access to the company's extensive travel content, enabling them to create new apps and build travel solutions.

Amadeus also powers innovation internally with Amadeus Lift, a bottom-up initiative that encourages employees to submit new ideas for incubation. And finally, there is the business incubator Amadeus Nexwave which will be the focus of this case study.

Amadeus Nexwave Business Incubator

Amadeus Nexwave's mission is to identify, incubate and grow new businesses that create better customer experiences for the travelers. Its roots trace back to 2019 when Amadeus recognized that its innovation efforts were predominantly B2B-focused, and decided to build a unit that puts travelers and their needs into the center of business model exploration and incubation. Since then, Amadeus Nexwave's corporate startups launched three products into the market:

– Amadeus Hey!, a comprehensive solution that enables travel providers to create better traveler experiences and increase customer lifetime value and loyalty. The technology behind Amadeus Hey! also powers Check-MyTrip, a B2C solution for travelers, which is used as a traveler lab (innovation sandbox) today.

– Amadeus Discover, a B2B platform that aggregates and distributes over 500,000 destination experiences such as theme parks, restaurants, and guided tours.

– Amadeus Travel Ready is a solution that supports airlines and passengers in an automated and digitized way at various checkpoints throughout the travel journey. It helps travelers to better manage the notification, collection, and verification of required travel documents.

Amadeus Nexwave currently has a staff of more than 100 employees and is a part of the corporate strategy unit. The Nexwave Incubation Office monitors and guides the strategy and operations of the corporate startups. Its responsibilities include portfolio management, governance, investment decisions, and marketing. Steve Kopp, one of the co-authors of this case study, leads the Nexwave Incubation Office.

The Story in Chronological Order

This is a case study about a business incubator that achieved best-in-class status. The authors ("we") describe how Amadeus Nexwave transitioned from a Lean Startup approach to the Lean Scaleup in four steps:

– Amadeus Nexwave sought an outside-in perspective on which of its corporate startups were scale-ready.

– We defined the next steps for each corporate startup on their way towards Scaling-Up.

– At that time, Amadeus Nexwave's validation approach was based on Lean Startup principles. Our discussions around scale-readiness showed why such an approach is not effective in a corporate context[76]. Consequently, we upgraded the Pre-Scaling from the Lean Startup to the Lean Scaleup.

– Jointly, we developed a customized business-building toolbox[77] to ensure consistency and quality when applying Lean Scaleup to corporate startups.

Amadeus' Business Graduation Scheme

Amadeus has an end-to-end business graduation scheme to categorize its business portfolio by size and maturity of the corresponding management systems. This scheme ranges from emerging business opportunities to mature and well-established businesses with modest growth rates and a fully industrialized management system.

Amadeus Nexwave is focused on emerging business opportunities. During the Pre-Scaling phase[78], new business opportunities are built on the Lean Scaleup framework and could be considered corporate startups in the terminology of this book; once they transition to the Scaling-Up[79] phase, they could be considered corporate scaleups. The scope of the business incubator covers the journey of corporate startups/scaleups from meaningful ideas via validation and scaling to initial revenues and industrializing their management system. Successful corporate scaleups with suitable revenues and an industrialized management system could be re-integrated into Core or merged into Joint Ventures.

---

[76] See chapters 2 and 6 for more detail.
[77] See below and chapter 9.
[78] See chapters 5 and 6.
[79] See chapter 9.

Changes in the Foundation

The first topic we tackled was language. Corporate startups should speak the same language as NOW. We replaced innovation jargon with clear, concise business language to facilitate communication and to foster engagement and adoption. Maturity stages in Pre-Scaling are no longer expressed in innovation jargon such as "problem/solution-fit" or "product/market-fit;" we use the terms Discovery, Business Foundation, Business Strategy, and Business Design[80].

Pre-Scaling: From Search Field to "Meaningful Idea"

Amadeus Nexwave has a number of standing search fields that relate to its traveler-centric mission and the long-term strategic growth priorities of the company. Within a defined search field, Amadeus Nexwave analyzes trends and generates ideas through internal ideation sessions and discussions with ecosystem partners. Simultaneously, Amadeus' units can propose ideas that are aligned to their growth strategy to be further explored or incubated. Corporate explorers then conduct a rapid "reality check"—a quick and focused initial validation.

The outcome of this process is a two-page document which summarizes initial validation data points and provides a substantiated view on the crucial dimensions of the meaningful idea. It allows for comparison of different ideas and supports the decision of whether a particular idea should be advanced to the Business Foundation stage. The document includes:

- The target customers.

- The problem statement, indicating which high-priority/high-value problem should be solved for these target customers.

- A rapid market analysis with indications about the market size and the competitive landscape.

---

[80] See chapter 6.

- An outline of the envisioned solution.

- Key unknowns and the critical next validations.

Pre-Scaling: Scale-readiness

Before upgrading to the Lean Scaleup, Amadeus Nexwave's corporate startups faced several challenges that often arise when companies apply the Lean Startup in a corporate context:

- The teams were familiar with all relevant canvases and thinking tools and utilized them, ran many experiments, and so on. However, they struggled in providing concise answers about the progress of their business-building mission.

- Amadeus Nexwave had not considered how corporate startups should connect and work with Core, particularly once they were getting closer to Scaling-Up.

- Decisive aspects such as the ecosystem preparedness were not addressed.

- For admission to Scaling-Up, the governance board required the corporate startups to achieve specific results, such as first revenues or a certain number of paying customers. However, Amadeus Nexwave struggled to translate these lagging indicators into deliverables that the corporate startups had to achieve.

To identify which corporate startups were scale-ready, we retrofitted the Lean Scaleup validation methodology described in chapter 6. We then visualized our findings in a bar chart showing the comparative maturity of the corporate startups, as shown in exhibit 4–2 below.

Using the Lean Scaleup's 4x4 validation grid, Amadeus Nexwave assessed scale-readiness for some of its corporate startups.

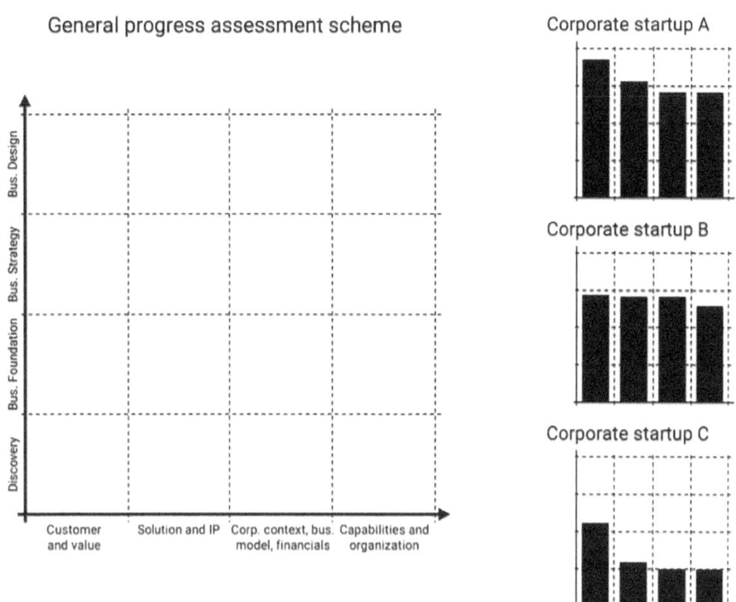

Exhibit 4–2: Assessing scale-readiness for corporate startups.

Using these insights, the recommendation for the governance board was as follows:

– Corporate startup A should be scaled up immediately. Scaling-Up should be done within one of Amadeus' business areas to compensate for a few missing pieces in the corporate context and to accelerate the journey.

– Transitioning corporate startup B to Scaling-Up required a leap of faith in a defined area. The governance board decided that the team could advance to the next stage upon providing proof points that de-risked this critical area. This was the first time Amadeus Nexwave took a leap of faith, moving away from the rigid way of dealing with deliverables expressed in lagging indicators.

Five pieces of work for a corporate startup that is close to Scaling-Up, but has one leap of faith.

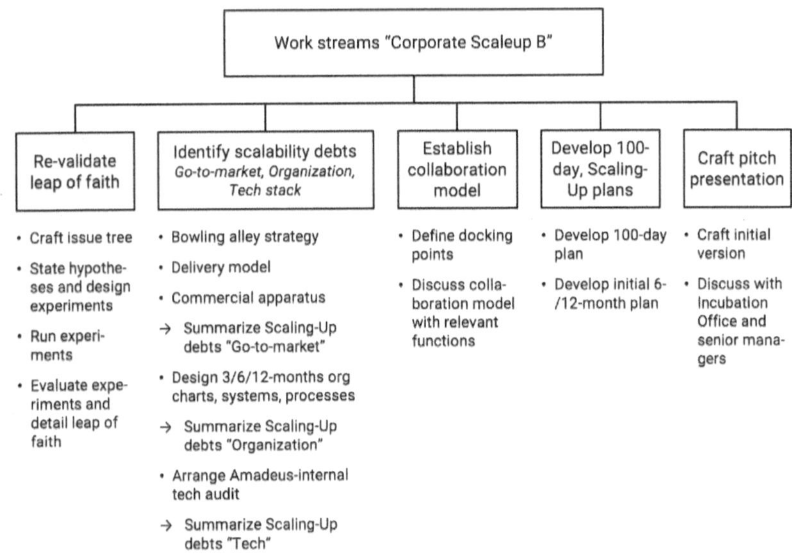

Exhibit 4–3: Preparing "Transitioning to Scaling-Up" with one leap of faith.

– Corporate startup C had not yet achieved a sufficient level of scale-worthiness and scale-readiness.

Pre-Scaling: Progress Monitoring

A typical challenge for corporate startups is to pinpoint where they are in creating a new business and communicating the status to their stakeholders in a language that they can understand. We addressed this challenge with a two-pronged approach:

– We broke down the validation, associated deliverables, and management thinking tools into 2-4-weeks sprints so that corporate startups and the Nexwave Incubation Office had a transparent game plan.

- We implemented a management process that generated a monthly progress scorecard for each team.

For the former part, we organized the deliverables for each Pre-Scaling stage in a logical sequence and defined the corresponding thinking tools that corporate startups must use. We decided to make this mandatory to ensure efficiency and quality in the management process. If each team were allowed to progress in their own way, the Nexwave Incubation Office would have to spend significant time to understand each team's thought process and to check if crucial parts were left unaddressed.

A second benefit is that corporate startups and the Nexwave Incubation Office can agree in advance on the agenda topics for upcoming meetings.

We call this outline "leading by questions" because it helps teams to identify questions they should work on in their current and the upcoming sprints. For the latter part, we implemented a management process with monthly meetings with the corporate startups and quarterly meetings with the governance board. Those monthly meetings help to align and discuss ongoing activities:

- Which are the relevant questions for this sprint?

- What are the most critical assumptions?

- Which experiments could reduce uncertainty?

- Based on experiment results: Should we progress, patch, or pivot?

- Where does the team need support?

- On a monthly basis, the Nexwave Incubation Office checks the status of the required deliverables and assigns traffic lights in a validation progress scorecard which are the primary communication document for the governance board, as illustrated in exhibit 4–4.

Amadeus Nexwave's Incubation Office creates a monthly progress update for every corporate startup, using required deliverables per business graduation stage.

Example: Business Strategy stage

Deliverable	Status	Already validated	Open validations
Validated customer and customer problem	●	• ... • ...	• ... • ...
Validated good market	◑	• ... • ...	• ... • ...
MVP co-created with and appreciated by customers	●	• ... • ...	• ... • ...
Corporate context established	◑	• ... • ...	• ... • ...
Economic Analysis, v2	◑	• ... • ...	• ... • ...
"Content" KPIs and traction metrics	◑	• ... • ...	• ... • ...
Validated capabilities acquisition (plan)	○	• ... • ...	• ... • ...
Validation plan for subsequent Business Design stage	○	• ... • ...	• ... • ...

Exhibit 4–4: Amadeus Nexwave's Pre-Scaling scorecard (Business Strategy stage).

Structure, Funding, Governance

Many business incubators struggle in aligning funding for individual corporate startups with the annual corporate budgeting cycles. An efficient bottom-up/top-down approach can be implemented when the provisions described above are in place. For the bottom-up part, Amadeus Nexwave's business graduation scheme provides the basis.

In Pre-Scaling, corporate startups receive metered funding tied to their maturity stage. This helps to determine how much funding an individual corporate startup needs in its current stage and in the near-term future. The sprint planning scheme and progress monitoring scorecard provide a good estimate of when the startup will reach its next milestone.

With the Lean Scaleup Pre-Scaling provisions, Amadeus Nexwave has an efficient and effective mechanism to determine funding needs.

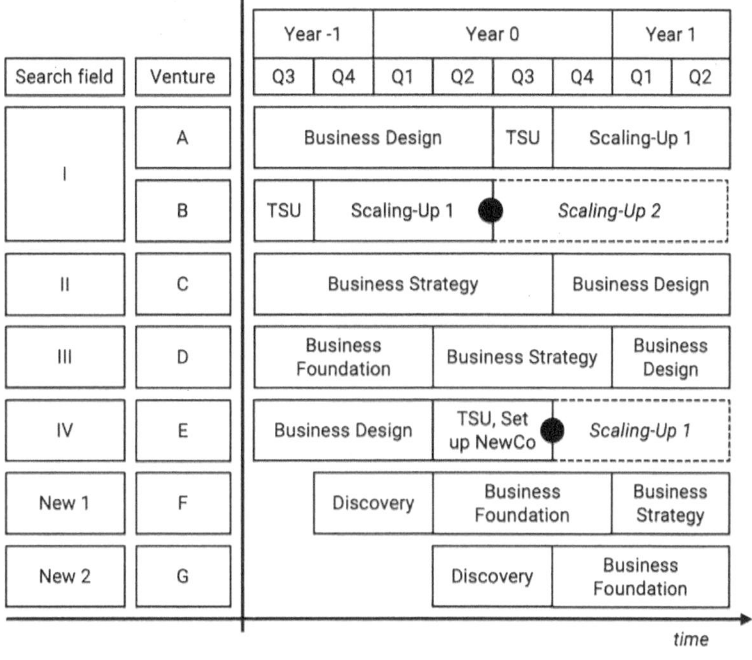

Exhibit 4–5: Amadeus Nexwave's bottom-up budgeting mechanism.

Corporate scaleups, however, require individual funding plans. Additionally, the Nexwave Incubation Office tracks when they transition out of business incubator as they will no longer receive funding. Amadeus Nexwave has come up with a formula to ensure that the transfer of corporate scaleups to business units does not negatively impact their EBITDA.

By adding up the individual budgets, the bottom-up budget requirement can be determined. This budget is then discussed with the governance board and stakeholders. The decided budget is then broken down to the individual corporate startups. In corporate setups, the approved budget is usually smaller than the total bottom-up funding request.

Amadeus Nexwave's policy is to be transparent and use actual figures, rather than inflating budget request so that the agreed budget fits the original estimate.

Governance is also a key element in the decision-making process for corporate startups, as seen in this case study. From the outset, Amadeus Nexwave knew the importance of having senior representatives from different business units being part of the decision-making group, the so-called Executive Incubation Board (EIB). That way, the business incubator and its startups are tightly connected to the company's strategy.

Over time, Amadeus Nexwave has evolved its governance to find the best setup for its decision-making needs. The most recent evolution was to level up and reduce the number of EIB members from 10 senior leaders from across the business units to four members of the Executive Committee. The EIB is supported by four members from the business units who oversee the startups on a more operational basis and by sponsors with vested interest.

This lean but high-ranked governance board allows the unit to be more aligned with the strategies of the business units. The key accountabilities of the current Executive Incubation Board are:

- Take start/stop/continue/transfer-decisions for individual corporate startups.

- Allocate budget and endorse investments.

- Review the performance of the portfolio of emerging business opportunities.

Business-Building Toolbox

During the implementation of the provisions mentioned above, we realized that Amadeus Nexwave could benefit from a knowledge hub to achieve excellence in new business development. This hub needed to solve four challenges:

- Establish a common language for internal stakeholders, the corporate startups/scaleups, and Amadeus Nexwave.

- Drive "Diligent Entrepreneurship." We found that in the past, teams often confused thinking tools with the thinking process. We wanted the teams to sweat over the questions that they were supposed to solve in each stage and have the right tools to answer them.

- Serve as a repository for best practices and progress monitoring reports. Corporate startups appreciate being able to see real-life examples from their environment and understand what "good looks like."

- Store all progress scorecards to maintain full transparency on the journey of each corporate startup and to refer back to individual cases for improving assessments and estimates.

To get up and running quickly, we implemented the new-business building toolbox on a software-as-a-service solution. Amadeus Nexwave found that such a knowledge hub is quite unique in the travel and tourism industry and an excellent way to demonstrate thought leadership when it co-innovates with external startups or with other incumbent companies.

Conclusion

As a conclusion, the below table summarizes all the changes that helped Amadeus Nexwave implement a best-in-class incubation approach:

Change	What it means in practice
Language	Avoiding innovation jargon and using business language to facilitate communication with Core.
Docking to Core	Adding Contextuality to the end-to-end process to leverage the relationship with Core.
Progress monitoring	Monthly scorecards that pinpoint a corporate startup's position in the Pre-Scaling part of the business graduation scheme.
Business-building toolbox	Knowledge hub to ensure diligent entrepreneurship, including the set of questions, deliverables and thinking tools that corporate startups need to answer.
Leaps of faith	From a rigid way to deal with deliverables to a more entrepreneurial approach.
Governance	Level up the governance body to the highest representatives of the organization, being supported by core members in more operational decisions.

Exhibit 4–6: Changes in Amadeus Nexwave's new-business building foundation.

About the Co-author

Steve Kopp is a visionary, result-oriented senior leader with over 25 years of experience in designing and building new digital solutions and businesses. He is an innovation and business expert in the travel and IT industries.

Steve has a key role in Amadeus Nexwave, the business incubator unit, as the head of the Incubation Office and Chairman of the Amadeus Executive Incubation Board. He is responsible for incubating new businesses, from ideation to scaling up. He leads cross-functional teams in portfolio management, business-building methodology, governance, marketing, and communications.

Prior to joining Amadeus, Steve held various design and innovation-related roles at SAP and Business Objects, where he had the opportunity to lead a multidisciplinary team, developed his analytical capacity, knowledge in IT, and mastery of user experience and product design.

Steve holds a master's degree in art history, and at the time he also explored his entrepreneurial skills by launching two startups in the publishing industry.

Vignettes from My Advisory Work

Scaling-Up

Without success in Scaling-Up, there is no business and hence, no "Return On Innovation," only "innovation theater" and "happy engineering." The previous case studies have not outlined this crucial, last part of the end-to-end journey to build a new business that ranges from a "meaningful search field" to a scaled-up business. This vignette describes **the methodology behind Scaling-Up**. It shows the example of a corporate venture, i.e., a greenfield startup that received a significant investment from a corporate.

The history of the corporate venture (CV) dates back to 2007, when three PhD graduates met while writing their PhD theses. They realized the potential of machine learning to tackle some of the shipping industry's major challenges such as fuel consumption. For instance, it is a known fact that when a ship's hull has accumulated marine growth, a vessel consumes up to 20 percent more fuel.

An AI-powered solution could assist in predicting the "fouling state" of a vessel's hull and suggest the optimal timing for cleaning activities. After several years of intense development and testing, CV's core machine learning technology matured. The company launched its first product in 2011 and quickly signed its first paying customer. Three years later, the corporate bought a majority stake with the intention of accelerating CV's growth. However, four years after the investment, the investor had not seen its ambitions fulfilled.

I was brought in to collect unbiased data about CV's position on the innovation end-to-end process and help to set it up for Scaling-Up success. While we found that CV was scale-worthy, there were loose ends in the scale-readiness.

For instance, we could not validate CV's growth strategy. Often, as in this case, transitions from one market segment to another are full of implicit assumptions and not properly validated. Additionally, the team lost its product strategy by responding to too many product requests. As a result, the product roadmap did not align with the market growth strategy and consequently, CV lost its product/market-fit and entered into turbulent operations that prevented successful scaling.

These and few more were important observations but not a reason to terminate the investment. They simply added up to the "operational and technical debt" which needed to be addressed.

On the market side of Scaling-Up, CV had to determine the sequence of market segments. As is often the case, this proved to be a significant challenge. To solve it, we used factors like:

- Proximity of customer segments.

- The ability to leverage available platform features.

- The availability of professional services.

- Sales-related aspects, such as the length of the sales cycle and the achievable price points.

On the product side of Scaling-Up, the most challenging task was to come up with a roadmap that supported the market ambitions. We found that CV had neglected two highly relevant aspects for Scaling-Up success: retaining and growing existing customers and winning mainstream customers in its initial market segments.

We conducted in-depth innovation interviews with existing customers and leads in advanced stages of the sales funnel to better understand what needed to be done. One group of interviewees expressed that they were less interested in sophisticated machine learning algorithms; they were more interested in clear and easy-to-understand decision support. Another group requested support with onboarding and rolling out the solution to capture its full value.

Consequently, the development team prioritized back-end reporting and decision support. Additionally, a service organization was added to the Scaling-Up setup.

Performance and Portfolio Management

F. Scott Fitzgerald once said: "The test of a first-rate intelligence is the ability to hold two opposed ideas at the same time and still retain the ability to function." While he likely did not have the C-suite of large companies in mind, his statement certainly applies to them. The two opposed ideas are "Exploit" and "Explore" (see chapter 3).

The previous case studies did not address the integration of the different goal systems of NOW and NEW into one overarching system. This vignette presents a real case from a leading logistics company.

The corporate startup (CS) originated from the company's innovation center and was spun out to scale externally. However, after two years of limited traction, CS's governance board decided to refocus in order to drive results. As a result, CS was rebranded and repurposed to serve a new customer group that Core had little presence in.

To accelerate progress, CS was granted access to corporate assets, including the corporate's back-end IT systems and global presence. In this process, CS' leadership negotiated two freedoms. CS was:

– Not obliged to use corporate assets if doing so negatively affected customers or CS's value proposition.

– Allowed to create its own performance management system, if this could be integrated into an overarching system.

To illustrate the second point, consider sales performance as an example. When CS developed a scalable go-to-market approach, it became clear that winning the target group required two things: expertise in online marketing and salespersons who could establish trust with customers. This was because CS's service was crucial to their value proposition and cost position.

However, CS's leadership discovered that the salespersons they needed were quite distinct from those in Core. Core's salespersons were "farmers" who nurtured relationships with existing customers, while CS required "hunters" to acquire new customers. Consequently, CS created new sales roles and a separate sales organization. To accelerate learning and progress, the sales organization was integrated closely with marketing.

At the same time, CS's leadership team understood that sharing the corporate customer relationship management system would be an invaluable growth enabler. Hence, CS worked with the heads of Core's sales functions to set up a process in which corporate salespersons could enter potential customers as leads in the system. To ensure that this process served both performance management systems, CS incentivized corporate salespeople only for a limited time, so that these were not tempted to get into the "farming mode" they were used to.

From a structural standpoint, CS's national salespeople reported to the local corporate organizations, and the revenue they generated was credited to those local organizations. CS's leadership invested heavily in their engagement and development to foster a sense of connection to the company. These provisions created a success. At the time of the strategic refocus, CS had 50 customers. Over the next four years, the startup expanded to 10,000 customers and the number of shipments grew fortyfold.

CS's CEO was wise enough to anticipate that the company's growth also meant that it would become more visible to NOW's senior management, and as a result, CS would need to align more components of its performance management system, not just sales performance, with Core. This had two practical implications:

– A North Star metric was defined that was relevant to both CS and NOW. CS' leadership team learned to be fluent in both corporate and startup KPIs. They spoke in corporate language in Core, and translated decisions into startup OKRs when they were back in CS.

– CS adapted its recruiting policy by focusing more on individuals who could navigate and facilitate deeper alignment with Core.

Chapter 5:
The Lean Scaleup Framework

Chapter 5
The Lean Scaleup Framework

Key Points in This Chapter

1. To increase the chances to succeed in out-of-the-box innovation and in new-business building, the NOW/NEW system problem must be solved. A system solution is necessary to solve that system problem.

2. The Lean Scaleup represents such a system solution. It is designed to "Reshape Core" by building adjacencies to the existing business. The framework has been co-created by leading companies and business schools and brings six fresh, big ideas.

3. The system solution is comprised of two parts: a bridge that connects NOW and NEW and four learnable skills. The bridge consists of three pillars that relate to leadership, methodology and people/culture. Each building block has four modules. In other words, the framework consist of 12 modules.

4. Collectively, these modules make up the "corporate infrastructure." Every role in out-of-the-box innovation and new-business building requires only a subset of these modules.

5. These modules are outlined in this chapter and shown in more detail in chapters 6-17.

**

29 out of 30 corporate startups fail to establish a business with USD 50m or more in annual revenues. Concepts may be cool, but new businesses pay the bills. To create and scale those new businesses, the NOW/NEW system problem[81] must be solved. The Lean Scaleup offers a solution. It is specifically designed to support the creation of new growth in spaces that

---

[81] See chapters 2 and 3.

are adjacent to NOW because in those spaces it is crucial to get the collaboration between NOW and NEW right.

The Lean Scaleup is designed to help companies "Reshape Core."
It supports out-of-the-box innovation and building adjacent businesses.

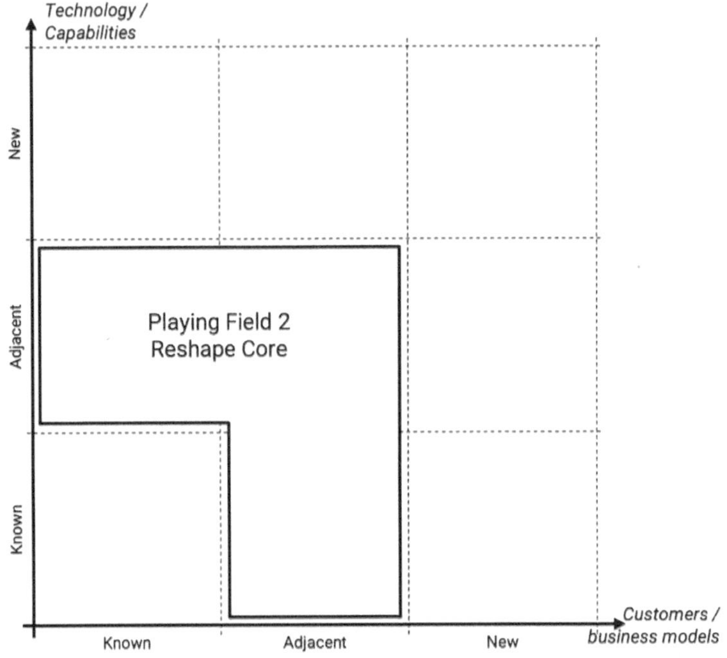

Exhibit 5–1: A framework to build adjacencies from out-of-the-box innovation.

Lean Scaleup: A Framework That Solves the System Problem

The Lean Scaleup is "a supporting structure around which something can be built," in other words, using the Cambridge Dictionary's definition, it is a framework. Its purpose is to provide guidance on how to succeed in out-of-the-box innovation, especially in building new, adjacent businesses. The solution consists of two parts.

The Lean Scaleup: a bridge connecting NOW and NEW and four learnable skills to succeed in out-of-the-box innovation and new-business building.

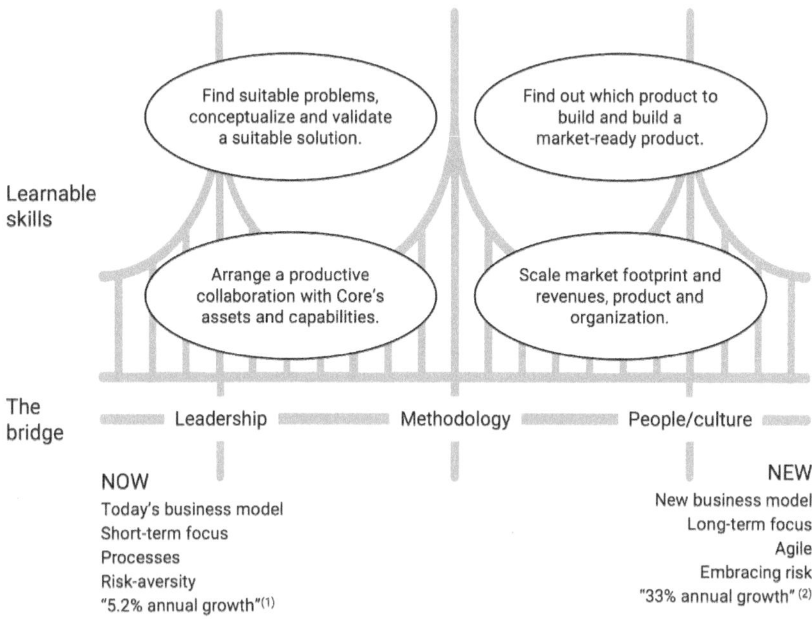

Exhibit 5–2: The bridge and the skills to succeed in out-of-the-box innovation.

The Bridge between NOW and NEW

The first part of the solution is a bridge between NOW and NEW with three building blocks:

- **Leadership.** Senior management's actions are crucial. For example, in allocating resources, in protecting the emerging business, and in establishing a one-company mindset.

- **Methodology.** This relates to the "how to," such as "how to design an effective end-to-end process" and "how to craft an effective collaboration model between Core and the corporate scaleup."

- **People/Culture.** This relates to, for example, creating a startup-like autonomy in the corporate context, selecting the right people on both sides of the fence, and creating a productive collaboration.

Four Learnable Skills

Once this bridge is built, the second part of the solution comes into play which consists of four learnable skills:

- Find suitable "problems worth to be solved" and navigate through uncertainties and assumptions to a satisfactory level of confidence that a solution to these problems can become a new business.

- Find out what products are needed for that solution and build an initial, market-ready product version.

- Organize access to corporate assets and capabilities for new-business builders to de-risk and accelerate the journey.

- Scale the market footprint and the corresponding revenues, advance the product, and grow the organization.

When I helped bp to design its "Scaling-Up factory" bp Launchpad, David Eyton, then a member of bp's Executive Team, described the Lean Scaleup as "a framework for effectively scaling promising concepts by utilizing the best ideas from the venture capital and lean startup world and adapting them to a corporate context."

The Lean Scaleup was the first framework for creating and scaling new businesses in a corporate context, and it remains the only one to this day.

Four Learnable Skills: The SCALE Formula

The four learnable skills mentioned above can be expressed in an easy-to-remember formula:

$$S = C * A * L * E$$

The letters in this formula spell out as follows:

- **S stands for success**, measured for example in new growth and in contributions to corporate transformation.

- **C stands for Contextuality.** A corporate startup/scaleup needs to be firmly embedded in the corporate context to receive the support it requires, mainly funding and access to corporate assets.

- **A represents a set of validated assumptions** about, for example, the size of the value pool, the company's right to win and the business concept's desirability, feasibility, and viability.

- **L refers to the initial launch,** i.e., the corporate startup's ability to drive the development of the product and the commercial activities to a point where it can launch the initial product and the new business model into the market.

- **E stands for the corporate scaleup's ability to expand** the initial footprint to a scaled-up business with all its operational activities.

Avoiding Failures

Corporate startups/scaleups rarely fail because their products are bad. They fail because they do not attract enough customers at the right price and time. This is for example the case when assumptions about customer behavior are not properly validated and is referred to as an A-failure in the SCALE formula. Chapters 6 and 19 contain guidance on how to avoid these failures. Advice on how to prevent C-failures can be found in chapters 6, 8, and 10-13, while chapters 6 and 19 address potential L-failures. Finally, chapter 8 illustrates how to prevent E-failures.

The formula says that success in out-of-the-box innovation and new-business building depends on four factors. If any of these factors is zero, success is not possible. No factor can compensate for failure in another. An important corollary is that technical excellence in building the initial product does not overcompensate for wrong assumptions about customers, value, and the go-to-market.

This formula does not guarantee success. A competitor may be faster and better than the corporate scaleup. However, the SCALE formula provides a good chance of success.

Lean Scaleup: The Benefits

As indicated in exhibit 5–1, the Lean Scaleup framework helps companies to increase the chances to "Reshape Core" via out-of-the-box innovation, especially new-business building. Additional benefits are:

- New growth.

- Business impact, measured by new revenue streams and contributions to the corporate transformation agenda.

- A healthy funnel of promising emerging business opportunities.

- Supporting corporate ambitions, for example by creating new businesses that contribute to the company's sustainability agenda.

- Improved Employer Value Proposition that attracts top talent, as a result from the above.

- Improved decision-making by increased transparency on the portfolio of emerging business opportunities.

- Higher efficiency for corporate startups/scaleups and their collaborators from Core.

- Reduced risk through systematic reduction of uncertainty.

- Guidance on how to build the corporate capability for new-business building.

Co-created by Leading Companies

The Lean Scaleup comes from real-world experience and collaboration. In 2017, I gathered an impressive group of companies and business schools for a think tank to crack the code on why it is so hard for companies to create NEW while winning NOW, and what a solution to the "out-of-the-box innovator's dilemma" might look like. Among the members of this group were Airbus, bp, Evonik, Philips, Robert Bosch, Swisscom, Telefónica, TÜV Rhineland, the London Business School and UC Berkeley.

The largest participant in this group, bp, serves as a striking example of how firms might improve their approach to new-business building. The participating senior vice presidents understood that without the ability to rapidly create new businesses, their company would be forced to pursue costly and risky M&A throughout its transition from an oil and gas company to an energy company. Due to the size of their transformational ambition, the company created bp Launchpad, a "Scaling-Up factory" that we designed according to Lean Scaleup principles.

Other participating companies also upgraded their new-business building processes using the Lean Scaleup. For instance, a manufacturing company enhanced collaboration between its corporate startups and Core's functions. A financial services company redesigned its non-incremental innovation space, while an aerospace company restructured its "beyond Core" validation framework.

Lean Scaleup: Six Big Ideas

The original co-creators of the Lean Scaleup framework came from a variety of industries, including oil and gas, banking, aerospace, chemicals, electrical, healthcare, telecom, and technology services. This diversity has resulted in a comprehensive and universal framework that incorporates best practices and emerging practices from many angles. The framework introduces six fresh and unique ideas.

The Lean Scaleup framework for out-of-the-box innovation and new-business building: 6 big ideas.

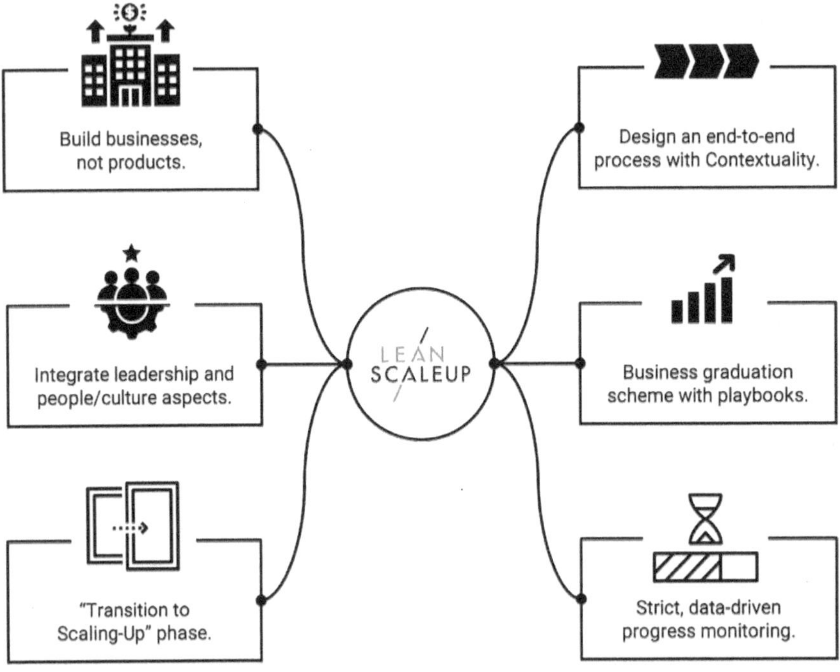

Exhibit 5–3: Six big ideas for scaling innovation and generating new growth.

Idea 1: Build Businesses, Not Products

I work with numerous companies on out-of-the-box innovation and new-business building. This provides me with a comprehensive understanding of the various approaches, companies use to address inherent challenges. Most of these approaches are based on the Lean Startup methodology and have maturity stages such as "problem/solution fit," "MVP," "product/market fit," and "scaling."

These approaches are product-focused, they are not business-focused. This brings two problems. First, teams tend to focus more on the product than on customer understanding. I have yet to find a customer that says: "I hope that this feature will help me to enjoy my subscription." **Customers care for having their problems solved. They do not care for products.**

Second, product-focused frameworks create internal challenges. Senior managers may be hesitant to provide funding and support since businesses, revenues, and margins are more important to them than products. And Core's functional heads cannot relate to product-focused teams since these do not care for their functional strategies.

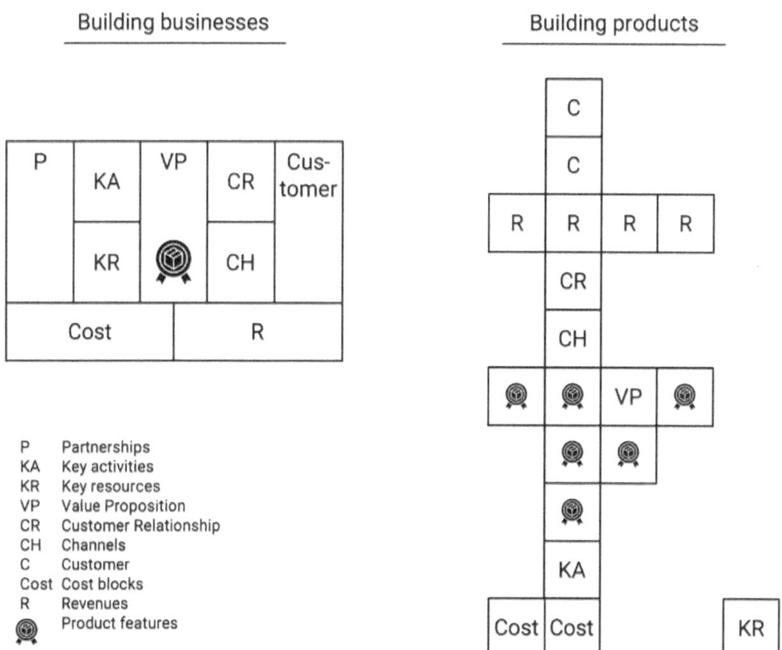

Exhibit 5–4: Frameworks should focus on building businesses, not products.

That is the reason why the Lean Scaleup framework thinks in building new businesses, not in products, from the very first steps on.

Idea 2: The End-to-End Process and Contextuality

Furthermore, most new-business building frameworks prioritize the early stages over the later stages and undervalue the corporate context. This results in **a significant gap in the end-to-end process and leaves corporate scaleups ill-prepared for the complexities of NOW**. Scaling-Up then becomes an arduous challenge, with seemingly insurmountable obstacles.

The Lean Scaleup provides an end-to-end process, from meaningful search fields to a scaled-up business. It also includes aspects that relate to the corporate context. "Contextuality" (see chapter 2) is equally important as the well-known dimensions of desirability[82], feasibility[83], and viability[84]. Contextuality brings a deep understanding of the corporate context into the new-business building process, ensuring that the teams move effectively and rapidly when they leave the protected space of their explorative unit.

Idea 3: Add Leadership and People/Culture Issues

Assuming the concept for a new business is sound, corporate startups/scaleups frequently lack senior management support, access to corporate assets and capabilities, and an effective collaboration at the working level. All these shortcomings can be attributed to an inadequate bridge between NOW and NEW.

It appears that many of the frameworks for out-of-the-box innovation and new-business building assume that senior managers will provide unwavering support to activities that initially are a mere distraction and

---

[82] Are customers willing to pay for the new product?

[83] Can we create such a product and deliver at an industrial scale?

[84] Can we create a sizable and profitable business from it?

Core's experts will naturally think outside the box, deprioritize their day-to-day duties, and make their expertise readily available.

In contrast, the Lean Scaleup recognizes the essential role of active senior management engagement and foresees **a gradual and managed engagement of NOW**. The framework also puts people/culture topics on an equal footing with leadership and methodology aspects. While **people may be collaborative, systems are not**. Therefore, collaboration must be embedded in the system and not left to chance.

Idea 4: A Business Graduation Scheme with Playbooks

A well-defined business graduation scheme with playbooks for every stage increases the chances to succeed in new-business building. The more detailed the approach, the better it supports corporate startups/scaleups, and the more effective the learning process is for building the corporate new-business building capability.

The Lean Scaleup provides such **a well-defined approach and operational playbooks**. In Pre-Scaling, corporate startups receive detailed guidance on what to do now and what to do next, broken down to the level of individual "sprints." In Scaling-Up, corporate scaleups benefit from operational playbooks that guide them in extending the market footprint, advancing the product, growing the organization without losing the startup spirit and developing the relationship with Core.

These playbooks also provide a solid foundation for learning, ensuring that the next concept for an out-of-the-box innovation has an even higher chance of success and can achieve it even more quickly.

Idea 5: Establish a "Transition to Scaling-Up" Phase

In most new-business building frameworks, scaling follows directly after validation. These frameworks seem to assume that once all validation checkboxes are ticked, Scaling-Up success will naturally follow.

However, **operational alignment between NOW and the corporate scaleup does not come overnight**. The Lean Scaleup provides actionable guidance for this critical transitional stage. Companies that already work with this module of the Lean Scaleup report that they were able to establish a solid setup for Scaling-Up success within two months.

Idea 6: Strict, Data-Driven Progress Monitoring

One of the key challenges companies face when they build new businesses is the difficulty to pinpoint the team's progress. Since **product-centric frameworks provide little insight into the maturity of the emerging business,** stakeholders often struggle in deciding whether to admit a corporate startup to the next stage and making the transition:

- From strategy and foresight to meaningful search fields.

- From a meaningful search field" to a meaningful idea.

- From a meaningful idea to scale-worthiness and scale-readiness.

- From validation to "Transition to Scaling-Up."

- From "Transition to Scaling-Up" to the first stage of Scaling-Up, which has a dual mission[85] and then to later Scaling-Up stages.

The Lean Scaleup offers a fresh solution to address these challenges. In Pre-Scaling, the solution is based on a scorecard with clear deliverables, in Scaling-Up on milestones. This approach supports rigor and effective decision-making while providing room for the necessary agility.

---

[85] See chapters 8 and 19.

The Lean Scaleup Framework from a High-Level Perspective

As mentioned above, a comprehensive new-business building framework needs to integrate effective methodology, impactful leadership actions, and an integrative people/culture setup. The co-creators of the Lean Scaleup found that every one of these dimensions has four modules.

These 12 modules make up the Lean Scaleup framework. The arrangement of modules, from left to right, loosely **aligns with the management challenges that arise during the conceptualization, validation, and scaling of an emerging business opportunity**.

The Lean Scaleup framework comprises 12 modules, with 4 modules allocated to each of the Methodology, Leadership, and People/Culture dimensions.

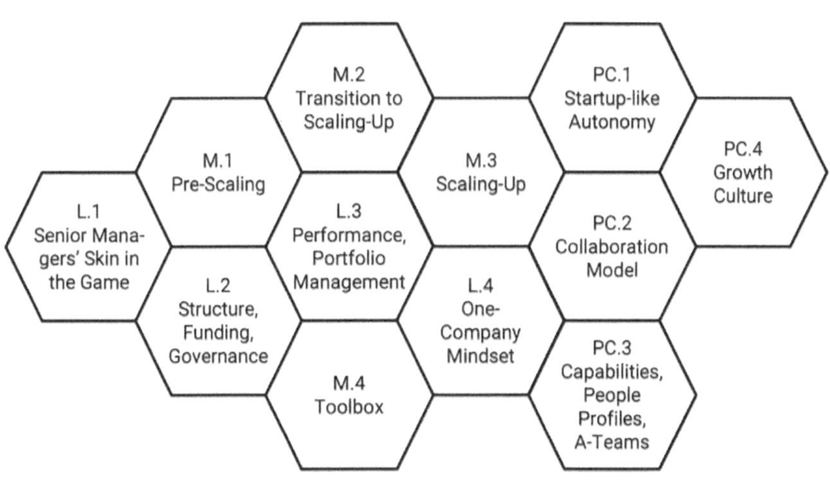

Exhibit 5–5: The 12 modules of the Lean Scaleup framework.

These challenges start with senior managers putting their "skin in the game" to create NEW and end with establishing a "growth culture" that supports the hypergrowth of a corporate scaleup over several years.

A Subset of These 12 Modules for Every Role

The 12 modules represent the corporate infrastructure. In practice, each role in out-of-the-box innovation and new-business building needs only a specific subset. Below are the relevant modules for the personas that I work with most in the new-business building context:

- **Heads of explorative units (e.g., business model incubators).** Senior managers' skin in the game; Pre-Scaling; Structure, funding, governance; Transition to Scaling-Up; Performance and portfolio management; Toolbox.

- **Senior managers.** Senior managers' skin in the game; Structure, funding, governance; Performance and portfolio management; One-company mindset; Transition to Scaling-Up; Startup-like autonomy; Collaboration model.

- **Leaders of corporate startups.** Pre-Scaling; Transition to Scaling-Up; Toolbox.

- **CEOs of corporate scaleups.** Senior managers' skin in the game; Structure, funding, governance; Scaling-Up; Startup-like autonomy; Collaboration model; Capabilities, people profiles, A-teams; Growth culture.

This chapter provides an outline of each module. For a more comprehensive understanding of the modules, please refer to chapters 6-17.

Methodology: Pre-Scaling

Pre-Scaling, the first phase of the Lean Scaleup's business graduation scheme, comprises four stages: Discovery, Business Foundation, Business Strategy, and Business Design. Each of these stages corresponds to a funding round, contains detailed playbooks, and has a defined progress monitoring process.

During the Discovery stage, numerous ideas related to a "meaningful search field" are generated and evaluated. Only a select few pass the evaluation and are "meaningful ideas." In the subsequent Business Foundation stage, an initial rapid reality check is conducted. A significant portion of "meaningful ideas" will not survive this stage. This intentional arrangement ensures that only significant ideas receive the resources for thorough validation, following the principle of "fail fast, fail forward."

In the subsequent Business Strategy stage, these ideas are validated to be scale-worthy and a Minimum Viable Product is co-created with potential customers to understand what product the corporate startup should build. At this maturity stage, the corporate startup must demonstrate the fit with the corporate context and that there is a good chance to create a sustainable competitive edge.

During the Business Design stage, the corporate startup has two objectives. First, the team must build the Minimum Marketable Product, the first version of the product that will be launched in the market, and demonstrate a rising interest in the market, i.e., a good product/market-fit. Second, it must design a new business with scalability in mind and demonstrate that this business concept is scale-ready.

The Lean Scaleup organizes validation content into four tracks: "customer and value," "solution and IP," "corporate context, business model, financials," and "capabilities and organization." These tracks and the four stages form a 4x4 grid with clearly defined deliverables in each of the 16 fields. This grid is the basis for data-driven progress monitoring.

The deliverables include four economic analyses[86], one in each stage with increasing levels of detail. These economic analyses prioritize top-line growth and cash flow, recognizing that emerging businesses do not yet

---

[86] I prefer to use this term instead of „business cases" since the latter generates the illusion of easy-to-validate assumptions and a level of detail that is not possible for out-of-the-box innovations and, in particular, business model innovations.

have the economies of scale to be directly compared at the bottom-line level with the existing business.

Methodology: Transition to Scaling-Up

After an emerging business opportunity has been validated to be scale-worthy and scale-ready, and after senior management has decided to invest into Scaling-Up, the Transition-to-Scaling-Up phase begins. This is typically a 2–3-month period in which the setup for Scaling-Up success is established. There are four work streams in this phase, which are described in more detail in chapter 7:

– Identify so-called scalability debts.

– Align NOW and the corporate scaleup.

– Develop a common game plan.

– Recruit key personnel for the Scaling-Up phase.

Methodology: Scaling-Up

Scaling up a validated new-business concept to a multi-million-dollar business is arguably the most challenging phase of new-business building within a company. Success in this phase is mandatory; without it, all previous activities are just a costly hobby, "innovation theater," or "happy engineering." The challenge comes from two angles: on the one hand time pressure, and other hand the need to implement multiple complex and interdependent activities simultaneously, as explained in chapter 8.

The Lean Scaleup organizes Scaling-Up in four tracks: "Strategy, Market, and Revenues," "Product," "Organization," and "Relationship to NOW." Milestones that cut across these tracks serve as triggers for funding rounds. When appropriate, they also prompt adjustments in the relationship to Core and changes to the growth strategy, such as acquiring other startups or entering into Joint Ventures to accelerate the journey.

The first track is about expanding the market presence by expanding within the initial market segment and entering subsequent ones. The strategic aspect of this track relates to acquiring the right type of customers and creating a defensible competitive advantage.

The Product track addresses the four types of product work that every corporate scaleup has. It is evident that close collaboration between the "Strategy, market, and revenues" and the "Product" teams is essential. Without it, the market expansion may lack adequate product support, or the product organization might develop features that are not relevant for expanding the market footprint.

The Organization track addresses how to maintain the startup spirit as the scaleup grows rapidly. Successful scaleups have growth rates that render top-down plans irrelevant. Such growth can only be supported by autonomous, yet aligned teams and a system that connects the objectives of the corporate scaleup with the key results that these autonomous teams are supposed to deliver.

Finally, the Relationship to Core track focuses on maintaining stakeholder perseverance and startup-like autonomy within the corporate context, while preparing for a changing relationship as the corporate scaleup grows and comes on the radar screen of corporate functions such as risk management, compliance, or financial controlling.

Methodology: Toolbox

As described in chapter 2, Core's senior managers and corporate new-business builders think, act, and speak differently. Without a shared language, corporate managers and corporate entrepreneurs can quickly find themselves to be "lost in translation." Establishing such a common language is one reason why companies that prioritize new-business building should have a toolbox, described in more detail in chapter 9.

Another reason is to guide corporate startups on their validation journey, via detailed instructions down to the level of so-called sprints in the

Pre-Scaling stages. And finally, with a defined progress monitoring in place, the toolbox can also help to improve planning for individual corporate startups and the portfolio of emerging business opportunities.

Leadership: Senior Managers' Skin in the Game

One of the challenges of out-of-the-box innovation and new-business building is to overcome the organizational inertia that comes with long-term successes. Senior managers who perceive a threat of disruption or an opportunity for growth outside of the existing business model must motivate the organization and direct the company towards new opportunities.

Neither presentation slides nor the establishment of a new business model incubator will be sufficient. Senior managers must go beyond that. They must be sending clear and compelling signals into the company that there is a NEW that will complement NOW.

The most effective way to achieve this is to put their skin in the game. This expression means that senior managers have a personal stake in the game. They demonstrate to Core that they accept the risks and put their track record on the line. Chapter 10 lists eight activities that send the right messages into the company.

Leadership: Structure, Funding, Governance

Success in new-business building requires a suitable structure, funding, and governance. With respect to the former, chapter 11 derives a reference model from Ford Motor Company's decision to split the company into two parts with a defined bridge:

- "Ford Blue" focuses on petrol- and diesel-powered vehicles and provides engineering and manufacturing capabilities for both businesses.

- Ford Model e" focuses on electric cars and mobility services which includes developing and industrializing connected-vehicle technologies and services for both businesses.

This chapter also covers funding and governance. A VC-type metered approach is the model of choice for providing financial resources to out-of-the-box innovation and new-business building. When Scaling-Up is done outside the company, external funding is also an option.

With regard to governance, chapter 11 outlines a 3-level governance model. When designing governance at the level of the individual corporate scaleup, it is important to consider the intended organizational home for the scaled-up business and the startup-like autonomy in the corporate context (see below).

Leadership: Performance and Portfolio Management

NOW and a corporate startup/scaleup have different markers of success. NOW's sophisticated Key Performance Indicators (KPIs) measure revenues, costs, productivity, process speed, throughput, risk exposure, customer satisfaction, and so on. Typically, the underlying time series are so extensive that they even allow for predicting the future. However, these dimensions are only partially relevant for corporate startups/scaleups since:

- They do not have a running business, only an emerging business.

- There are many unknowns that do not allow for defining structured processes.

- They have KPIs which are not relevant for NOW[87].

These points show that new-business building requires two sets of KPIs. The art is to find the overlap and to communicate accordingly, depending on the audience. One crucial element in this context, explained in more detail in chapter 12, is a KPI that relates to both NOW and the corporate scaleup. Such a so-called North Star metric is a powerful concept that:

---

[87] For example, Airbus' satellite imagery platform UP42 has KPIs that relate to new-partner acquisition, the diversity of partner products, and active customer usage.

- Aligns NOW and the corporate scaleup.

- Helps to establish the one-company mindset (see below).

- Helps to secure support from the relevant operative business units.

Leadership: One-Company Mindset

Senior managers understand the importance of communication. A big part of their success is based on reducing the complexity of a challenge, crystallizing the essence of what needs to be said, packaging this essence into easy-to-understand stories and then delivering these stories in a way that ensures buy-in from the internal audience.

However, they often underestimate how much, how systematic, and how persistent they need to communicate out-of-the-box innovation and new-business building. One particular audience is Core. Senior managers need to craft powerful messages that show a perspective for those people who will not transition to NEW.

Ford's CEO did this when he pointed out that the existing and the emerging business both support the whole company, although in different ways. And for Fujifilm's then-CEO Shigetaka Komori, the one-company mindset was foundational to build new businesses in time before the existing business model collapsed[88]. Chapter 13 provides more information about this module of the Lean Scaleup framework.

People/Culture: Startup-like Autonomy

One of my clients, the head of a "Scaling-Up factory" of a leading Engineering company counted 800 corporate rules that govern his company. It is simply not possible to build a new business which competes against fast-moving corporate startups from other incumbents and VC-backed

---

[88] The case study in chapter 4 provides more detail.

greenfield startups by following a playbook that was defined for a slow-moving, siloed large organization.

Corporate scaleups need a so-called startup-like autonomy. This is a form of autonomy that resembles, to some extent, the independence of a greenfield startup but within a corporate context. If this autonomy is not established, the corporate scaleup will face a two-front war: one front is the market and the other one the internal one within the company to secure necessary permissions, protection, and resources. An effective startup-like autonomy consists of six key components that are explained in chapter 14.

People/Culture: Collaboration Model

A well-defined and operationalized collaboration model is crucial for a corporate scaleup to get access to Core's assets and capabilities. In large-scale transformations like in the Ford example mentioned above, the collaboration model is structurally embedded into the organization.

In contrast, the collaboration model for a single corporate scaleup involves identifying which Core functions the corporate scaleup requires to fulfill its mission, followed by discussions with the relevant functional heads over contributions, responsibilities, risks, and sharing of risks and rewards.

One unique collaboration model is when the scaleup pays for functional support. While this may seem straightforward, there are potential pitfalls. More detailed insights into collaboration models between Core and a corporate scaleup are in chapter 15.

People/Culture: Capabilities, People Profiles, A-Teams

To create sizable and profitable new businesses successfully, different people profiles are required at various stages. Discovery, the first stage of Pre-Scaling, requires people with a blend of ethnographic analytical prowess and business creativity. The remaining Pre-Scaling stages require pragmatic teams that approach validation with a scientific and product-building with a customer-centric, data-driven mindset.

Finally, Scaling-Up requires individuals and teams capable of delivering results under immense pressure. They should persevere through challenges, adapt, remain determined, and stay motivated in ambiguous situations. For more detailed information on capabilities, people profiles, and team composition, refer to chapter 16.

People/Culture: Growth Culture

Exceptional corporate scaleups have one thing in common: they foster a specific company culture. This culture must be capable of sustaining hypergrowth over many years and remain resilient even as new individuals are hired, who, in turn, hire more people. Chapter 17 shows eight factors that characterize a so-called growth culture.

Chapter 6:
Pre-Scaling

Chapter 6
Pre-Scaling

The Lean Scaleup framework comprises 12 modules, with 4 modules allocated to each of the Methodology, Leadership, and People/Culture dimensions.

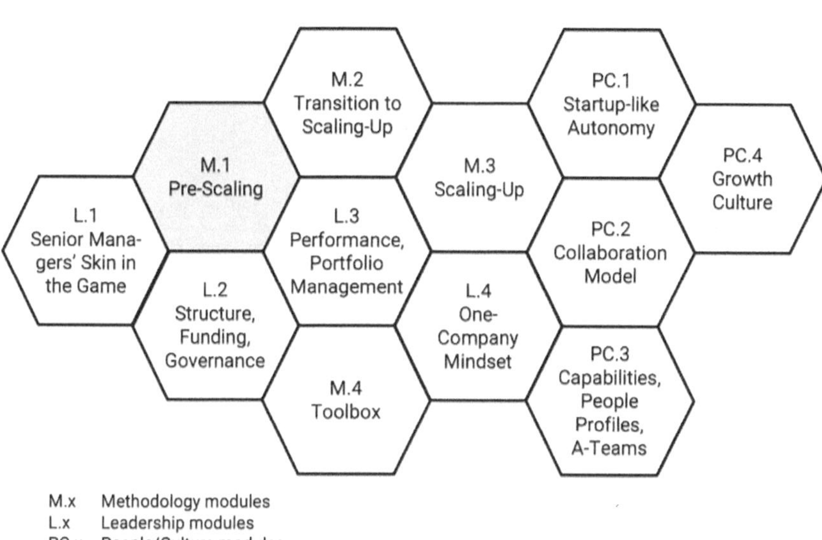

Key Points in This Chapter

1. Every out-of-the-box innovation, especially new-business building, is based on underlying assumptions. Some of them are explicit, while others are implicit. To ensure a solid foundation for success, it is vital to validate these assumptions.

2. The Pre-Scaling phase is dedicated to the validation mission. The Lean Scaleup organizes validation scope and sequence in four tracks and four stages. The resulting 4x4 grid enables a data-driven progress monitoring of corporate startups and an effective management of the portfolio of emerging business opportunities.

3. Tracks and stages are designed to (1) think in building new businesses, not products, right from the outset and (2) engage NOW in a gradual and transparent manner, without surprises or disruptions.

4. Typical validation frameworks have a "push" mindset. They assume that if the value proposition of the intended solution is strong enough, a clever go-to-market can drive the innovation into the market. Such frameworks undervalue customers' innovation adoption, which is a vital aspect of product/market-fit. Validating innovation adoption is an integral part of the Lean Scaleup's Pre-Scaling module.

**

After just 23 days of operation and a USD 300m investment, CNN closed its streaming service, CNN+[89]. Could this expensive failure have been avoided? While I do not have insider information, my advice to CNN would have been to take a methodical, step-by-step approach to validating and scaling their new business.

Before committing to substantial investments, it is important to rigorously test assumptions across four dimensions:

- Customers and value.

- Solution and Intellectual Property.

- Corporate context, business model and financials.

- Capabilities and organization.

CNN could have reduced risk in their business model and their market launch by following a well-planned sequence of market niches. This would have enabled them to continuously test their assumptions about customers' innovation adoption and make necessary adaptations.

---

[89] See https://bit.ly/3wXaObI.

Those tests must be both inexpensive and quick, enabling the collection of many data points to assess the validity of the assumptions. As Amazon's founder and CEO Jeff Bezos said[90]: "We understand the value of failing early and iterating until we get it right. When this process works, our failures are relatively small. And when we discover something that truly resonates with customers, we double down on it, aiming to turn it into an even bigger success."

In the case of CNN+, one assumption that could have been rapidly and cost-effectively tested is about customer's "skin in the game." They could have said: "We believe that X percent of market niche Y will visit CNN+ after seeing an add on CNN, and Z percent will provide their email and phone number in exchange for a free 3-month subscription." Such an approach could have allowed CNN to assess market readiness and iteratively refine their go-to-market strategy before committing substantial resources.

Unfortunately, the CNN+ story is not unique. Many companies have ambitious goals for growth outside of NOW. However, in too many cases, the underlying assumptions are wrong, which leads to inevitable failure. It is like trying to build a skyscraper on shaky ground—it is bound to collapse.

Like skyscrapers, new businesses require a solid foundation to ensure their long-term success. Since new businesses are by definition new, it is not possible to predict the solidity of the foundation in advance. Instead, it must be uncovered through a data-driven process in which corporate startups demonstrate to the corporate investor that the foundational assumptions are strong enough to support ambitious goals.

This process consists of two parts. First, a Discovery phase in which meaningful ideas are identified within meaningful search fields. Second, a systematic and thorough step-by-step validation of the underlying assumptions, including those related to the corporate context. Only when the assumptions have been validated, further investment can be justified.

---

[90] See https://bit.ly/3yMheLe.

The Lean Scaleup module that covers the aspects above is referred to as Pre-Scaling. The Pre-Scaling phase consists of four stages: the Discovery stage mentioned above and three subsequent stages, Business Foundation, Business Strategy, and Business Design. These four stages are also the first four stages of a comprehensive end-to-end business graduation scheme. At the same time, they are the foundation of early-stage funding and portfolio management.

This chapter provides a detailed description of the Lean Scaleup's Pre-Scaling module. Many corporate startups may find similarities to their existing practices. However, attention to detail is crucial for successfully building new businesses.

For instance, corporate startups often fail to recognize that validating the corporate context is more than just checking a "strategy-fit" checkbox. Similarly, they often fail to recognize that understanding customers' barriers to innovation adoption is as important as having a superior value proposition. Chapter 19 offers guidance on these subtle yet crucial details.

Validation

Pre-Scaling starts with the Discovery stage and defining meaningful search fields. These establish the limits for innovation efforts by specifying which kinds of ideas are not in focus. Senior managers and out-of-the-box innovators should collaborate in defining these fields to ensure the NOW/NEW alignment. Corporate explorers then generate many innovation ideas inside these boundaries. These ideas can come from a variety of sources, such as market research, interviews, intrapreneurship programs, open innovation initiatives, collaborations with external startups.

After these ideas have been evaluated and meaningful ideas have been found, a corporate startup develops a business model concept, validates its underlying assumptions, and builds the first version of the product that will hit the market. These activities are organized in a three-step process, as explained below.

Validation, the process of confirming assumptions, can be challenging for corporate stakeholders due to two reasons. First, when discussing emerging business opportunities with corporate startups, there is often a lot of innovation jargon. Second, compared to NOW's well-structured processes, the stream of validation activities may appear to be disorganized.

Corporate startups must adopt a scientific mindset for validation and communicate accordingly to engage their stakeholders. This scientific mindset is built on four steps:

- Establish assumptions by asking: "What would need to be true?" (or alternatively: "We believe that…") and prioritize them.

- Design meaningful and effective experiments[91], define the success threshold and anticipate the outcome of the experiments.

- Run the experiments, evaluate results, and compare these with the anticipated outcome.

- Determine if the experiment's results match expectations. If so, the corporate startup can proceed with confidence. Otherwise, they must adjust the assumptions or discard the idea.

In other words, **validation is the process of transforming assumptions into learning**. The key is to understand the amount of learning required to progress on the so-called affordable loss principle (see chapter 16).

When Can You Safely Stop Validating?

When can you confidently conclude validation? This is a question that I often discuss with corporate startups and their stakeholders. There is no one-size-fits-all answer to this question. I typically use two criteria.

---

[91] See David Bland, Alexander Osterwalder: Testing Business Ideas; Wiley, 2019

First, have we learned enough? In the context of new-business building, learning refers to the ability to predict experiment outcomes with increasing accuracy, as explained above. For instance, when a corporate startup wants to test the most effective messaging for a business model innovation, they might run ads on Google and LinkedIn and measure click-through rates. If the team expects a 40 percent click-through rate and achieves a 38.35 percent rate, they have learned enough.

Second, did potential customers put their skin into the game? This expression refers to something of value, such as money, time, or reputation. For example, when the corporate startup finds that a potential customer is willing to invest time to co-create the Minimum Viable Product, this could be considered as skin in the game. **A corporate startup should not put its skin in the game, i.e., invest significant resources and budgets, before there is skin in the game from the target market.**

Avoiding Validation Bias

Validation should be carried out with objectivity and optimism, "with a cold eye and a warm heart." The corporate startup and the stakeholders want the idea to succeed, but they should not deceive themselves by misinterpreting facts. Below are **six common biases that can lead corporate startups to misjudge reality**:

- Recency. Putting too much weight on recent events.

- Anchoring. This means to base judgment on the first information given.

- Regression. This refers to seeing cause-effect relationships when there are only correlations.

- Hindsight. In retrospect, events seem more predictable than they were.

- Halo. This means liking or disliking someone or something.

- Attachment. The tendency to stick to past behaviors and opinions.

Mastering the Art of Validation

The sweet spot in corporate new-business building is at the intersection of three elements: an emerging business opportunity that addresses a high-value/high-priority problem in the market, leverages Core's assets and capabilities, and is attractive for the corporate investor.

The emerging business opportunity should solve big customer problems, leverage corporate assets and create a business that the corporate investor can invest in.

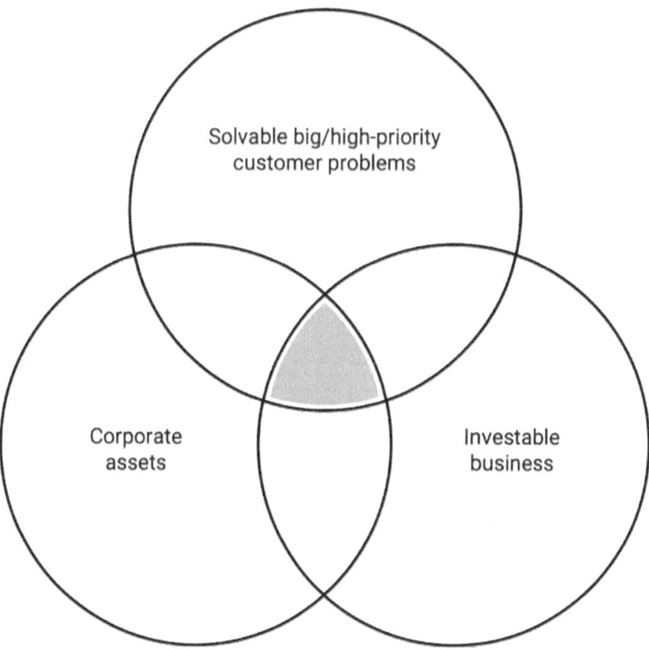

Exhibit 6–1: The sweet spot in corporate new–business building.

The challenge arises when corporate startups recognize that there is not sufficient time to conduct all validation activities. Consequently, validating emerging business opportunities requires the ability to prioritize effectively. I believe there are two key dimensions to prioritization.

Speed

Corporate startups race against time. They must not stretch the patience of corporate stakeholders, and they must find their way to market before the space is occupied by competitors. To achieve this, they must focus on validation items that are essential to advance to the next stage of the company's business graduation scheme, i.e., the next funding round.

Consequently, speed is more important than perfection. However, not all corporate startups operate under this concept. To illustrate, let me share one example from my advisory work. A senior manager at a manufacturing company asked me to assess a corporate startup that made little progress. Their documents seemed to be in order. The presentations spelled out the assumptions they wanted to test. These assumptions related to measurable outcomes. The documents were visually appealing, almost stunning.

From my perspective, the team was striving for excellence and ensuring the accurate completion of all tasks. They worked on the company's most significant ambition and were concerned about answering the stakeholder's critical questions during the next status update. They feared making mistakes and were worried that additional customer interviews might reveal flaws in their assumptions. As a result, they became stuck in analysis paralysis and concentrated on perfecting their current work instead of obtaining additional and more comprehensive customer feedback.

Learning

Effective corporate startups are assumption hunters. They consistently ask themselves: "Which assumptions must be valid so that we can advance with a reasonable level of confidence?" Although many corporate startups are skilled in this area, it is quite common that they encounter challenges when it comes to prioritizing validation tasks.

Typically, corporate startup teams use spreadsheets to list assumptions, with each row representing an assumption and columns indicating factors such as validation expenses and validation time. This approach works in predictable environments, but it is inadequate when there is insufficient data. In such cases, learning—the ability to predict the outcome of experiments—must be the top priority.

The team should ask: "Which of these assumptions offers the most learning?". Learning can only occur with firsthand data. Corporate startups must go outside of the building and engage in direct interactions, as Steve Blank, the founder of the Lean Startup movement, suggests. He said: "In a startup, no facts exist inside the building, only opinions[92]."

What Comes First – Customer Problem or Solution?

Most innovators agree that creating a new business begins with addressing a superior customer experience. Amazon's founder Jeff Bezos and Apple's founder Steve Jobs have repeatedly stated that innovators should start from that angle and work backwards to define the product and the required technology, rather than starting with the technology and trying to figure out how to market it.

The Lean Scaleup is flexible regarding whether the customer or technology should be the starting point. The latter can also serve as a solid foundation, as many examples show. Take NVIDIA as a first example. Founded in 1995, the company initially produced graphics cards for the PC industry. It then recognized broader opportunities in areas such as 3D rendering for PC games and computer-aided design. By delivering three times the performance of its competitors, NVIDIA built a strong brand and took market share from industry heavyweight Intel[93].

---

[92] See https://bit.ly/3Vl2wnB.
[93] See chapter 2.

The company then discovered that university researchers used its products to run complex compute challenges. It invested in making its products programmable, laying the foundation for the widespread adoption of its chips for AI workloads. Today, NVIDIA is valued at more than USD 2tn.

There are even more routes that corporate startups could take that do not start with customer experience:

- Procore and Uber started with identifying what was broken in the construction industry and the taxi industry, respectively.

- Tesla started with a focus on individual battery-powered mobility as a customer benefit.

But here is the crucial point: It is imperative to provide firsthand evidence of problem/solution-fit. Corporate startups that start with technology or other angles must ensure that their intended solution aligns with high-value/high-priority customer problems. Desktop research or brainstorming target markets are not insufficient in this case. While this statement may appear simplistic, it is unfortunately true. The most common regret of corporate new-business builders is that they failed to fully comprehend their customers' needs, expectations, and pain points[94].

Care about Innovation Adoption

The Japanese use the word chindōgu for solutions that cause more problems than they solve. A chindōgu creates more friction than value. To customers, this friction can come in many dimensions:

- Downsides and disadvantages of adopting the innovation.

- Ambiguity about implementation and roll-out.

---

[94] See https://mck.co/455QoZU.

– Personal reputational risks for the decision-makers.

– Implementation effort and costs.

– Risks related to investment and running costs (i.e., promised advantages do not materialize).

– Productivity loss while switching to the innovation.

– Fees to exit existing contracts.

– Efforts to change existing habits and behaviors.

– Efforts and costs to train staff.

Exhibit 6–2 on the next page displays the forces that determine how fast customers will adopt the innovation. On the hand, there is the market push of the corporate startup. On the other hand, there is the restraining force, which includes objective factors and perceptions that prevent customers from adopting the innovation[95].

Many corporate startups focus on finding a repeatable, efficient, and scalable go-to-market process, but they neglect to deeply understand the barriers that prevent customers from adopting their innovation.

Validating the latter is mandatory in Pre-Scaling. This is because the barriers to switching from existing practices to the innovation may be too high for customers, resulting in high customer acquisition costs or even failure for the corporate startup. Consequently, the Lean Scaleup's Pre-Scaling module includes a thorough analysis of the customer's switching barriers in the Business Strategy and Business Design stages.

---

[95] The quality of the product/market-fit (see below) is determined by these forces.

Understanding innovation adoption and the customer "barriers to switch" from the existing practice to the innovation is vital for innovation success.

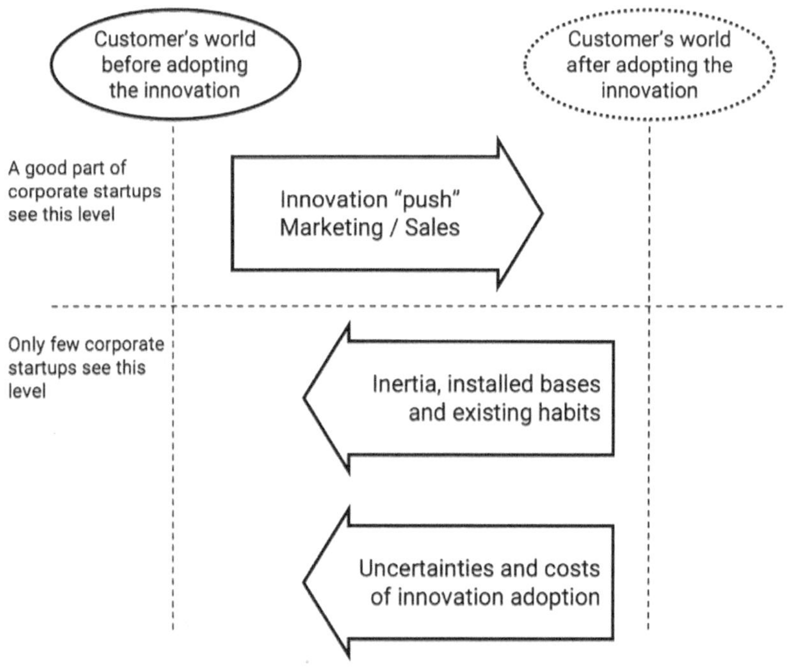

Exhibit 6–2: Three forces influence innovation adoption.

Build Businesses, Not Products

New-business building is about creating businesses, not just products. Let me exemplify this point with a historical case study.

In 2015, Hewlett-Packard (HP) decided to enter the emerging smart-watch market[96]. The company believed it had the assets and capabilities to

[96] See https://bit.ly/47HTmEj.

create a new business, including engineering skills, the ability to miniaturize electronic components, a global scale, and a low-cost supply chain that allowed for large-scale production. Furthermore, HP had already proven its ability to launch innovative watch-related products with a digital watch that included a calculator.

The company launched a corporate startup to develop the first Minimum Marketable Product in an envisioned smartwatch business. The team collaborated with a renowned designer and demonstrated that it could master the technological challenges and achieve first sales: HP sold 5,000 units and generated USD 1.2m in revenues.

While these revenues paled in comparison to HP's annual revenues of USD 111bn at that time, stakeholders saw them as a promising indicator for a potentially sizable business and agreed to take the next step. The team recruited more engineers and collaborated with more designers. HP sold around 15,000 watches, generating USD 8m in revenue. This progress encouraged stakeholders and the new-business team to think even bigger. In the following year, they sold 80,000 units of the third-generation watches, generating USD 12m in revenue.

Senior management then decided to discontinue the emerging business opportunity. They recognized that the company could continue collaborating with even more designers and producing even more watches, but it could not create a scalable business. HP's watches—unlike, for example, the Apple Watch—were characterized by small production runs. Therefore, increasing production volumes would reduce the margin because elevated costs could not be offset by economies of scale.

Such a product-centric approach to building new businesses is not uncommon. Companies can end up like HP: repeatedly launching new waves of products, but not building a sizable, scalable new business. To avoid this trap, the Lean Scaleup's Pre-Scaling module is business-centric, not product-centric[97].

---

[97] See chapter 2 for a more comprehensive explanation.

The following section outlines what needs to be validated, while the subsequent section deals with the sequence of validations.

What Needs to Be Validated: 4 Tracks

To streamline the validation process, the Lean Scaleups organizes the individual validation topics into four tracks:

– Customer and value.

– Solution and Intellectual Property.

– Corporate context, business model and financials.

– Capabilities and organization.

The validation activities in these tracks are described below. Every *italicized item* represents one validation item.

Track 1: Customer and Value

Value is the focal point in my definition of innovation, which is "capturing the value from meaningful insights via new offerings." Value is defined by the customer, not by the company. Therefore, accurately *defining the customer* is crucial since several key validation items rely on it, such as:

– Finding the right partners for innovation interviews.

– Understanding value and a superior value proposition.

– Estimating the market size.

– Assessing the quality of the problem/solution-fit.

– Understanding the customer's barriers to adopting the innovation.

– Assessing the quality of the product/market-fit.

To generate revenues, the corporate startup must offer a solution to a *high-value/high-priority problem* that customers are *willing to pay for*. To efficiently acquire these customers, this solution must have a *superior value proposition*, i.e., it must solve that customer problem better than any alternative (which might come from a different angle).

Additionally, the corporate startup must ensure that *value creation* and *value delivery* are effective, efficient, and scalable. This can often be achieved by incorporating *value enablers*, such as ecosystem partners, into the business model. Finally, the team must provide evidence that the *market is large and attractive enough* for the corporate investor and that it can *capture the value*.

To summarize, this track comprises six validation areas:
– Customer and problem.

– Value proposition.

– Value creation.

– Value delivery and value capture.

– Value enablers, in particular ecosystem partners.

– Value potential, especially size and attractiveness of the market.

Track 2: Solution and IP

Value propositions are based on products. This *product* will be conceptualized and co-created with pioneer customers in three steps:
– Pretotype (a rapid demonstrator or mock-up).

– Minimum Viable Product.

– Minimum Marketable Product.

Understanding the customer's existing situation and the *adjacent technology* into which the product will fit is an important validation topic since this relates to the barriers to innovation adoption. The adjacent technology may be production machinery if the product is a physical product, or it might be software used by the customer. The product and the surrounding elements that make up the superior value proposition must be feasible from both a technical and an *Intellectual Property* (IP) perspective. Therefore, an initial IP landscaping, a detailed IP analysis at a later point and a carefully crafted IP strategy before transitioning to Scaling-Up are mandatory items in Pre-Scaling.

To summarize, this track consists of three validation headlines:

- Product.

- Adjacent technology.

- Intellectual Property.

Track 3: Corporate Context, Business Model, Financials

Corporate startups work in a corporate context. Thus, Contextuality is an essential, non-negotiable success factor for corporate new-business building, as explained in chapter 2. Initially, the corporate context is relevant in defining meaningful search fields, in identifying meaningful ideas and in discussing suitable high-level business model options.

At a later stage, *alignment with functional strategies*, and *acceptable risks* need to be validated. In the final stages of Pre-Scaling, the potential *synergies with Core's operating model* and the *collaboration areas during Scaling-Up* need to be investigated.

This track also encompasses the *business model and financials*. Unlike other frameworks which put the business model in close proximity to customer validation, the co-creators of Lean Scaleup believe that in a corporate context, new business models should be discussed within the corporate context. There are two main reasons for this.

First, the intended business model might not be feasible for NOW's infrastructure. For example, some of my corporate startup clients were not aware that NOW's systems and policies, such as those in accounting, financial management, contract handling, and service level management, were not suitable for the service-centric business models they pursued.

Second, most companies mandate that corporate startups adhere to Core's methodologies and terminology for *economic viability analyses*[98], formulating financial projections, and addressing *risk, legal, and regulatory issues*. For instance:

- If the innovation involves physical products, balance sheet implications must be considered.

- For service-centric business model innovations, Core's finance units typically expect economic viability analyses to include cannibalization effects and to be articulated in established terminology.

In summary, this track consists of three validation areas:

- Business model, commercial model, and financials.

- Corporate context.

- Risk, legal and regulatory issues.

Track 4: Capabilities and Organization

Building a new business often requires new capabilities, both to validate assumptions in Pre-Scaling and during Scaling-Up. These capabilities may be domain-specific, such as a deep understanding of the new market, or topic-specific, such as expertise in digital technologies. Consequently, during Pre-Scaling, it is crucial to validate the *availability of capabilities* and corresponding recruiting channels.

Designing an effective Scaling-Up organization brings *people-related challenges*. Specific individuals with industry expertise, an entrepreneurial mindset, and corporate acumen are vital for Scaling-Up success. For example, the

---

[98] I suggest to not use the term "business case" since it generates mental images of well-defined and easy-to-validate assumptions and a high level of precision that is hardly possible in out-of-the box innovation.

demand for AI experts in Germany has increased tenfold in 2023[99]. Consequently, validating *talent acquisition for key positions* is imperative in the late validation stages.

Furthermore, the scaleup's *operating model* and *organization* will differ from Core's. Creating a lean, scalable structure without precedent requires careful validation before transitioning to Scaling-Up. Lastly, it is critical to validate *HSSE* (health, safety, security, and environment) provisions, including *cybersecurity*.

To summarize, this track consists of three (validation) headlines:

- Capabilities and people.

- Operating model and organization.

- HSSE and cybersecurity.

Four Maturity Stages and the 4x4 Grid

This section explains the four stages of Pre-Scaling which are at the same time the first four stages of the Lean Scaleup's business graduation scheme. At the stage level, the process is comparable to traditional phase/ gate processes that are used for managing incremental innovation. However, there are three fundamental differences:

- The content differs due to the context of out-of-the-box innovation.

- The unfamiliar content and uncertainties require an agile approach.

- Usually, there will always be an uncertainty that requires an entrepreneurial decision to move forward.

---

[99] See https://bit.ly/3wG2lcl.

To facilitate effective communication between NOW and NEW in Pre-Scaling, the Lean Scaleup uses plain language rather than innovation jargon such as product/market-fit or traction. The co-creators of the Lean Scaleup discovered that the majority of stakeholders are able to comprehend the logic of the following four-step approach:

- Discovery. "First, we need to find a promising idea for a future business."

- Business Foundation. "Then, we need to validate that this idea has a solid foundation."

- Business Strategy. "Next, we must convince ourselves that there is a strategy that will ensure a sustainable competitive advantage over the next three to five years."

- Business Design. "Finally, we need to design a business that can create and deliver the value proposition at scale and at cost".

These four stages are related to funding rounds (see chapter 11) because they reduce uncertainty about the emerging business opportunity and justify larger investments. Some of my clients consider these four stages to be value inflection points. At the end of the stages, the value of an out-of-the-box innovation has increased because it can be backed by validation.

The stages are designed to engage NOW in a transparent and gradual manner, without surprises or disruptions. The Lean Scaleup's co-creators found that this is the most effective way since Core's functions typically do not have spare capacity for dealing with an unexpected innovation.

Overlaying the four tracks mentioned in the previous section with the four stages described below provides a 4x4 grid that:

- Guides the corporate startup on what they need to deliver to get to the next funding round.

- Provides a solid basis for progress monitoring, as detailed in the Amadeus Nexwave case study in chapter 4.

- Is the basis for an effective management of the portfolio of emerging business opportunities, as described in chapter 12.

The Lean Scaleup's 4x4 validation grid guides the corporate startup and provides a solid basis for progress monitoring and portfolio management.

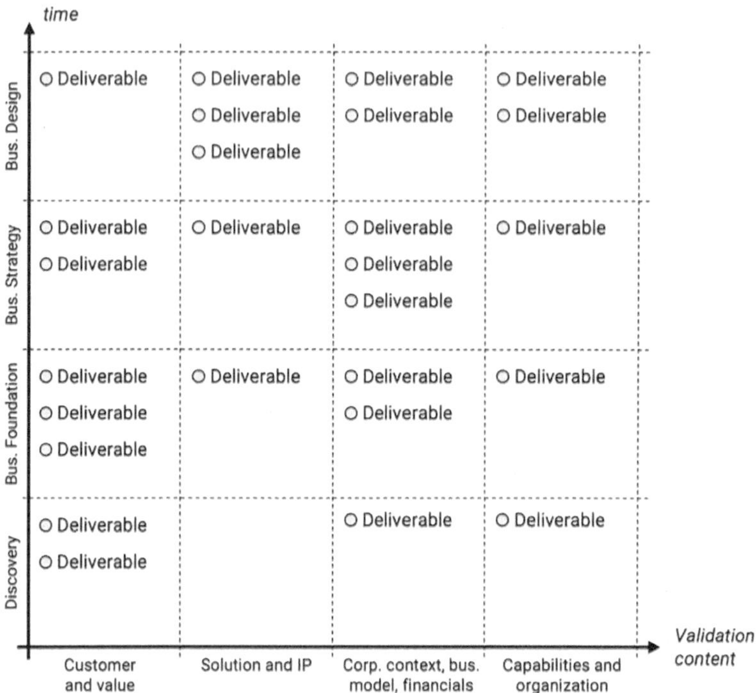

Exhibit 6–3: The Lean Scaleup 4x4 validation grid.

In the following descriptions, each *italicized item* represents a validation deliverable.

Stage 1: Discovery

The end-to-end process of building a new business within an organization starts with meaningful search fields. While there may be many potential search fields, usually only a small number of them are meaningful with respect to the company's specifics. The selection of these fields depends on various criteria, such as:

- Changes in customer behaviors and needs.

- Megatrends in the VUCA environment (see chapter 2).

- Corporate assets and capabilities that could be an "unfair advantage."

- Breaking industry orthodoxies ("you can have either … or …").

- New business models enabled by digital technologies.

- New capabilities that the company must build.

- New technology that might be a basis for a superior value proposition.

Typically, companies have an abundance of ideas to pursue. However, it is crucial to find the few *meaningful ideas*. Customer desirability is one selection criterion. However, a corporate startup must think more broadly. Simply solving a customer problem is not enough. It must find problems worth to be solved. To evaluate those problems, the following eight questions are helpful:

- Problem Qualifier: Is the problem a good and sizable problem?

- Competition: Who else tries to solve the identified customer problem?

- Superior value proposition: What are the reasons to believe that the company's intended solution provides more value for the customer than solutions from these competitors?

- Unfair advantage: What does the company bring to the table that could accelerate and de-risk the innovation journey?

- Go-to-market hypothesis: What are the reasons to believe that the business model innovation can be efficiently brought to the market?

- "Reason to dream:" What is the approximate size of the market?

- Major cost blocks and uncertainties: Which will be the biggest cost blocks and what could be showstoppers?

- 3-year environment scan: Which changes in the business environment could accelerate or slow down the adoption of innovation?

The Lean Scaleup offers a valuable tool that integrates all aspects into a single canvas. Additionally, the so-called Meaningful Idea Canvas serves as a gateway to two pivotal thinking tools utilized in subsequent stages: the Lean Canvas and the Business Model Canvas.

The Lean Scaleup's "Meaningful Idea Canvas" summarizes the key points for evaluating if an idea is meaningful. It leads into commonly used canvases.

Pain areas	Innovation idea	Superior Value Proposition	Unfair Advantage	Customer segment
Problem qualifier	**Market engagement hypothesis**	**Competitors**	**Go-to-market hypothesis**	
Major cost blocks and uncertainties		**3-year environment scan**	**Size of the prize, revenue model and "reason to dream"**	

Exhibit 6–4: The Lean Scaleup's Meaningful Idea Canvas.

Once a meaningful idea checks enough boxes and no showstoppers are found, it can move to the next stage.

Stage 2: Business Foundation

It is hard to compensate for poor early decisions with good late decisions. For example, it is hard to make money in real estate if one overpays in the beginning. Of course, things can be improved by making good decisions along the way, but the effects of poor early decisions tend to persist.

That is why the Lean Scaleup places great emphasis on validating that a meaningful idea is a solid foundation for a future business. This foundation has three key elements:

- *Problem/solution-fit.* This means that a corporate startup has identified a high-value/high-priority customer problem and initial evidence that customers view the intended solution as a solution to that problem.

- A *superior value proposition*, meaning the intended solution provides more value to the customer than any other solution aimed at solving the customer's problem.

- *Customers' willingness-to-switch* from their current solution to the innovation. By understanding which factors prevent customers from adopting the intended solution and removing those obstacles, corporate startups increase their chances of success.

I often discuss with corporate startups how to gauge the level of interest from potential customers at this early stage. In addition to measuring the amount of skin in the game, the following checklist can help assess the quality of the problem/solution-fit for a particular customer:

- Value points. Potential customers articulate a problem and its business impact or share compelling needs to change or the metrics by which success will be measured.

- People points. At least one person per customer company agrees to serve as an internal champion. This individual shares who the most influential stakeholders are, invites them to meetings and collaborates with the corporate startup on a pitch deck to sell the corporate startup's solution internally.

- Competition points. The customer shares the pros and cons of the current solution and shares which other solutions are being considered.

- Product points: The customer shares the specific capabilities the solution must have and the adjacent technologies that a solution must integrate with.

- Buying process points: The customer shares details about the buying process.

It is obvious that these points are based on real customer interviews[100] and experiments. These must be thoughtfully designed and carried out with a scientific mindset. Simply brainstorming or relying on desk research is insufficient for achieving that level of clarity.

However, there is another important aspect to consider. Abstract discussions about new business models, value propositions or potential products often fall short because of misunderstandings. Therefore, in-depth conversations require tangible, rapid, and cheap artifacts. Such an artifact, known as a *pretotype*[101], serves two purposes:

- It ensures that the customer and the corporate startup are on the same page and do not get "lost in translation."

- It supports initial feasibility assessments, answering the question: "Can we make such a product on an industrial scale at a reasonable cost?"

Investing significant financial and human resources into a new business concept is only justifiable when the market potential is substantial enough. Therefore, the corporate startup must conduct an initial *market sizing*. This analysis aims to determine whether the segment of the market that aligns with the problem/solution-fit, known as the *Serviceable Addressable Market*, is large enough to satisfy the corporate investor's appetite.

If the corporate startup succeeds in creating a sizable new business, it will inevitably reshape industry value chains and ecosystems. Consequently, they must have an idea on *how the superior value proposition should be created and delivered at scale*[102].

---

[100] See chapter 19 for more guidance.

[101] This is not a typo. Pretotypes prioritize learning over engineering, see also https://bit.ly/3HskFrO.

[102] In other words, a precursor to the corporate scaleup's operating model.

To avoid "lost in translation," corporate startups should work with pretotypes in the Business Foundation stage.

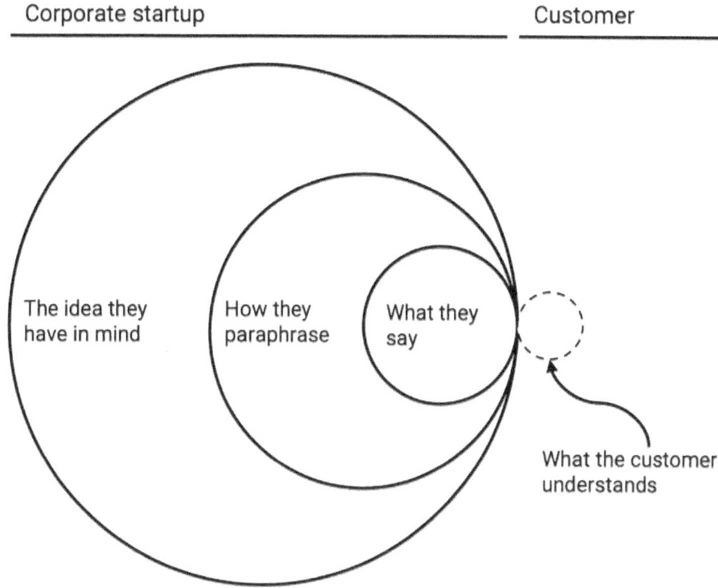

Exhibit 6–5: Pretotypes ensure that corporate startup and customers are in sync.

Lastly, establishing a strong business foundation requires an *initial validation of the corporate context*. At this stage, this alignment is about reaching a fundamental consensus on the investment rationale, the suitable business model options, the associated risks, and an *initial economic viability analysis*.

Stage 3: Business Strategy

The Business Strategy stage has three main goals:

– Co-creating the Minimum Viable Product (MVP) with potential customers.

– Finding the proof points that there is a winning strategy.

– Aligning with the corporate context.

Co-creating the MVP with potential customers helps the corporate startup to understand which product they should build in the next stage. The MVP is a demonstrator with some working functionality that highlights some aspects of a future product that customers see as a superior solution to their problem. It is used only in controlled environments, such as co-creation sessions. Customer interaction is more important than engineering in co-creating the MVP. Chapter 19 provides guidance on how to get the MVP right.

Second, the corporate startup must develop and validate a winning strategy. If there is no validated winning strategy, the chances for Scaling-Up success are limited. The winning strategy consists of two parts:

– The market growth strategy.

– Building a sustainable competitive advantage during Scaling-Up.

The *market growth strategy* identifies the initial market segment, the so-called *beachhead*, and the subsequent market segments, the so-called *bowling alley*. **Crafting a solid market growth strategy is hard validation work. It is much more than educated guesses about market segments that might also be interested in the intended solution. This is one of the points where many corporate startups stumble.**

The second part of the winning strategy is the sustainable competitive advantage. Analyses of successful (corporate and greenfield) startups show that these have one or more sustainable competitive advantages[103]. Building up such a sustainable competitive advantage must be embedded into the business, operating and mental models of the corporate startup, as indicated in the exhibit below[104].

---

[103] See https://bit.ly/3xBv9TW and https://bit.ly/4cTqEEv.
[104] Adapted from Jim Barney, Resource-Based Theory, Oxford University Press, 2007.

is to *define the business model* with a lean, scalable *operating model*, a lean scalable *organizational design*, and a scalable *commercial infrastructure*. This includes a clear view on the *target organization for the first few months*, the *key positions that need to be staffed first*, and ideally, a shortlist of potential candidates.

The second line of action is to demonstrate a *repeatable sales process with traction*, commonly known as achieving a good product/market fit. In this context there is a pitfall that many corporate startups are not aware of: **with its first customers, the corporate startup has achieved product/pioneer-fit, not product/market-fit** and hence it must validate that it can win "mainstream customer segments" efficiently, as explained in chapter 19.

Finally, on the industrialization side, the team needs to have at least a *clear view on how to ensure production at scale* when the business model innovation builds on physical products. In this case, the technical design for the MMP and the value creation—suppliers, parts specifications, their manufacturing processes, and the company's manufacturing process—need to be worked out with a reasonable level of detail.

Furthermore, the corporate startup has to *prepare the decisions that are to be taken in the subsequent Transition-to-Scaling-Up stage* described in the next chapter. Apart from the points already mentioned, a *detailed economic analysis* and a *substantiated Scaling-Up budget* are required. Finally, before launching the MMP into the initial market, a deep-dive IP analysis needs to confirm *freedom-to-operate*, and future IP management to be defined.

Focus on Leading Indicators, Not on Lagging Indicators

Quite often, corporate stakeholders assess a corporate startup's scale-readiness on metrics such as revenue or number of customers. However, these metrics do not provide insights that benefit both the team and their stakeholders since they are "lagging indicators."

In management theory, there is a crucial distinction between these lagging indicators and so-called leading indicators. The former measures the outcome one aims to achieve and is a result of past actions. The metric is clear, but it is only visible in hindsight. A leading indicator measures the effectiveness and efficiency of actions taken to achieve that lagging indicator and predicts future success. For instance, the number of prospects in the last four weeks is a lagging indicator, whereas the number of sales calls is a leading indicator for that lagging indicator.

Focusing on leading indicators forces the corporate startup to focus on factors it can control and identify actions that will have the greatest impact on achieving the desired lagging indicators. This approach also enables stakeholders to evaluate whether the team's successes were fleeting or whether, with systematic and diligent effort, those initial successes can be replicated and scaled.

Chapter 7: Transition to Scaling-Up

Chapter 7
Transition to Scaling-Up

The Lean Scaleup framework comprises 12 modules, with 4 modules allocated to each of the Methodology, Leadership, and People/Culture dimensions.

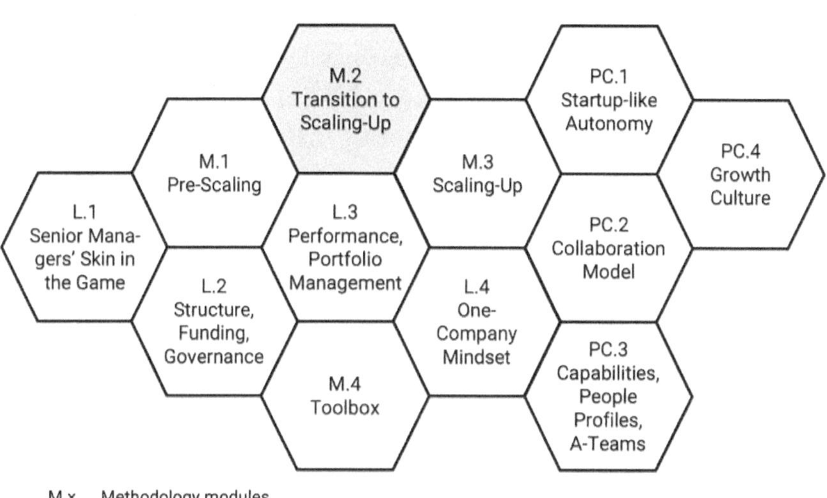

Key Points in This Chapter

1. Many new-business building frameworks lack a transitional phase between validation and scaling.

2. These frameworks seem to assume that at end of Pre-Scaling, NOW is perfectly prepared to support Scaling-Up.

3. The Transition-to-Scaling-Up phase has four work streams: (1) identify scalability debts, (2) determine the organizational home for the corporate scaleup, (3) design the interplay between Core and the corporate scaleup, and (4) develop a shared game plan.

* *

One of my clients, a senior vice president of a technology commercialization unit, made a remark that I found particularly insightful. His unit had invested over USD 100m in numerous corporate scaleups and corporate ventures. He said: "We were too focused on initial revenues. The moment we booked first sales, we rushed into Scaling-Up. However, most of our corporate scaleups and corporate ventures hit a roadblock because neither they nor NOW were adequately prepared."

Most new-business building frameworks have no dedicated transition phase between Pre-Scaling and Scaling-Up (as discussed in the previous and next chapter, respectively). It appears that these frameworks assume that once validation is done and initial revenues are achieved, NOW is perfectly prepared to support Scaling-Up.

However, this assumption is far from reality. The lack of operative alignment between NOW and NEW is one of the key reasons why out-of-the-box innovation concepts do not scale. Another one is timing:

- Premature Scaling-Up is a "silent killer." 3 out of 4 internet startups fail because they scale up too early[106]. They overspend on marketing, hire the wrong people, hire too soon, become distracted by the demands of their initial customers, and so on.

- Arranging collaboration and support from Core requires respecting the planning cycles of the relevant operative units and functions.

Alignment to ensure Scaling-Up success is required at two levels. At a high level, senior management must align NOW and NEW, as described in chapters 10-13. The second level is the operational level. This chapter outlines the necessary steps to achieve this objective.

---

[106] See https://bit.ly/48o4GXV.

The Challenges in Operational Alignment

When a corporate scaleup seeks access to corporate assets and capabilities to create an unfair advantage, prior operational alignment is required. To illustrate the challenges, let us consider two examples: aligning a corporate scaleup with Core's sales functions and with corporate IT.

Core's sales functions are a valuable asset for a corporate scaleup. They have access to customers, skilled sales professionals, effective customer relationship management systems, tools for creating commercial proposals, and so on. However, from the perspective of the salespersons, innovation does not fit their fine-tuned and well-oiled sales approach[107]. It goes without saying that salespersons enjoy discussing "what comes next" with customers. However, selling new business models is likely to result in a decrease in sales productivity, which is not a good thing for them.

Corporate IT can be another valuable asset for a corporate scaleup when they want to access transactional data. However, the view from the other side is different. Core's IT functions invest large sums to run operational systems and build new ones. They manage the portfolio of IT initiatives using processes that ensure flawless execution of their mission-critical role in NOW. Therefore, the corporate scaleup must align with these processes.

Four Work Streams

Achieving this operational alignment requires a series of meetings which should cover four work streams:

- Identify scalability debts.

- Determine the organizational home for the corporate scaleup.

---

[107] See chapter 19 for a detailed explanation and ideas for overcoming this challenge.

– Design the interplay between Core and the corporate scaleup.

– Develop a shared game plan.

When a company is more mature in new-business building, these alignment discussions can become an integral part of NOW's annual planning and budgeting processes.

Identifying Scalability Debts

At the end of Pre-Scaling, a corporate startup usually has a somewhat repeatable sales process and a first version of a market-ready product. Often, this MMP is built on modern technologies, which are not aligned with the technology platforms mandated by corporate IT. For example, one of my corporate startup clients built its MMP on Amazon Web Services, while corporate IT mandates Microsoft Azure.

This is one example of what I call a scalability debt. These are gaps between the current maturity of the corporate startup and full scalability. The Lean Scaleup does not suggest that a corporate startup should have full scalability before being admitted to Scaling-Up, for two reasons:

– This would extend the Pre-Scaling phase. During this time, a competitor with a good-enough product may enter the market and achieve a first-mover-advantage.

– During this period, the emerging business opportunity would have its organizational home in a structure designed for exploration and validation, but not for rapidly growing business operations. Such a structure is not suitable for investors—neither for the corporate investor, nor for co-funding business units, or for external investors—who should fund the subsequent Scaling-Up phase.

These scalability debts must be addressed during Scaling-Up. When I discuss scalability debts with corporate startups, six topics are frequently on the list:

- Go-to-market and customer acquisition.

- Customer adoption (i.e., how fast customers begin to use the innovation productively).

- Customer success (i.e., customers see the value of the innovation), which is a key factor for customer retention.

- Tech stack.

- Organization (for example staffing of key positions).

- Preparedness of external partners to create and deliver the value proposition.

Determine the Organizational Home for Scaling-Up

In essence, scaling a corporate scaleup can be done in-house or externally, with the latter often referred to as a spin-out. Upon closer examination, the former offers three potential avenues for consideration. This implies that there are four potential options:

- Inside an operative business unit.

- Inside the company but outside of the operative units in a Scaling-Up function.

- Inside the company but outside of the operative units in a dedicated organizational unit (for example, a "Digital Solutions" unit).

- Outside the company, in a separate legal entity that is initially entirely owned by the company.

The first option typically poses significant challenges for the corporate scaleup, as it will face constant short-term pressures in a process-driven context. However, if there is overwhelming customer acceptance, this approach may be the best choice.

Dimension	Company-inside when...	Company-outside when...
Relation to Core	Natural extension or dependency on existing products or business models.	Disrupting core business. A multi-vendor solution is part of the innovation.
Customers	Overlap with existing base. Existing customers are references for bowling alley.	New customer groups. Existing base is not key in winning new customers.
Assets and capabilities	Heavy leveraging of corporate assets and capabilities.	Significantly new capabilities. Significant capabilities from external partners.
Go-to-market	Close collaboration with Core's sales functions feasible.	Only a few synergies with NOW's go-to-market.
Value of corporate brand	An asset to accelerate the journey.	Possible failure can harm corporate brand.
Value for NOW	NOW creates significant value with solution.	Solution weakens NOW's value proposition.
Talent	Internal talent and strong employer brand to attract talent.	Millennial / Gen-Z talent required.
Funding	Sufficient internal funds for funding Scaling-Up.	External funding needed. Allowing external investors.
Risk view	Willingness to carry risk alone.	Risk should be shared.
Intellectual Property (IP)	IP should remain within the company.	Willingness to share IP with external partners.
Financial rationale	New revenue streams.	New revenue streams. Increased market cap.

Exhibit 7–1: Deciding on the organizational home for Scaling-Up.

For example, during the Covid-19 pandemic, one of my corporate startup clients developed a solution that solved a pressing challenge for the company's customers. Consequently, Scaling-Up was arranged within the relevant business unit.

The second option may be a good choice when technical scaling needs to fit an existing production infrastructure and close collaboration between the corporate scaleup and Core's manufacturing function is mandatory. The corporate scaleup must ensure that technical scaling does not overshadow the go-to-market, as this would slow revenue growth. Furthermore, this option has inherent disadvantages when it comes to attracting top talent.

The third option may be the right one when senior management wants to send a transformational signal into Core. Although the new unit is still part of Core, it has the remit to be different. Typical arrangements include growth resources that individual scaleups can use, such as fast-track procurement processes, rapid recruitment capabilities, or a dedicated scalable technology stack. This option has two challenges:

– Recruiting and retaining top talent on the corporate payroll may be challenging.

– Core might be jealous that this units receives disproportionate management attention, which could hinder effective collaboration.

The fourth option offers two significant advantages: it is generally easier to attract top talent and it allows for the admission of external investors to individual scaleups or parts of the new-business portfolio. However, there are also two major drawbacks to this approach:

– Negotiating the details of the carve-out with NOW's senior management can be time-consuming.

– This setup usually does not contribute to a one-company mindset[108].

---

[108] See chapter 13.

Design the Corporate Scaleup/Core Interplay

There are four main issues that relate to the interplay between Core and the corporate scaleup during the Scaling-up phase. First, mitigating the downside for relevant Core functions. When supporting a corporate scaleup, key metrics of the supporting function, such as employee productivity and revenue growth, may suffer. **If these adverse effects are not mitigated, Core's functions and units might not fully embrace their role in Scaling-Up.**

Second, designing the startup-like autonomy within the corporate context. To rapidly scale up, a corporate scaleup needs the flexibility to operate with fewer corporate constraints while still adhering to defined guardrails. This is a critical factor for success and is discussed in chapter 14.

Third, the composition of the governance board. A lean governance board with the necessary skills and an entrepreneurial mindset is crucial for success. This governance board should have an earmarked Scaling-Up budget release it pro rata when pre-defined Scaling-Up milestones are achieved. Chapters 8 and 11 provide more information on these issues.

Fourth, embedding Scaling-Up milestones into the goal systems of corporate functions and operational units. Without this integration, supporting Scaling-Up is not a goal for Core's middle managers and functional experts and they may not embrace their role as supporters.

Develop a Shared Game Plan

In this workstream, there are typically five key activities involved. First, developing an initial Scaling-Up roadmap, as explained in the next chapter. Given the remaining uncertainties, it should not be expected that this roadmap will remain unchanged during a multi-year Scaling-Up journey.

Second, developing a 100-day operational plan to create momentum and to build trust between Core, the corporate scaleup and its governance board. This period sets the tone for the next years. Without this momentum, the Scaling-Up ambition may lack determination and energy.

Third, recruiting key personnel. As explained in chapter 16, exceptional scalers possess a unique personality profile. If individuals with these characteristics are not available within the company, external recruiting or hiring interim managers should be considered.

Fourth, selecting the CEO. The ideal candidate should possess a strong entrepreneurial drive and a deep understanding of how Core operates. Chapter 16 dives deeper into the profile of this role and outlines the challenges that NOW's senior managers face when they should become the corporate scaleup's CEO.

Fifth, orchestrating the first Scaling-Up stage in the case that the corporate scaleup should collaborate with Core' sales functions. In this case, the first Scaling-Up stage has a dual mission. The first mission is that the corporate scaleup must significantly increase revenues and the number of customers. The second mission is to operationalize sales-related activities for these functions. This refers to what salespersons need for high sales productivity, such as sales presentations, tools for crafting commercial proposals, compelling materials to attract prospects, case studies with early customers, pre-sales support and so forth.

Chapter 8:
Scaling-Up

Chapter 8
Scaling-Up

The Lean Scaleup framework comprises 12 modules, with 4 modules allocated to each of the Methodology, Leadership, and People/Culture dimensions.

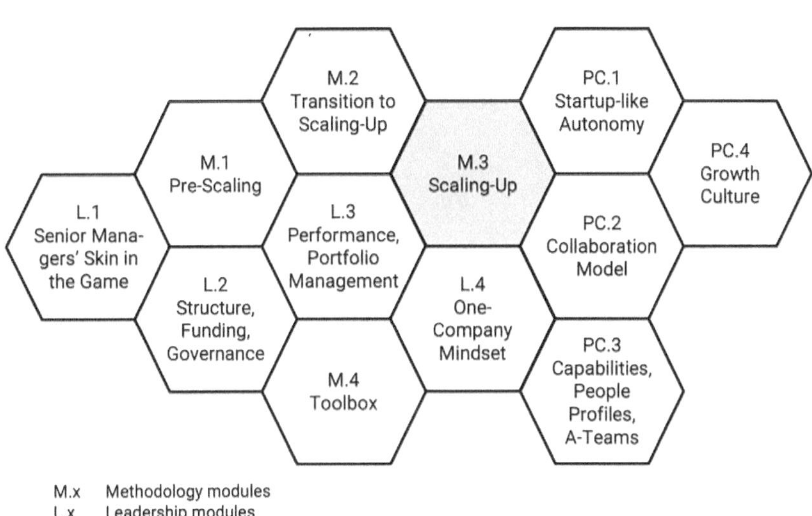

Key Points in This Chapter

1. Scaling-Up is a vital phase in out-of-the-box innovation. Without success in this phase, all previous activities are just a costly hobby or "happy engineering."

2. A solid setup for Scaling-Up success requires a thorough validation in the Pre-Scaling phase and a Transition-to-Scaling-Up phase, as described in the previous two chapters.

3. Scaling-Up plays out on four tracks: (1) strategy, market, and revenues; (2) product; (3) organization; (4) relationship to NOW.

4. In the first track, it is as important to build strategic moats that protect the corporate scaleup's growth as it is to drive revenue growth. An early expansion into subsequent markets may not be effective.

5. The second track involves four types of product work. A corporate scaleup's product team must be aware of these and not just be a "feature factory."

6. The third track chapter is about organizational growth while maintaining the startup spirit. A growth culture is mission-critical; this issue is—due to its importance—addressed in a separate chapter (chapter 17).

7. As the corporate scaleup grows it becomes more visible to corporate functions such as corporate risk, compliance, and ESG. The corporate scaleup should anticipate and adjust accordingly.

**

A senior manager from a corporate technology and innovation function asked for my help in understanding why a corporate scaleup did not progress as expected. They had developed an AI-solution that solved a major problem for an entire industry. However, after acquiring a few initial customers, their growth plateaued.

The corporate scaleup's CEO developed a growth plan that included additional funding. However, the governance board did not approve the plan. They had difficulties in understanding whether this plan and the next round of funding would enable significant progress. After conducting a short assessment, I concluded that some missteps had been made. My report included nine points:

– Premature Scaling-Up. They began Scaling-Up after the first customer was signed. However, in many cases—like in this one—this is premature. They were not scale-ready.

– Premature hiring. The leadership team anticipated a surge in demand and hired additional personnel. However, the new hires increased the cost base and did not align with the company's existing culture, which negatively impacted morale.

– Losing focus. The corporate scaleup agreed to many product requests from potential customers to close the deals. This made it increasingly difficult to prioritize product work and maintain alignment between the go-to-market and the product teams.

- Confusing leadership with management. Initially, the leadership team was able to handle all functional roles. However, due to increasing tensions between the go-to-market market and product teams, they found themselves in constant firefighting mode.

- Lack of cohesion. The corporate scaleup had a remarkable long-term vision. But the leadership team failed to create a roadmap with 12-18-months steps that could be easily understood by the corporate investor and integrated into NOW's mindset and planning systems.

- Ineffective marketing. The marketing plan was "more of the same." Their messaging spoke to technology leaders in their target market, but it did not speak to mainstream customers.

- Unclear funding situation. The size of the funding request came as a surprise to the governance board, and they were not convinced by the arguments. To secure his funding request, the corporate scaleup's CEO had to align with NOW's annual budgeting cycle, which resulted in the postponement of many plans.

- Non-scalable infrastructure. The corporate scaleup focused too much on firefighting and neglected to build a scalable organizational and technical infrastructure. As a result, they were not prepared to handle additional business even if they received additional funding.

- Losing agility. The leadership team believed that hierarchies and proper execution of their plans were necessary to regain and maintain control. They were at risk of losing their startup spirit and everything that enabled them to achieve their initial successes.

What Is Scaling-Up?

Scaling-Up is an essential phase of the innovation journey from a meaningful idea to a scaled-up business that generates new growth and contributes to the company's transformation. This phase involves rapidly growing sales and operations, with growth rates exceeding 100 percent annually[109]. Such growth requires a rapidly growing organization as well.

This phase begins when a corporate startup has been validated to be scale-worthy and scale-ready and it has also passed the Transition-to-Scaling-Up stage, as described in the previous two chapters. It ends when a "sizable business" has been created. There is no general definition about what sizable means. One of my clients, a German engineering company with USD 80bn in annual revenues, sets the bar at USD 10m in annual revenues while other clients set it at USD 20-50m.

Although this newly created business is much smaller than NOW, it has characteristics, such as a repeatable go-to-market process, that allow further growth by re-integrating it into one of Core's operative units or by turning it into a new business unit. It can also grow as a stand-alone entity within the corporate group or be folded into a joint venture.

Why Is Scaling-Up So Hard?

Scaling-Up is incredibly hard. Only one out of five corporate startups that launch its first product into the market create a USD 50m business[110].

Many companies recognize the need to create new businesses. But they do not devote the same attention to scaling the emerging business opportunities that they have created.

---

[109] See https://chartmogul.com/reports/saas-growth-report/2023.
[110] See chapter 2.

Rapid Growth, Time Pressure, Super-Complex

Scaling-Up requires focus, determination, discipline, and tenacity. However, most importantly, it demands dedication to the customer and the humility to accept that early wins do not guarantee long-term success.

The best corporate scaleups grow twenty times as much as the average Fortune 500 company[111]. Apart from mastering this extraordinary growth, they face constant time pressure:

- Competitors may copy their business model.

- The patience of the corporate investor is limited.

In addition to these two challenges, Scaling-Up requires a professional management of complexity. A number of issues contribute to this complexity, for instance:

- Since the business model is new, there are no processes, playbooks, or best practices. The corporate scaleup must "build the parachute while it falls down."

- It must manage several moving parts at once, such as retaining customers, entering new markets, developing products and services, hiring and training new employees, managing increasing business volume, and so on—and it must make sure that these parts fit together.

- As the headcount of the corporate scaleup grows rapidly, maintaining the culture established in the early stages of Scaling-Up is a challenge.

Uncertainties Require a Specific Budgeting Logic

Even with the most rigorous and professional validation, there are still inherent uncertainties and unknowns in Scaling-Up. Examples include identifying the most effective strategies for acquiring mainstream customers or determining the optimal approach for delivering exceptional customer

---

[111] See https://bit.ly/46OgBgj.

service at scale. Therefore, scaling up an emerging business opportunity is about learning, not about executing a plan.

Effective funding mechanisms must take these uncertainties and unknowns into account. The Scaling-Up budget, which the corporate scaleup secured in the Transition-to-Scaling-Up phase, is only an estimate. It is not uncommon for a corporate scaleup to exhaust the allocated budget while at the same time key metrics provide reasons to be optimistic.

Therefore, it is good practice to establish a "secondary budget" to mitigate those situations. This additional funding can be released on short notice by the governance board, outside of NOW's lengthy budgeting cycles. It should be linked to Scaling-Up milestones and reduced over time—for example, 20 percent of the relevant Scaling-Up budget in the first year and 10 percent in the next two years.

Scaling-Up Requires Special People Profiles

Mastering the dynamic, complexity and uncertainty of Scaling-Up requires special people. These individuals are neither the visionaries, strategic thinkers, and empathetic listeners who excel in the Discovery phase, nor assumption hunters with a scientific mindset required for the subsequent stages of the Pre-Scaling phase.

A successful corporate scaleup requires individuals who excel in multitasking and enjoy a degree of autonomy while being aligned with an overarching purpose and vision. Chapter 16 provides more detail about the people profiles needed to succeed in Scaling-Up.

How This Chapter Is Organized

Corporate scaleups build out-of-the-box innovations and new businesses in many categories. The example above falls into a category that could be called AI solutions. Other areas for new growth that my clients pursue are, for example:

- Service-centric business models.

- Smart physical products.

- Circular business models in the Sustainability context.

- Digital platforms and marketplaces.

- Smart agents in B2B2C scenarios.

This list is not exhaustive. Considering this diversity, I think it is impossible to provide a one-size-fits-all guidance for Scaling-Up. However, it is possible to highlight the factors that make the difference between winning and losing, the main challenges, and the most crucial aspects when dealing with them.

Therefore, the content of this chapter is organized along the four "swim lanes" that every corporate scaleup must master in parallel:

- Strategy, market, and revenues. The corporate scaleup must expand its customer base and revenues with a clear strategy to avoid losing focus. This section covers market-facing challenges. Questions related to how a scaleup should structure its go-to-market functions are addressed in the "Organization" section of this chapter. The issue of collaborating with Core's sales functions is addressed in chapter 19.

- Product. The corporate scaleup must also advance its product, from a Minimum Marketable Product (MMP) to a product that solves multiple problems for multiple market niches. This section contains product-related issues. Questions that relate to how to organize the product function are addressed in the "Organization" section.

- Organization. As the corporate scaleup expands its market presence and product offerings, it must also grow its organization. This section discusses challenges such as how to grow the organization without losing the startup spirit and how to balance agility and standardization. Additionally, this section addresses the right metrics and organizing the go-to-market and product functions, as mentioned above.

– Relationship to NOW. As the corporate scaleup grows, the relationship with NOW will change. It gets on the company's radar screen and the importance of corporate compliance, risk management, and financial control becomes more pronounced. This section outlines the key points and provides guidance on how to design a productive collaboration.

The final section in this chapter, "Scaling-Up stages and milestones," shows how these four swim lanes can be used to define clear Scaling-Up milestones that are the basis for an effective, lean governance and staged, so-called metered funding.

Strategy, Market, and Revenues

What makes the difference in market success, assuming that a corporate scaleup had been validated as scale-worthy and scale-ready? One answer stood out when I discussed this question with the co-creators of the Lean Scaleup: an effective strategy.

An effective strategy means to do four things right. First, to stick to a validated growth path and to know what not to do. Less successful corporate scaleups react to many market impulses and engage in sales activities in many market niches. They end up losing focus and hardly achieve repeatability and scalability in their go-to-market approach.

In contrast, successful corporate scaleups follow a validated growth strategy. To expand their market presence, they build a sequence of market successes, where each step leverages the product features and customer base of the previous market niche.

When a corporate scaleup in the early stages of Scaling-Up is solely focused on acquiring as many customers as possible, it is very easy to become distracted by market temptations. But what is the point of building new features for a potential customer from a low-margin market? Although they might win that customer, but they would require significant marketing resources to attract additional customers from such a market. This turns market growth into swimming against the tide—despite swimming hard, progress will be limited.

Strategic Moats and a Sustainable Competitive Edge

An effective strategy means secondly to protect growth by creating strategic moats that ensure a sustainable competitive edge. Successful scaleups apply eight patterns[112]:

- Network effects where the value increases with every new participant.

- Privileged access to mission-critical resources like patents and locations.

- Economies of scale.

- Switching costs, i.e., prohibitive costs for replacing a current solution.

- Counter-positioning, i.e., driving new business models that incumbents cannot copy due to anticipated damage to their existing business.

- Data, i.e., collecting and connecting more and better transactional data for superior insights.

- Process excellence, meaning superior knowledge and expertise about how to run business processes.

- Culture and brand.

The Crucial Role of the End Game

An effective strategy means thirdly to be clear about the customer and contract structure that the corporate scaleup should build. The optimal structure depends on the intended pathway-to-value after successful Scaling-Up.

---

[112] This relates to greenfield and corporate scaleups. See https://rb.gy/cwzxv7 and https://bit.ly/3Qfu89J.

For example, if the corporate scaleup should be re-integrated into Core, the customer and contract structure should be designed to fit—or deliberately designed to complement—the existing business. In other cases, when for example the corporate scaleup should be spun out and financial investors be admitted, they should aim for long-term contracts and be selective of the markets it targets.

M&A to Accelerate Scaling-Up

An effective strategy means fourthly to be open to acquiring other startups or scaleups to accelerate Scaling-Up. This strategic move might be effective in three situations:

- Rolling up similar businesses. Adding startups or scaleups with complementary verticals or geographies helps to gain credibility and accelerate the journey to achieve economies of scale.

- Capabilities to support the growth strategy. This is an attractive move if subsequent markets demand a piece of technology that would take some time to develop.

- Market access. Acquiring local champions in a subsequent market niche helps to accelerate the bowling alley strategy.

Winning the First Batch of Customers

Initial customers of a corporate startup's MMP typically have the capability and resources to scout innovative solutions and to integrate these into their infrastructure. The theory on the adoption of new technology[113] says that these so-called pioneers make up an average of 2.5 percent of the total market. Winning the first batch of customers beyond the initial one is a significant challenge. In my experience, two approaches are effective.

---

[113] Geoffrey Moore, Crossing the Chasm, Collins, 2014.

First, keep on developing. The first option is to keep developing. This does not mean that the product team should isolate itself. On the contrary, it is mandatory to talk to technological leaders in the market, form relationships, receive feedback, and stay current with market developments. However, in the long-term, following the product vision may be more important than developing customer-specific solutions.

Second, intersect the market. It is not uncommon for corporate scaleups to identify niche opportunities in overlapping markets where customer needs align with the product's current maturity. By selling to these segments, they can increase their revenues without diverting attention from long-term product and market goals.

Winning Two Thirds of the Market

To drive market presence and revenue growth, a corporate scaleup must win the largest segment of the markets it operates in. These so-called mainstream customers account for two thirds of the entire market. Customers from this segment have different priorities when they buy new technology. They request:

- Deep support and documentation.

- Services that support onboarding, training and change management.

- Partnerships in their industry.

- A relevant ecosystem.

- A solid Return On Investment calculation.

These mainstream customers ask for product features that go well beyond the MMP, such as:

- Well-designed user interfaces.

- Decision support.

- Support for secondary processes such as tax or ESG reporting.

- Pre-built integrations.

- Functionalities to manage the user base.

- Efficient data entry and data visualization modules.

- Support for third-party software.

To identify pioneer and mainstream customers, I recommend investigating the events that target customers attend and the media they consume. For example, the corporate scaleup mentioned in the beginning of this chapter found pioneer customers at AI-related conferences, while they met mainstream customers at general industry events.

When to Expand from the Initial Market

The list above shows that product complexity increases, and service elements may be needed when the corporate scaleup wants to succeed with mainstream customers or conquer subsequent market niches. This raises the question when the corporate scaleup should expand from its original market, the so-called beachhead market.

It may be better to focus on conquering the initial market before expanding into other segments. Expanding into lukewarm market segments too early could slow down momentum, negatively impact the network, generate below-average product reviews, drive up costs, and dilute the corporate scaleup's messaging.

However, if the corporate scaleup focuses a little longer on its beachhead market, fine-tunes the customer experience to match the expectations of mainstream customers in that market, the quality of the product/market-fit could reach a point where several crucial things happen:

- Customer acquisition costs decrease.

- Customer retention increases.

- Customers' willingness-to-pay increases.

- Press coverage and social mentions increase.

- NOW's appreciation of the corporate startup increases.

All these positive developments could then make other customer segments envious to get access to the corporate scaleup's product—which is an excellent starting point for then executing a carefully crafted bowling alley strategy.

Valleys of Death

The co-creators of the Lean Scaleup found that in Scaling-Up there are several "Valleys of Death" that relate to challenges in the go-to-market approach, depending on three revenue thresholds. Between:

- USD 1m and USD 10m, the challenge is to professionalize the sales process and to scale sales efforts.

- USD 10m and USD 30m, the challenge is to implement sustainable growth practices, in particular the scalability of sales-related and sales-supporting activities.

- USD 30m and USD 50m, professionalizing customer retention becomes as important as customer acquisition.

Dealing with Slowing Growth

As the corporate scaleup grows into other market segments, the market message dilutes. At the outset of Scaling-Up, they targeted one clearly defined market with a solution to one well-defined problem. But after initial successes, the market message needs to care for multiple niches with related, but slightly different problems. Take these two companies as an example:

- In 2020, Slack's key message on its corporate website was: "Slack replaces email in your company." In 2024, it is: "Made for people. Built for productivity."

- Zoom's message was: "Zoom for video, conference rooms & phone." It is now: "One platform to connect."

The dilution of the market message might be one factor that contributes to a slowing growth. This does not mean that the end of the corporate scaleup's growth story is near. But it is crucial how a corporate scaleup's leadership team reacts in such a situation. My piece of advice is to develop a "healthy paranoia." The numbers could be interpreted as declining efficiency in a marketing channel or an underperforming sales region. It might be tempting to assume that some tactical fixes will reignite growth.

But the real reason—and implicitly expressed in a diluted market message—may be a decrease in product/market-fit. With excellent product/market-fit, most activities produce the desired results; when it deteriorates, many things that used to work do not work anymore.

If fixing the symptoms does not bring the corporate scaleup back on a solid growth path, it may be wise to take a step back. Failing to acknowledge that the issue is fundamental, and that product/market-fit must be reestablished could be a significant failure.

Product

After the concluding dinner of a one-day workshop with a corporate scaleup, I stood at the bar with their Chief Technology Officer (CTO). I had asked him when product-related issues spun out of control.

He said: "As we expanded our team from a dozen to over thirty developers in just a few months, our promised deliveries were no longer functioning properly. Individual modules passed the tests, but when we integrated them, all kinds of problems arose. As delays increased from days to weeks and then to months, our development plan fell apart. Hiring more engineers did not resolve the problem. The office was buzzing around the clock, but we could not deliver on time."

This story is not about people profiles. The CTO had ten years of experience. His team had impressive CVs; some had previously worked for Big

Tech companies. All team members were accustomed to building products under pressure using modern tools and methods.

However, I find that this CTO's situation is not unique. Successfully scaling the product is just as challenging as scaling the market footprint. Additionally, keeping both sides in sync as the corporate scaleup grows from one market niche to the next adds another layer of complexity.

Four Types of Product-Related Work

Product work in Scaling-Up differs significantly from product work in Pre-Scaling. Prior to Scaling-Up, product work involves conceptualizing a superior solution to a high-priority customer problem, understanding which product to build through several iterations of a Minimal Viable Product (MVP), and ultimately building a feature-poor MMP that pioneer customers from the initial market use in their environment.

In Scaling-Up, there are four categories of product work, each of them adding different value points:

- Feature work extends the product's functionality.

- Growth work accelerates product adoption and usage, thus increasing customer retention. This includes creating internal tools for first-level and second-level support or self-service solutions for customers.

- Product/market-fit expansion work expands the product into adjacent markets to support the bowling alley strategy.

- Technical scaling work establishes a scalable, high-performing, solid and secure platform that unlocks new levels of feature, growth, and product/market-fit expansion work.

If the technical team of a corporate scaleup is not clear about these different types, it cannot prioritize effectively. This can lead to suboptimal processes, incorrect measures of success, a suboptimal technical portfolio, and misalignment between product and go-to-market teams. Any one of these issues can cause problems, but when they occur together, they can put the entire ambition at risk.

While new features may be exciting, they are just one of the four types of product work. I have witnessed corporate scaleups that:

- Emphasized feature work when they should have done growth work to ensure retention of the first customers.

- Focused on growth work when they should have prioritized feature work to win early adopters from a new market segment.

- Prioritized growth work and feature work when they should have worked on expanding product/market-fit, thus hampering the execution of the market growth strategy.

- Preferred the first three items over technical scaling, thus limiting the ability to launch new things rapidly.

Look for Scale, Not Customer-Specific Solutions

Finding new customers can be challenging for corporate scaleups, and they may be tempted to create customer-specific solutions in response to specific feature requests. However, following too many of these temptations can lead them away from the product vision. Therefore, it is important to consider whether creating a specific solution for one new customer brings the corporate scaleup closer to its goals.

Scaling-Up is not about solving one specific customer problem at a time to generate short-term revenues. The goal is to create a profitable, high-growth business with a solution for many customers. While the corporate scaleup's product may be niche, it should not be a collection of customer-specific features.

In my opinion, it is essential to establish guidelines for dealing with requests for customer-specific solutions. For instance, one of my corporate scaleup clients decided that if a custom solution's business value was less than USD 5m, it would decline the request.

But even when the business value of a custom solution exceeds a certain threshold, it is still a matter of careful consideration. A customer-specific, sophisticated digital solution can be sold with a seven-figure price tag, which means that only a few customers are needed for a USD 20m business. But here is the point: any customer who spends millions on a software expects a certain level of support and service. Such a situation might lead a corporate scaleup away from its ambition and bring it closer to become a software house that develops customer-specific solutions.

Product Strategy

In Pre-Scaling, a corporate startup should say "yes" whenever a potential customer invites them to explore. However, in Scaling-Up, this could have the opposite effect, leading to many half-baked projects. Therefore, it is essential for product strategy that product teams learn to say "no."

The product strategy challenge lies in the fact that it is eyeing products that are used externally, but it is intended for internal audiences. These audiences include the corporate scaleup's leadership team, members of the product team and to some degree also corporate stakeholders. The product strategy serves a distinct purpose for each of these audiences. For instance, the former must establish the direction and ensure horizontal and vertical coherence while the product team requires clear, reliable, yet flexible decision-making guardrails for prioritization.

The product strategy should instill mindfulness when it comes to product features. Some features may be products in disguise and permanently thinking about what should—not could (!)—be added to the feature base is an important part of product strategy.

Atomic Units of Engagement

The deeper reason why I recommend mindfulness in product feature work is the observation that all great products are built around "atomic units of engagement[114]." These are the simplest, most repeatable actions that users

---

[114] See https://www.focusedchaos.co

perform. For the e-commerce solution Shopify, these are product selection and purchases; for Facebook, these are posts and reactions.

When product teams consider adding new features, they should be clear on the reason why. When discussing with product teams why a certain feature should be developed, I often hear arguments like:

– Cross-selling other products.

– Creating a new revenue stream.

– Establishing feature-parity with a competing product.

– Driving upsells.

– Reducing customer churn at renewal time.

– Minimizing the number of abandoned trial accounts.

These are all valid points. However, I see two areas for concern. First, product teams often neglect to consider how to enhance and safeguard the core of their product, the atomic units of engagement. Too many features hide the product core which increases the time until the customer sees the value, decreases customer engagement rates, lowers customer retention rates, and may lead to growth problems.

Second, each new feature incurs so-called feature shadow costs. There is no zero maintenance. Features must be constantly maintained, updated, and supported, regardless of the number of customers using them. Terminating unpopular features is easier said than done since sometimes these are heavily used by a few power users. Removing those features can upset this important customer segment.

Product Metrics

Why do smart product teams build products with little impact? Often, the answer lies in the metrics that the product team uses. An approach that organizes product metrics into a pyramid[115], comparable to Maslow's hierarchy of needs, helps to establish clarity.

At the base of the pyramid, there are metrics related to the health and reliability of the product, such as load times and the number of security incidents. Without a certain performance level in this dimension, a corporate scaleup's product will never be successful.

One level above are customer satisfaction metrics. These metrics measure how well the product solves customers' problems. Examples of metrics in this category include Net Promoter Score, customer service metrics, and social media/listening metrics, including sentiment analysis.

Metrics on level three track the number of customers and users, growth, customer onboarding and retention, and product usage intensity. Examples of metrics at this level include:

— Number of new users.

— Conversions from free to paid plans.

— Churn rates.

— Renewal rates.

— Daily Active Users.

— Number of user actions.

— Time to complete tasks.

Finally, the top level of the pyramid addresses business metrics. These metrics include, for example, monthly recurring revenues, average revenue per user or account, and customer lifetime value. This level should also contain the crucial North Star metric, as explained in the next section.

---

[115] Adapted from https://rb.gy/a3zhjj.

Product metrics should cover 4 levels.

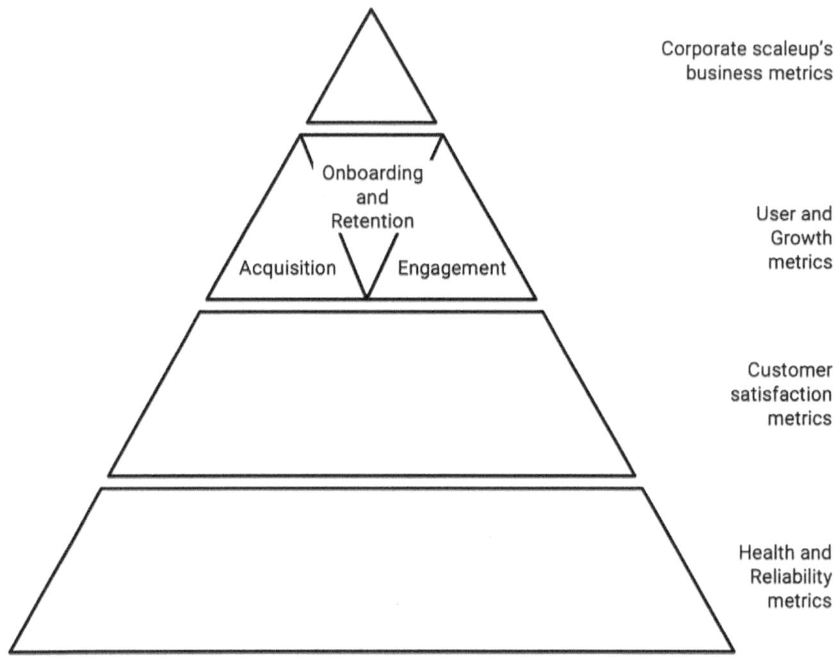

Exhibit 8–1: Product metrics hierarchy in Scaling-Up.

Organization

A corporate scaleup's organization, people, and culture can make or break the ambition. Therefore, there are four modules in the Lean Scaleup framework that relate to these issues, which are discussed in more detail in chapters 14-17. This section focuses on the organizational challenges and the hard factors such as metrics, recruiting, and the organizational design of the go-to-market and product functions.

Challenge 1: Autonomy and Alignment

At the outset of Scaling-Up, the corporate scaleup has a few initial customers who use the MMP. Let us assume that the revenues generated are USD 500k. When the goal is to build a USD 10m business in three years, the compounded annual growth rate (CAGR) is more than 170 percent; when the goal is to build a USD 30m business in five years, the CAGR is more than 150 percent.

Annual top-down plans are inadequate in such an environment. To create and manage such growth, it is imperative to unleash the entrepreneurship of autonomous teams while ensuring that their activities align with overarching goals. As a general guideline, the more aligned the teams of a corporate scaleup are, the greater the autonomy they can have.

Balancing alignment and autonomy requires a transparent and straightforward mechanism that connects the key results and the corresponding activities of teams from different parts of the organization with overarching objectives[116]. Installing such a system, aligned with a North Star metric that is also relevant for NOW (see below), is a foundational piece for aligning the corporate scaleup with NOW.

Two important aspects of team autonomy are easy to spot. The first is the team's ability to make two-way-door decisions. In his 2017 letter to shareholders[117], Amazon's founder Jeff Bezos outlined his framework for categorizing decisions. He distinguished between two types of decisions: those that are irreversible and one-way, and those that are reversible and two-way. He said: "As organizations get larger, they tend to use heavy-weight type-1 decision-making processes on most decisions, including type-2 decisions. The result of this is slowness, unthoughtful risk aversion, failure to experiment sufficiently, and consequently diminished invention."

---

[116] One method that has gained widespread adoption is the OKR method, see https://en.wikipedia.org/wiki/Objectives_and_key_results

[117] See https://bit.ly/3MIdUFk.

The second indicator of team autonomy is the level of trust. While autonomy/alignment systems like OKRs are necessary, they are not sufficient without trust. A sign for a lack of trust is when team leaders micromanage their teams. They may see their behavior as ownership, but it can lead to frustration and resentment among team members who are expecting entrepreneurial freedom.

Challenge 2: Agility and Standardization

Autonomous teams should be small and responsible for an end-to-end product or an outcome for internal or external customers. In addition, the team should be self-sufficient, comprising individuals who possess all the necessary capabilities.

The work style of autonomous teams is highly agile. They work in short cycles, so-called sprints, and integrate learnings from customer interactions into future cycles. This approach allows teams to deliver results much more rapidly than if they were working in functional silos.

In addition to agility, a corporate scaleup also requires structured processes for scalability. Streamlined business processes such as go-to-market, product development, operations, and customer care must be installed during Scaling-Up. **The key is to identify when to switch from agility to process and to have reliable metrics that show if the process is effective.**

For instance, when a corporate scaleup wanted to implement a semi-automated recruiting process, their metric was how long it takes newly hired salespersons to win the tenth customer. However, they found that this metric was increasing. Consequently, they turned back some of the automations they had put in place.

Challenge 3: Structure and the Startup Spirit

As the corporate scaleup grows, managing communication between staff members becomes increasingly difficult. There are 45 potential lines of direct communication with a staff of 10, but more than 1,225 with a staff of 50. Therefore, additional structures are necessary at some point.

I advise my corporate scaleup clients to think of organizational structures as communication architectures. Structures optimize communication among certain parts of the organization while potentially hindering communication with others. For instance, if the product team is part of the engineering group, communication between the product team and engineering functions may be optimized, but this may impede communication between the product team and the marketing function.

This applies to the external environment as well. For example, a corporate scaleup organized its sales unit by product groups to improve communication with technical product groups and the salespersons. But this approach made it more difficult for customers who purchased multiple products because they needed to interact with different salespersons.

Challenge 4: Finding the Right Approach to Planning

Although annual top-down plans are not suitable for hypergrowth corporate scaleups, planning is still necessary. When I discuss with CEOs of corporate scaleups about an effective planning approach, I frequently find that a storytelling approach with a focus on the first unit of time and less detail on the subsequent units can be very effective.

For instance, when planning for the next year, the corporate scaleup's leadership team describes what success looks like 12 months from now. Then, they break this down into quarters, with the first quarter receiving more attention than the remaining three. The team can then repeat this process for the months in the first quarter and, if desired, for the weeks in the first month.

This approach provides a detailed plan for the upcoming period and bullet points for the subsequent periods. Detailed plans beyond that point may not be accurate anyway for a rapidly growing corporate scaleup. However, establishing a shared narrative and short-term goals is highly beneficial as it ensures that all team members are aware of their key results required to achieve the aspired objectives.

Challenge 5: Perfection versus "Good Enough"

A corporate scaleup is in a constant race against time and to achieve growth. Hence it must focus on what matters most—growth per time unit. Growth comes from solving customer problems or saving resources in internal workflows. In this mindset, there is little room for perfection. When working with corporate scaleup teams, I often pose the challenging question: "What is the hack? What is the 20/80-Pareto-principle action we can take to resolve the issue at hand?"

Another approach I use to avoid low-impact work is the "order of magnitude test." When discussing how to solve a defined problem, I ask: "What would you do if you need to find a solution for a challenge that is ten times as big as the one you are discussing?" This helps the team to understand that onboarding 100 clients instead of ten or sending out 20 commercial proposals instead of two per week is a different ballgame.

Metrics

Scaling and growth are two fundamentally different concepts. The latter means generating more revenue with a proportional increase in resources and costs, while the former is about significantly increasing revenues while keeping the underlying cost base low. Just as with any other business-relevant aspect, Scaling-Up requires effective metrics. In my view, **a corporate scaleup should have at least five sets of metrics**:

- Financial metrics, such as revenues and revenue growth, profit margins, and free cash flow. These provide insights into the financial health of the corporate scaleup and indicate whether it is scaling or just growing.

- Health of the customer base and how well it attracts new customers is the second set of metrics since these are leading indicators of future revenues. This set of metrics includes, for instance, customer acquisition costs, customer lifetime value, churn rate, and traction.

- A third set of metrics relates to operational efficiency and effectiveness. Metrics in this set, such as employee productivity, provide insights into the corporate scaleup's operational scalability.

- A fourth set of metrics should be product-related, as explained above.

- Finally, there should metrics that are relevant for NOW as well since these quantify the value that the corporate scaleup brings to NOW.

Metrics from the fifth category are essential to create the one-company mindset that is described in chapter 13. A great example of such a so-called North Star metric[118] comes from a beverage company that launched a direct-to-consumer business model innovation. Its North Star metric was the "number of points-of-sales."

Talent Recruiting, Onboarding, and Retention

A corporate scaleup must overcome three talent challenges:
- Finding A+ players.

- Hiring the best candidates through an excellent recruitment process.

- Effectively onboarding these new hires.

Falling short on one of these challenges can lead to problems, but falling short on all three can destroy the scaling ambition. This is because with a rapid growth in staff, new employees can outnumber the originals overnight. When "new people hire new people to hire new people," improper management of this dynamic can permanently alter corporate culture.

One example of an A+ player is Charlie Ward, who worked as an engineer at Amazon. While Amazon was testing delivery process options, he

---

[118] See also chapter 12.

realized that the discounting and promotions algorithm was overly complex and had become an impediment. Charlie Ward saw that the DVD rental team had built a subscription capability, so he put these together and suggested a new subscription for free shipping. Today, Amazon Prime has over 230 million customers in 17 countries and is a USD 40bn business[119].

Amazon's recruiting process[120] finds people like Charlie Ward and wins them for the company. It is a radical alternative to the home-grown approaches of many corporate scaleups. These typically fall short in two areas:

- Interviewers' skills. Interviewers play a crucial role in recruiting. But most interviewers in corporate scaleups lack the training to accurately assess a candidate's potential job performance.

- Interview process. Internal discussions about candidates often lack clarity, leading to confirmation bias and other decision-making traps that may feel right but ultimately result in poor choices.

Time pressure can partially explain suboptimal recruiting processes. On average, a Silicon Valley startup spends nearly 1,000 hours recruiting 12 software engineers[121]. In other words, the average hire costs two workweeks in recruiting efforts. This takes time away from an already understaffed team that struggles to meet deadlines.

Successful corporate scaleups invest into onboarding new hires and talent retention since it increases staff retention by 82 percent and productivity by over 70 percent[122]. This is a wise investment. Let us take Silicon Valley startups as an example. The average startup has an annual average employee churn rate of 25 percent[123]. So, if one of these startups wants to grow its staff size from 100 to 200, it needs to recruit 125-150 people and not 100. It is

---

[119] See https://www.yaguara.co/amazon-prime-statistics.
[120] Colin Bryar, Bill Carr, Working Backwards, St. Martin's Press, 2015.
[121] See https://rb.gy/4vrx6s.
[122] See https://rb.gy/1kp74v.
[123] See https://rb.gy/jeqosl.

challenging to achieve, let alone sustain, hypergrowth if a corporate scaleup must continually replace departing team members.

Go-to-Market Functions

This part of the text focuses on the two primary sales approaches used by corporate scaleups: product-led growth and sales-led growth. Chapter 19 includes guidance on how to collaborate with Core's sales functions.

In product-led growth, the product is the primary driver for customer acquisition and retention. Customers can try the product before purchasing and experience the value of the product. This self-service approach enables customers to explore the product at their own pace, eliminating in many instances the need for direct sales involvement. Product-led growth offers various benefits and advantages, such as:

- Low Customer Acquisition Costs.

- Increased customer satisfaction since customers can make informed decisions.

- Faster time-to-value since customers can use the product immediately without requiring lengthy sales cycles.

- Viral growth since satisfied customers can become brand advocates.

- Deep insights into customer behaviors, enabling the corporate scaleup to make data-driven decisions about product optimization.

Product-led growth requires a seamless customer experience. This in turn necessitates a collaborative effort inside the corporate scaleup to understand the user journey, optimize customer onboarding, and continuously use data and user feedback to iterate and improve.

Sales-led growth relies on personal touch and expertise to drive conversions. This approach requires salespersons who engage actively with prospects and negotiate deals. Sales-led models are generally more appropriate when the products are complex and when the product encapsulates technology that needs to be explained.

Some corporate scaleups use hybrid approaches that combine elements of these two models. This approach involves prioritizing a self-service model to attract customers. However, when high-value companies engage, revenues plateau, or specific circumstances arise, a sales team reaches out.

In my view, most corporate scaleups could do better in customer onboarding. Underperformance in this area jeopardizes customer retention and the opportunity to sign larger, longer-term contracts. To address this challenge, they must design an onboarding journey that ensures that customers adopt the product as a mandatory tool for their work. Customer success teams play an important role in this context. Apart from onboarding individual customers, they help to remove obstacles in the onboarding process such as:

- Lack of clear instructions.

- Inadequate resource.

- Overwhelming information.

- Lack of personalization.

Product Function

There are two criteria for product success: it helps the customer to solve a high-priority problem and it helps the corporate scaleup to move its business forward. However, designing an effective product organization is challenging, despite these intuitive and straightforward decision criteria. I have observed that product teams struggle in one or more of five ways.

First, a focus on output (but not outcomes). Some product teams prioritize their timeline above all else. These teams are often evaluated on their ability to deliver features on time. Because user research and product discovery can be time-consuming and implementing learnings from these activities can impact their timeline, they prefer to stick to the plan.

Second, the race for the next feature. These teams believe that if they deliver that next feature, another deal could be closed. This may lead to a permanent scramble for releasing the next feature which can be exhausting for developers as they constantly need to get up to speed in new domains.

Third, a focus on business metrics. Some product teams focus on business metrics[124]. However, no customer cares about these metrics. When product teams focus on business outcomes, they can lose sight of the leading indicators that they can—and must—influence.

Fourth, a lack of customer research. Product teams can become disconnected from their customers and maybe even think that they know more about the customer's problems than the customers themselves. Consequently, they do not have in-depth conversations with their customers—and they risk building features that no one wants.

Fifth, assuming that customer discovery has ended with validation. Some product teams seem to have lost their desire to deeply understand customers when they enter Scaling-Up. However, these teams miss the point. As the customer bases grows it becomes even more important to understand what the team should build.

When I see one or more of these symptoms, I advise to build a strategic system of experimentation. This includes determining the appropriate metrics and developing a portfolio of experiments. To maximize the effectiveness of the metrics, they should adhere to the following principles:

- Include the North Star metric.

- Use leading indicators.

- Be relevant for customers as well as for the corporate scaleup's growth.

- Be actionable.

- Focus on high-value and actionable learnings.

To avoid the trap of small-step/quick-win experiments, the experimentation portfolio should have some big bets as well. These need to be sequenced to avoid low-confidence hypotheses. This way, small experiments can help to validate bigger hypotheses.

---

[124] The highest level in exhibit 8–1.

Relationship to NOW

A key point of this book is that the relationship between NOW and the corporate startup/scaleup must be designed intentionally. Significant topics have been divided into individual chapters for clarity and ease of reference[125]:

- Validation in the corporate context.

- Creating the setup for Scaling-Up success.

- Defining an effective collaboration model.

- Creating a startup-like autonomy in the corporate context.

- Funding and governance.

In addition, I find that in practice, corporate stakeholders and the corporate scaleup's leadership team need to discuss two other issues to make the relationship productive.

The Problem with "The Plan"

In NOW, senior managers succeed when they develop effective plans to reach defined goals and ensure flawless execution of that plan. Hence it is understandable that, when they take a seat on the governance board of a corporate scaleup, they assume that this approach is also suitable for NEW.

However, NOW is fundamentally different from NEW, as described in chapters 2 and 3. I have witnessed many difficult discussions between a corporate scaleup's leadership team and their governance board. Sometimes members of governance boards call me to help the team deliver "the plan."

---

[125] See chapters 6, 7, 12, 14 and 15.

The issue with "the plan" often begins in Pre-Scaling, when stakeholders urge corporate startups to think big. They request ambitious goals that capture the attention of senior management. And many corporate startups comply by setting ambitious goals and "the plan" for achieving them.

However, the corporate scaleup and its governance board may soon realize that the initial plan does not align with reality. For instance, if revenues and customer numbers are not growing as projected in the spreadsheet, a more realistic assumption would have been[126] that successful corporate scaleups have captured only 10 percent of their Serviceable Obtainable Market halfway through Scaling-Up.

In these situations, I recommend revisiting the key assumptions behind "the plan" and to align on the nature of the governance meetings. One example for the latter point is a corporate scaleup which began every governance meeting with a list of the things it needed most, rather than providing a routine progress update.

The Problem with the Three Years

"What if you are successful? What if you create a sizable business? How would that change NOW's view?" When I ask CEOs of corporate scaleups these questions, I usually get disbelieving looks. Is this not the objective of the entire game?

Of course. However, with these questions I challenge my clients to consider how NOW's perspective will evolve as it grows. NOW's stakeholders in ESG (Environmental, Social, Governance), compliance, risk management, controlling, IT, and so on will take notice of a rapidly growing corporate scaleup and seek to apply NOW's standards to it.

One of my clients, who heads a corporate Scaling-Up unit once stated: **"We have three years. After that, NOW will evaluate everything we do**

---

[126] See https://rb.gy/mwfzt6.

according to NOW's standards. We need to work hard now to negotiate from a position of strength later."

Scaling-Up Stages and Milestones

The Lean Scaleup foresees that funding for the end-to-end process for out-of-the-box innovations and new-business building are tied to specific milestones and deliverables. Following this principle, the corporate scaleup and their governance board should define milestones that—at the same point in time—cut across the four Scaling-Up tracks:

- Strategy, market, and revenues (for instance, USD 10m revenues and first customers in a defined subsequent market).

- Product (for example, AI-based prediction engine added to the product).

- Organization (e.g., Chief Revenue Officer recruited, and staff grown to ca. 50 people).

- Relationship to NOW (for example, some defined components from NOW's financial controlling system added to the corporate scaleup's controlling system).

When the corporate scaleup reaches them, budgets for the subsequent Scaling-Up phase are automatically released. This eliminates the need to go through lengthy and complex approval processes each time they require funding and helps them to focus on what matters most: building a new business.

Chapter 9: Business-Building Toolbox

Chapter 9
Business-Building Toolbox

The Lean Scaleup framework comprises 12 modules, with 4 modules allocated to each of the Methodology, Leadership, and People/Culture dimensions.

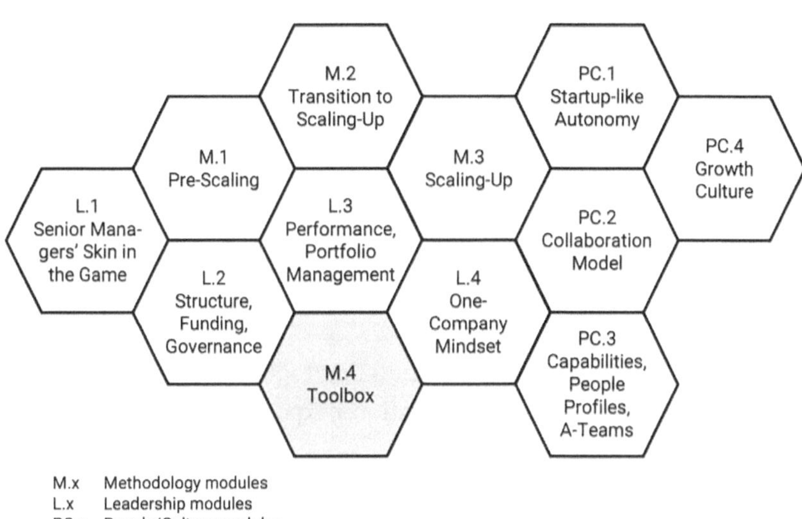

Key Points in This Chapter

1. A business-building toolbox can help to address four challenges: (1) increase the communication between NOW's senior managers and out-of-the-box-innovators; (2) provide guidance for corporate start-ups; (2) increase validation quality; (4) establish a learning system for Pre-Scaling work.

2. It can also serve as a knowledge hub for corporate startups, innovation portfolio managers, and leaders of business model incubators.

3. It is necessary to determine whether deliverables and thinking tools are mandatory or optional. In my view, they should be mandatory.

4. A business-building toolbox is an excellent spot to store company-internal best practices and progress monitoring scorecards.

5. Finally, the toolbox can be an information portal for NOW's senior managers.

* *

There are two cost-effective yet impactful strategies for improving out-of-the-box innovation and new-business building: establishing a common language between NOW and NEW and ensuring that all corporate startups use effective tools. Both can be supported by a business-building toolbox.

Why Is a Business-Building Toolbox Needed?

To demonstrate how a business-building toolbox can be designed, I use the Lean Scaleup toolbox for illustration purposes. It effectively addresses four common challenges:

- The communication between NOW's senior managers and functional experts and corporate startups needs to be increased.

- Corporate startups need clear guidance on their current tasks and their two next steps.

- The validation quality needs to be ensured in an efficient way.

- Pre-Scaling should be a learning system with continuous improvement.

What Is the Lean Scaleup Toolbox?

The Lean Scaleup toolbox supports corporate startups and business model incubation units in Pre-Scaling. It increases quality and speed in validation and connects senior managers with corporate startups.

A SaaS Platform

From a technical perspective, the Lean Scaleup toolbox is a software-as-a-service solution built on one of the most prominent productivity and workspace cloud solutions. Typically, companies customize the look of their toolboxes to match their corporate design. Some companies use the toolbox on its native platform, while others have migrated the content to a different tool in the company's cloud.

A Knowledge Hub

A primary function of the Lean Scaleup toolbox is to be a knowledge hub for corporate startups, innovation portfolio managers, and leaders of business model incubators. For this group, the toolbox provides:

- The definition of validation tracks and validation stages and the associated funding rounds[127].

- The deliverables that the corporate startup must provide in order to be admitted to the next round of funding.

- The thinking tools, such as canvases, checklists, and templates, that the corporate startup must use to document the deliverables.

- The composition of the corporate startup teams at each stage to ensure that the required capabilities are available.

- Recommendations on which team member should work on which deliverable at each stage.

- The sequence of activities that the corporate startups must perform to generate the deliverables, broken down to the level of individual sprints.

---

[127] See chapter 11 and the Amadeus Nexwave case study in chapter 4 for a detailed explanation how the toolbox supports budgeting.

The Lean Scaleup toolbox guides corporate startups in their work by outlining "sprints" and thinking tools (*Excerpt from Business Strategy stage*).

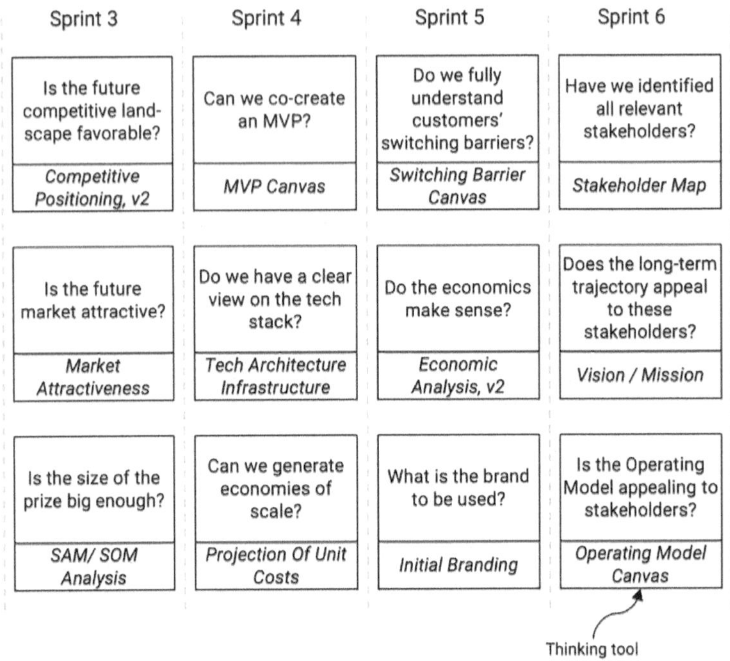

Exhibit 9–1: A toolbox guides corporate startups on how to design their sprints.

Deliverables and thinking tools should be mandatory to enable:

– Efficiency in progress monitoring.

– Comparability of individual corporate startups as a basis for effective portfolio management.

– A solid foundation for continuous improvement.

A Best Practice Repository

The toolbox illustrates deliverables and thinking tools with best practices and illuminating examples from earlier corporate startups. This provision:

- Shows a corporate startup team "what good looks like."

- Improves the onboarding of new team members.

A Progress Monitoring Database

Chapter 6 explains how the Lean Scaleup helps companies track the progress of their emerging business opportunities. The core component is a monthly scorecard, which employs a traffic light system to assess the completion grade of validation deliverables. The Lean Scaleup toolbox stores these monthly scorecards for every corporate startup with two goals:

- Documenting a corporate startup's journey, especially how fast they moved compared to the original assumptions.

- Improving planning by generating relevant statistics.

An Information Portal

The toolbox also serves as an information portal for NOW's senior managers and functional experts. It provides them with:

- Explanations and definitions to ensure a common language, delivered via short "explainer videos" and "cheat sheets".

- A high-level overview over the current corporate startups, including the estimate when the next stage of Core engagement is expected.

The Lean Scaleup Toolbox at Work

Amadeus, a leading travel software company, uses the Lean Scaleup toolbox in their business model incubator Amadeus Nexwave. More details can be found in the case study in chapter 4.

Chapter 10: Senior Managers' Skin in the Game

Chapter 10
Senior Managers' Skin in the Game

The Lean Scaleup framework comprises 12 modules, with 4 modules allocated to each of the Methodology, Leadership, and People/Culture dimensions.

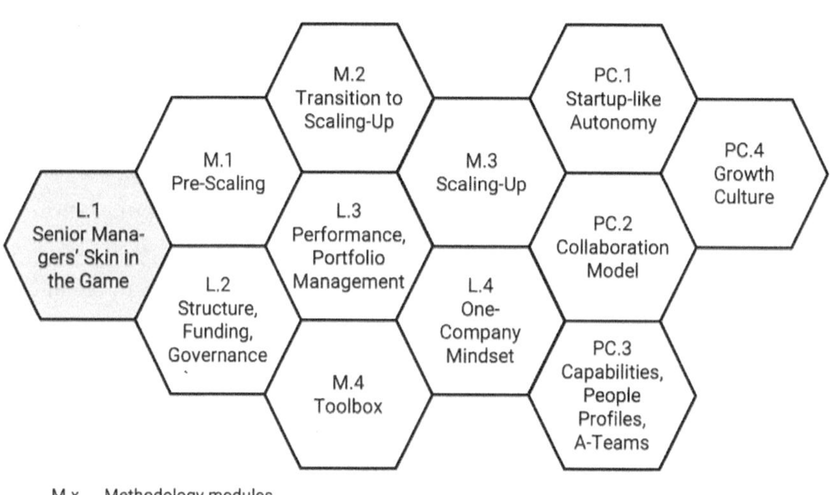

Key Points in This Chapter

1. When senior managers are serious about out-of-the-box innovation, they must invest in the outcome, involve themselves and be affected by how it turns out. They must have "skin in the game."

2. Only when corporate explorers and corporate startups/scaleups see that senior managers have skin in the game, they have the confidence to fulfill their respective missions at pace.

3. There are eight actions to demonstrate that senior managers have skin in the game. They build on the right mindset: be realistic, humble, curious, consistent, and open for a new corporate identity.

4. At the end of the day, these eight actions are about taking not-so-easy decisions.

5. Out-of-the-box innovation could be a capital market story. It may provide the chance to have the company's CFO put skin in the game as well.

* *

Ørsted is a prime example of a successful corporate transformation. It transitioned from a fossil-energy to a green-energy company and has been ranked the world's most sustainable energy company four times in a row[128]. During its transformation, Ørsted learned how to run NOW and NEW in parallel while significantly improving its financial performance.

The predecessor of the company, DONG, was formed in 2006 through the merger of six Danish energy companies and five power generation and distribution companies. The resulting energy company operated across the entire value chain, with 85 percent of its electricity coming from fossil fuels. At the time, it accounted for a third of Denmark's carbon emissions.

In 2008, mounting societal pressure to address climate change prompted DONG's senior management to embark on a transformational journey. They anticipated that this pressure would challenge and eventually erode the existing business model. To create and scale a new, sustainable business model, they decided that by 2040, the energy mix should be flipped to 85 percent green and 15 percent fossil energy. A significant portion of the green energy should come from offshore wind farms.

It is crucial to recognize that at that time, offshore wind was a nascent technology, lacking economies of scale and therefore relatively expensive. Furthermore, the future scale, cost reduction potential, and commercial viability of the industry were uncertain. In other words, this decision carried significant risks. The transition away from fossil fuels presented significant challenges, not only from a commercial risk perspective:

– Staff members viewed fossil fuel energy as the company's core capability. They were proud of running power plants with world-class efficiency.

---

[128] See https://bit.ly/3R2PRmP.

- Media and external stakeholders considered the transformation to be overly ambitious.

- There were concerns about whether the company, with such an important role in the Danish economy, could handle the uncertainties of the transformation, considering its engineering background and dependence on the established business model.

Nevertheless, senior management executed their plan with determination. They closed coal power plants and avoided new investments in fossil assets. The company increased investments in offshore wind, acquired wind farms and purchased wind turbines at a scale larger than the existing global fleet. It acquired a wind turbine installation company to have direct control over this crucial part of the value chain and admitted institutional investors to invest in the increasing number of wind parks.

Four years into the transformation, the global gas market experienced a decline. DONG saw its revenues falling and its stock downgraded to BBB+ with a negative outlook, which is only slightly above the rating of a speculative investment. Any further downgrade would result in an unsustainable increase in the cost of capital, jeopardizing the entire transformation. Again, many analysts and critics questioned the soundness of the ambition.

To weather the storm, the company divested further assets from its legacy fossil business and brought in new investors to fund the future growth of a renewable energy business. While these external investors helped to keep the transformation ambition alive, they also increased pressure to deliver financial performance.

It became clear that the company needed to create a tipping point for the entire ecosystem, including governments and suppliers, to scale up the industry. DONG set an ambitious target which can be compared to John F. Kennedy's "we choose to go to the moon" moment[129]: the cost of offshore wind electricity should be lowered to EUR 100 per MWh within

---

[129] See https://bit.ly/3wSuGwL.

a decade. This goal sparked a wave of innovation within the ecosystem. Just four years later, offshore wind energy was cost-competitive with coal and gas power.

During this process, DONG's senior management undertook a restructuring of the historic upstream oil and gas business, with the objective of generating cash to provide the funding required for further scaling offshore wind. In 2016, after improving its financial performance, the company went public with its unique story of being a global leader in offshore wind and a pioneer in decarbonization and sustainability.

One year after the initial public offering (IPO) and following the divestiture of the remaining oil and gas production assets, the company changed its name to Ørsted. In 2019, it achieved its goal of flipping its energy mix, 21 years ahead of schedule. In the twelve-year period since the company initiated its corporate transformation, it has reduced its carbon emissions by 86 percent while almost doubling its operating profit.

The Bird's Eye Perspective on Leadership's Role

From the perspective of a senior manager, it is often more straightforward to adhere to a proven formula for success than to venture beyond the existing business and operating model. NOW is simpler, less risky, easier to control, and problems are more obvious. NEW is complex, harder to control, carries more risk, and problems are often hidden.

This perspective is understandable. The Ørsted case study above demonstrates that reshaping Core via out-of-the-box innovation and building a new business (combined with M&A, in this case) is a complex change initiative. **It demands more from senior managers than simply running the day-to-day business. They must think more, explore what is working in NEW and address the inherent tensions between the important and the urgent throughout the process.**

However, corporate explorers seeking to identify new value pools, corporate startups striving to find out how to capture that value, and corporate scaleups aiming to generate new growth need a solid and consistent backing from senior management. They must feel that senior management is invested in the outcome, that they are directly involved and will be affected by how it turns out. This backing will help them to deliver their respective missions at pace.

Leadership's Role in Out-of-the-Box-Innovation

As explained in chapter 5, the Lean Scaleup provides senior managers with guidance to succeed in out-of-the-box innovation and new-business building. The key factors for success are to build a bridge between NOW and NEW and to implement four learnable skills.

The bridge is constructed from three pillars: an effective methodology, a focus on people and culture, and impactful leadership actions. With respect to the latter, there are four key points that must be addressed. Each of these represents one module of the Lean Scaleup:

- **Senior managers' skin in the game.** When corporate explorers and corporate startups/scaleups see that senior managers is aligned and provides the necessary support, they have the confidence to create new businesses at pace. This module is addressed in this chapter.

- **Structure, funding, and governance.** Corporate explorers and corporate startups/scaleups need a suitable organizational home and an effective mechanism for further funding if they make good progress. Chapter 11 provides additional details.

- **Performance and portfolio management.** Chapter 12 explains how to enhance the company's goal system with future-proofing metrics and how to manage a portfolio of emerging business opportunities.

- **One-company mindset**. The fourth module, described in chapter 13, covers how senior managers can help middle managers and staff to understand that the company is not NOW company with some out-of-the-box activities but one company that has NOW and NEW elements.

The Right Mindset

As described below, senior manager's skin in the game can be seen by eight senior management actions. They all build on the right mindset, which is essential for success. When I discuss the right mindset with senior management teams, five topics are frequently on the agenda:

- Be realistic. Senior managers should not artificially inflate the out-of-the-box ambition with excess urgency. Staff members have only a limited "absorptive capacity."

- Be humble. Neither high-paid consultants nor corporate explorers and corporate startups are able to identify which idea will become a new, sizable, and profitable business. The truth can be uncovered through professional Pre-Scaling, as outlined in chapter 6.

- Be curious and open-minded. In VUCA business environments[130], disruption and the associated threats and opportunities can come from many angles. Senior managers should listen to the findings of foresight teams and strategy dialogues between operative units and out-of-the-box innovators[131] to spot weak signals of disruption.

- Be consistent and persevere. When NOW experiences two consecutive bad quarters, corporate startups do not come up with a great idea, or corporate scaleups struggle with creating significant growth, Core pays close attention to senior management's actions. A reduction in ambition

---

[130] See chapter 2.
[131] See chapters 13 and 20.

is most likely perceived as a signal that out-of-the-box innovation is not that important after all.

– Be open to create a new corporate identity. As the case studies about Ørsted and Fujifilm[132] show, the company will have a new identity when out-of-the-box innovation is successful. The question "what business are we in?" must be on the agenda of every strategy process.

With this mindset in place, there are eight decisive senior management actions, depicted in exhibit 10–1, that will convince out-of-the-box innovators and Core of senior management's seriousness and determination.

Establish a Clear Mandate and Legitimacy

Out-of-the-box innovation requires a clear mandate. The "reason why," or the underlying purpose, may be intrinsic or extrinsic, as illustrated by the case studies of Ørsted and Fujifilm, respectively. Effective mandates have five characteristics. They are:

– Easy to understand.

– Are specific and not just general statements about, for example, corporate transformation or future-proofing the company.

– Go beyond mere profit maximization.

– Have a clear rationale for deciding between short-term wins and long-term ambition.

– Provide wiggle room to adjust over time.

---

[132] See chapter 4.

To convince the company of the importance of growth via out-of-the-box innovation, senior management must have skin in the game.

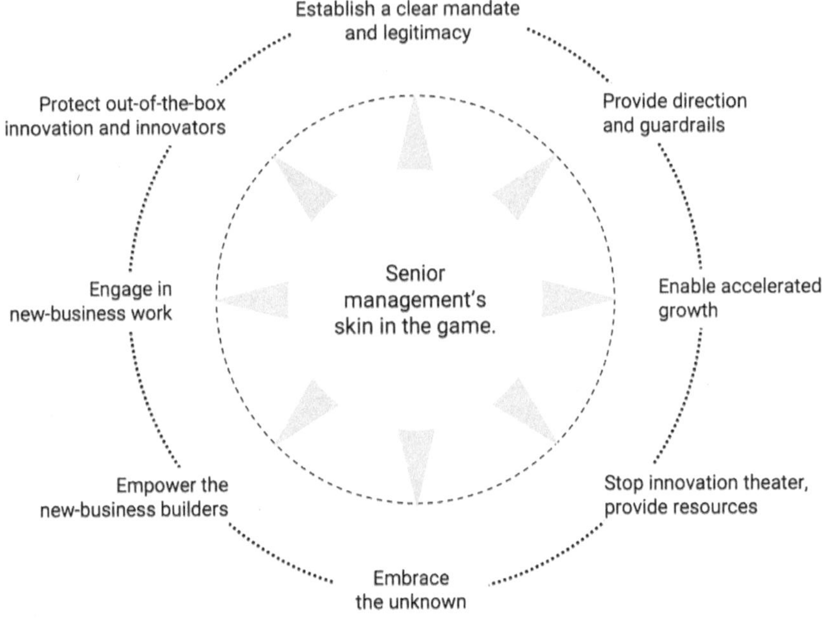

Exhibit 10–1: Senior management actions that show they have skin in the game.

Provide Direction and Guardrails

Out-of-the-box innovation needs guardrails. Often, however, these are not clearly visible, and corporate explorers and corporate startups/scaleups are left on their own to figure out what to do.

Here is one example from my advisory work in the automotive industry. The company's senior managers asked their business model incubation teams to launch corporate startups in the search field "autonomous vehicles in a logistics context." The team discovered that the customers in these business models would not be the existing dealers, but rather the customers of today's customers. In other words, scaling these business model innovations would create a significant channel conflict.

Senior managers cannot ask a corporate scaleup to solve such a fundamental dilemma for the entire company. Unfortunately, such situations are often discovered too late in the process. They result in disappointment for both senior managers and new-business builders. Therefore, senior management must play an active role in defining meaningful search fields as explained in more detail in chapter 6.

Enable Accelerated Growth

In order for out-of-the-box innovation to be successful, it is necessary to make adaptations to NOW in order to enable the startup-like autonomy described in chapter 14. In my advisory practice, I have observed two lines of actions. The first is one is to remove growth constraints.

For instance, when I discussed new-business building with one of my clients from the plastics industry, it became evident that the ability to provide potential customers with product samples within 24 hours was a key factor for success.

Step by step, the company then removed impediments to achieving that goal. It integrated the customer relationship management system with the laboratory management system, which was then integrated with the portal of a logistics company. The company even installed a pick-up box for the logistics company, eliminating the need for additional human interaction in the shipment process. With these changes, the company can handle 50 product sample requests per week, a tenfold increase on previous levels.

The second approach is to speed up decision-making. As explained in chapter 14, most companies apply a heavy-weight decision-making process to reversible two-way-door decisions. Consequently, the time required for decision-making and the time between decision-making and implementation are extended. Applying two-way-door decision-making in defined areas reduces corporate bureaucracy and enhances the company's agility in areas where collaboration with corporate scaleups and their startup-like autonomy is essential.

Stop Innovation Theater, Provide Resources

Often, there is a misalignment between meaningful search fields and the portfolio of R&D projects and out-of-the-box initiatives. This misalignment absorbs significant resources and funding and creates "innovation theater" and waste. Two examples may illustrate this point:

- A corporate startup of a financial services company spent six months developing what they called a "minimum viable product" without significant customer input. They created a prototype for a product that nobody wanted.

- A corporate startup of an automotive company developed a sophisticated radar device. After investing several years and millions of dollars it became evident that they had no solid plan for marketing the product.

Stories like the ones above speak loudly and clearly about waste. Senior managers must ensure that there is no waste of:
- Money that hurts the company's bottom line.

- Resources when engineers build something that has no customer value.

- Opportunity, because the company could use the money and the resources to create new growth instead.

Senior managers must focus out-of-the-box innovation to ideas that align with the company's meaningful search fields. They must insist on rapid reality checks in the Discovery and Business Foundation stages. The corresponding resources that are freed by stopping innovation theater will then help to resource the right out-of-the-box-initiatives.

One final observation on this issue: it seems to me that it is usually easier for senior managers to commit financial resources than human resources. This is because top talent is often fully absorbed in the NOW or other "Reshape Core" initiatives[133]. Unfortunately, money alone cannot create an unfair advantage by leveraging corporate assets and capabilities.

Embrace the Unknown

Building new business is, by definition, new. It is outside the box of today's business, operating and mental model. Initially, it may not be clear where the company should play, what the rules of that game are, what role the company should play, and how it can win. With all these unknowns and risks, out-of-the-box innovation is always outside the comfort zone.

Ideally, senior managers would understand NEW as deeply as they understand NOW. However, this is unrealistic since new businesses require new capabilities and senior managers' time to learn is limited. One effective solution to this dilemma is to appoint external experts in an advisory role to the relevant governance boards. This ensures that senior managers and corporate startups/scaleups have access to the insights they need to mitigate risk and accelerate the journey.

However, it is not only the content that presents a challenge for many senior managers; it is also the process. The work style of validating and scaling out-of-the-box innovations differs from established practices in NOW. There, they manage well-defined processes and drive incremental innovation

---

[133] See chapter 3.

that have many knowns and business cases that build on assumptions which can easily be identified and validated.

They may perceive the activities of corporate startups/scaleups as undirected and maybe even random. As one of my clients said: "The real clashes occur when agile new-business builders run into corporate processes." This challenge can be addressed by adopting the Lean Scaleup that provides a staged, end-to-end business graduation scheme with clear deliverables and meaningful scorecards, while allowing for agile work within the stages.

Empower the New-Business Builders

One of my senior manager clients said: "We can only build new businesses under two conditions. First, one of the company's founders is demanding it. Or, second, when there are corporate mavericks who are passionate about their idea. They get tarred and feathered on Friday but come back on Monday even more determined to turn that idea into a new business."

In situations like the one described above, the company risks losing top talent and the insights that they have gained. The tensions between NOW and the corporate mavericks are inevitable, as described in chapter 3. Senior managers should keep two things in mind:

- Every company experiences these tensions when it aims at creating new revenue streams.

- Since future-proofing the company is senior management's "job number one," they must find the optimal solution for an inevitable dilemma.

Apple's founder Steve Jobs said[134]: "It does not make sense to hire smart people and then tell them what to do. We hire smart people, so they tell us

---

[134] See https://bit.ly/3ySJlIH.

what we need to do." Leaders of corporate startups and CEOs of corporate scaleups are typically smart people. As they work to "Reshape Core," they will inevitably bump into the limits of existing business, operating, and mental models. Senior managers should listen to them.

Two effective ways to empower these individuals are to grant them a startup-like autonomy within the corporate context, as detailed in chapter 14, and to ensure that "failure" from taking calculated risks does not result in a career-limiting setback. In such an environment, these smart people build new businesses so that the company will thrive in the next decades.

Engage in New-Business Work

Senior managers can demonstrate that they have skin the game by investing their personal time. In Pre-Scaling, they should invest their time in defining the meaningful search fields and dive deeper into the meaningful ideas that corporate explorers discovered. During the Transition-to-Scaling-Up and the Scaling-Up phases, senior managers must establish and maintain operational alignment between the corporate scaleup and NOW.

The transitional phase is crucial because it sets up the foundation for Scaling-Up success. Senior managers can best support by investing their time to ensure that:

- The corporate scaleup is set up in the best organizational home.

- Negative impacts on operational units that come from supporting corporate scaleups are mitigated.

- An effective governance board is established.

- Appropriate Scaling-Up milestones are defined and integrated into the goals of relevant corporate functions.

- Funding for Scaling-Up is earmarked and prepared for release upon achieving these milestones.

- Effective collaboration models are defined.

- Suitable individuals are selected for key positions.

Protect Out-of-the-Box Innovation and the Innovators

Due to the inherent uncertainty in out-of-the-box innovation and new-business building, failures and setbacks will happen. For instance:

- A meaningful idea cannot be validated.

- A corporate startup is not able to build the Minimum Marketable Product that delivers the envisioned value proposition.

- In executing the bowling alley strategy, the corporate scaleup cannot create an impact in subsequent market segments and growth stalls.

This is part of the game, and therefore unavoidable. **Even the most rigorous validation methodology, the most professional work of corporate startups/scaleups, and the highest level of senior management engagement cannot guarantee success.** The issue is how NOW's senior managers will respond to these failures and the likely repercussions within the company.

They have two options: They view such a failure as a negative point in the track record of the responsible new-business builders, potentially even as a career-limiting event. Alternatively, they may view it with a growth mindset[135].

In my view, the key factor for how to view failures and setbacks is the decision-making context. A clearly defined risk, such as when certain assumptions could not be validated and when a corporate startup aligned with the governance board to take a leap of faith, is not a failure.

---

[135] See chapter 17.

However, when, for example, a corporate startup does not validate crucial pieces such as customers' switching barriers[136] or when a corporate scaleup deviates from a validated growth strategy[137], these failures are a bug and not a feature of out-of-the-box innovation.

Senior managers must protect the new-business builders in the former case. If they do not do it, they risk that the company's top talent will stay on the safe road of NOW, abstain from creating NEW or even leave the company. In addition, senior managers must address negative publicity that may arise from such an event within the company. If they choose not to address the situation, they will only reinforce the skeptics and critics.

A third element of protection is to safeguard the entire ambition from negative impacts that originate in NOW's context. These could include two bad quarters in a row or a CEO change. That is the reason why out-of-the-box innovation must be baked in NOW's system, by connecting NOW and NEW and by implementing four learnable skills[138].

Coming Up: Aligning NEW with the CFO

At first glance, Core's finance function may not seem compatible with out-of-the-box innovation. The former prioritizes capital efficiency, revenue growth and predictable margins while the latter prioritizes learning efficiency and funding corporate startups/scaleups as long as they demonstrate progress.

The finance function's focus on capital efficiency makes it challenging for NOW to pursue high-risk/high-reward options. Those options are not

---

[136] See chapter 6.
[137] See chapter 8.
[138] See chapter 5.

supported by the CFO per se; support typically requires senior management sponsorship. Given this context, it is understandable that out-of-the-box innovators may not view the financial function as strong supporters. However, I argue that if out-of-the-box innovators present a compelling opportunity, the CFO can become a powerful advocate.

Changing the Conversation

Although the role of a CFO varies from company to company, maximizing shareholder value is a common goal. This provides an opportunity for out-of-the-box innovation to change the conversation and add value to the CFO's ambitions.

When discussing budgets, corporate new-business builders have two options. They can view funding as a single line item in the corporate budget scheme, which puts these budgets immediately in competition for resources. Or they can position new-business building budgets as a capital market story in which the valuation of the corporate startups/scaleups drives the company's market capitalization and Price/Earnings ratio[139].

---

[139] In the Pharma industry, valuation of the product pipeline is an established practice.

Chapter 11: Structure, Funding, Governance

Chapter 11
Structure, Funding, Governance

The Lean Scaleup framework comprises 12 modules, with 4 modules allocated to each of the Methodology, Leadership, and People/Culture dimensions.

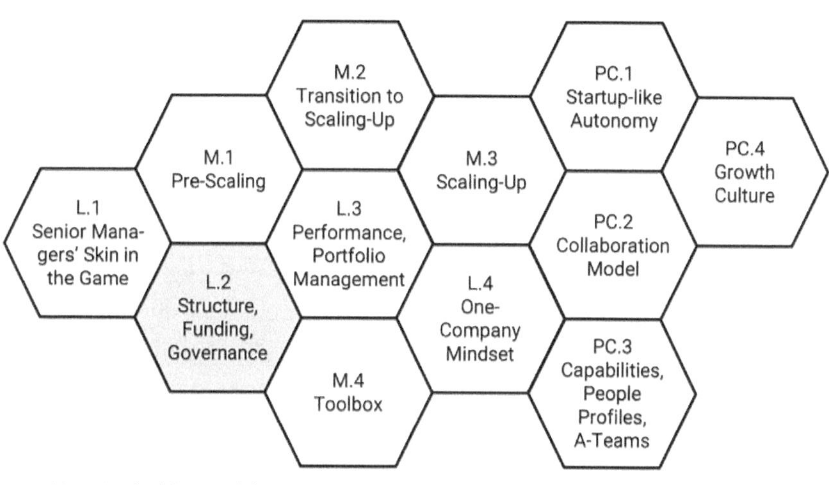

Key Points in This Chapter

1. The funding and governance schemes of NOW must not be altered since this would put its mission—safely delivering the margins for its shareholders and funding NEW—at risk.

2. Ford Motor Company's decision to split the company into a NOW unit and a NEW unit with a defined bridge provides a reference model for how to set up NEW structures inside the company.

3. Typically, companies do not make such substantial decisions. Rather, they create structures that relate to parts of this reference model. Six questions help to find the optimal structure(s).

4. Out-of-the-box innovation should be funded at three levels: the ambition, the portfolio and the individual corporate startup/scaleup.

5. Most companies overlook that those functions that support Scaling-Up require extra funding to compensate for the inevitable decrease in their NOW-related KPIs.

6. The funding of corporate startups/scaleups should be ringfenced and depend on achieving milestones. The governance board of corporate scaleups should be equipped with a "learning buffer" to address unforeseen challenges.

7. Governance should be consistent with the three-level funding setup.

**

To ensure future success, the company must optimize and exploit its existing business and operating model, while simultaneously exploring, validating, and scaling new business opportunities. As explained in chapters 2 and 5, NEW needs a distinct organizational home with a bridge that connects it with NOW.

One of the building blocks of this bridge is made up from four modules that relate to key leadership actions. Determining and implementing the optimal structure, governance, and funding arrangements is one of these elements. It is addressed in this chapter.

Do Not Touch Playing Field 1

In any company, NOW's daily operations are structured and governed by processes, procedures for managing exceptions and committees that decide on cross-silo topics. Incremental innovation is typically managed by a phase/gate process with clearly defined decision-makers at each gate.

Funding for operational expenses and incremental innovations is arranged through annual budgeting cycles.

In other words, Playing Field 1[140] has a clear structure, an established funding apparatus, and a defined governance scheme. Out-of-the-box innovation and new business building must not alter these provisions, as they ensure NOW's mission to safely deliver the margins that ensure support from investors and funding NEW.

However, the situation is different in Playing Fields 2 and 3. There, the innovation content is by definition new to the company. Playing Field 1's governance and funding apparatus will not be effective due to:

– The level of uncertainty.

– The level of agility required to cope with this uncertainty.

– Collaboration with external partners who require a workstyle which does not fit the process-driven, risk-averse setup of the company.

– A long-term time horizon that contrasts sharply with Playing Field 1's short-term focus.

– A potential for cannibalizing the existing business.

A Reference Model for NEW's Structure

The automotive industry is undergoing a significant transition. In the future, vehicles will be smarter, more connected, software-defined, and powered by batteries, hydrogen, or other forms of energy. In March 2022, Ford Motor Company (Ford) announced[141] that it would split its auto busi-

---

[140] See chapter 3.
[141] See https://ford.to/3KjceAV.

ness into two separate but interconnected divisions with discrete profit and loss statements.

The first business, "Ford Blue," focuses on petrol- and diesel-powered vehicles and provides engineering and manufacturing capabilities for both businesses. The second business, "Ford Model e," targets electric cars and mobility services and provides industrialized connected-vehicle technologies and services for both businesses.

When explaining the decision, Ford's CEO Jim Farley said: "It is about harnessing a century of hardware mastery to help build the future." He emphasized that Ford took a clean-slate approach when designing Model e's business, operating and mental models. In other words, to create NEW, Ford has established a separate structure that is at eye level with NOW and with the remit to be different.

If we consider Ford Blue to be NOW, the company's setup outlines a reference model for structuring NEW inside the existing business. NEW:

- Has a clear mandate to build and scale out-of-the-box innovations.

- Is led by a senior manager with a seat at the company's leadership table.

- Receives the same senior management attention as NOW.

- Operates in a dedicated organizational unit with dedicated resources and is the organizational home for out-of-the-box innovations.

- Manages the end-to-end process, including the inflows into the process, the relevant ecosystem, and innovation service providers.

- Owns and manages the portfolio of emerging new-business opportunities, including the budgets for validating a large number of corporate startups and earmarked budgets for a few corporate scaleups.

- Collaborates with Core across a defined bridge to leverage corporate assets and capabilities, and, where appropriate, to re-integrate scaled-up businesses back into Core.

Frequently Used Structural Models and Their Challenges

Most companies have innovation vehicles that cover aspects of this reference model. Below are the innovation vehicles I frequently encounter and the challenges I help them solve.

The *innovation center* is a structure that is located within NOW. The unit's primary objective is to identify adjacent or new technologies and explore business opportunities that arise from commercializing these technologies. Innovation ideas focus, for example, on new materials, physical devices, and digitally enhanced solutions such as smart surfaces.

In practice, this structure encounters two main challenges. First, its engineers often lack the mindset and expertise for proper validation of emerging business opportunities. Second, the transition from early-stage to late-stage validation and the subsequent stages is often challenging because it involves shifting the focus from technology to business and requires different people, as described in chapter 16.

Incubators are structures that could be inside or outside of NOW. Their purpose is to provide intrapreneurs and early-stage corporate startups with the resources they require to succeed, including training, access to corporate stakeholders, and a physical working space.

Two challenges often arise: when the incubator is external, it is often difficult to establish the corporate context; when it is internal, the teams' view of the potential success of an idea is often overly optimistic, and teams tend to fall in love with their idea rather than with a customer problem.

Accelerators are structures that could be inside or outside of NOW. They provide services to late-stage corporate or greenfield startups similar to those of an incubator. They also support Pre-Scaling and the initial stage of Scaling-Up by facilitating access to corporate assets and capabilities.

The main challenge for accelerators is to motivate Core's stakeholders to go beyond a general interest in innovative technologies or business concepts. Chapter 19 provides insights on how to get technical pilots right.

The *digital lab* is a NOW-internal structure. It supports the company's digital transformation by using technologies (such as blockchain or AI) to:

– Optimize Core.

– Increase customer experience and customer insights.

– Create ideas for new businesses such as, for example, data-driven or service-centric business models.

The main challenge for digital labs are comparable to those of an innovation center. Staff is often too technology-focused and the handover from technology to business-building is often challenging.

A *project house* is a structure located inside or outside of NOW that addresses business opportunities which require co-innovation from partners across the value chain or ecosystem. The main challenge for these structures is to maintain alignment from a diverse group of companies over a long-time horizon.

A *Scaling-Up factory* is a structure that is set up outside of NOW to support corporate scaleups or corporate ventures in Scaling-Up. It provides growth resources, infrastructure, and access to corporate assets and capabilities. Some companies use such a structure as an organizational home for corporate startups that do not have an apparent re-integration path.

The challenge for these structures is to maintain alignment with NOW, as their corporate scaleups/ventures are at risk of falling off the radar screen.

Venture builder is a term with two meanings. It can refer to either a NOW-internal or external structure or to a third-party service provider[142].

---

[142] In the latter case, synonyms are "company builder" or "venture studio."

These units regularly launch (corporate) startups, conduct Pre-Scaling, provide interim resources for Scaling-Up, and recruit a team to take over.

Both types of venture builders often use approaches that fall short on the corporate context, as explained in chapter 2. The primary challenge for external venture builders is to get access to corporate assets and capabilities to de-risk and accelerate the journey and to ensure re-integration after scaling.

Corporate Venture Capital units are NOW-internal structures that invest into promising greenfield startups. The motivation for these investments can be manifold:

– Hedging bets on new technologies or business models.

– Obtaining access to breakthrough technology.

– Accelerating growth by subsequent integration into Core.

– Accelerating a greenfield startup's Scaling-Up by granting access to corporate assets and capabilities.

In the context of new-business building, the primary challenge for these units lies in the third and fourth aspects. Core often perceives these units as mere "deal makers." In practice, this perception makes it even more challenging to establish a productive collaboration between a greenfield startup and Core than it would be for a corporate startup.

Finding Effective Structures

Based on my experience working with clients from various industries, I have found that six key questions are helpful to design a NEW structure that should cover some aspects of the reference model.

Question 1: In which Playing Fields should the structure operate? When the structure's focus is on Playing Field 2, then leveraging cross-business-unit potentials, corporate assets and corporate capabilities is critical. These are strong arguments to place the structure inside NOW, but outside of Core's operational functions and units. In certain situations, for example when corporate startups/scaleups should access corporate IT systems, it may even be mandatory for the structure to be Core-internal.

However, if the focus is on the far edge of Playing Field 2 or on Playing Field 3, the structure should be NOW-external. This is because the need for accessing Core's resources is limited and the most important interactions will be with other companies. When the corporate startup/scaleup builds new businesses that could cannibalize the existing business, it is mandatory to place the structure outside of NOW because otherwise the "corporate immune system" would react strongly and hamper the ambition.

Question 2: What is the strategic mandate? NEW's structure needs a clear mandate. Problems frequently occur when there is a lack of clarity:

– Vague objectives such as "driving corporate transformation" makes it challenging to assess the value that the NEW structure generates.

– When corporate priorities change and NEW's structure is inflexible, it may lose cohesion with Core.

Question 3: Which part of the innovation journey should be covered? On the end-to-end-journey from meaningful search fields to a scaled-up business, companies position their innovation vehicles on various parts of the process, as mentioned above.

Question 4: Where is the primary source of critical capabilities? When the company is the primary source of critical capabilities, NEW's structure should be inside NOW, but outside Core's operational units, and outside NOW in other cases. When the company pursues innovations in competitive arenas that transcend traditional industry boundaries, NEW's structure should be outside of NOW, since the need to collaborate with ecosystem partners requires agility and rapid decision-making.

Question 5: Where do ideas come from? There are many examples of NEW structures set up to be an organizational home for company-internal ideas. There are also many examples of structures that provide a home for beyond-Core ideas that arise from open innovation and greenfield-start-up-related activities.

Ideas related to the former case are often closer to NOW, and therefore it might be more appropriate to locate the NEW structure inside. In the latter case, the ideas are typically more distant, and so there is an argument for locating the structure outside of NOW.

Question 6: What is the intended future organizational home? If the main objective for a scaled-up business is to be re-integrated into Core, then corporate stakeholders' expectations must be considered and met early on. This is an argument to place NEW's structure inside. However, if the corporate scaleup should by partially funded by external investors or even be publicly listed, the structure should be placed outside of NOW.

The 1-Pager Mission Statement

Since these questions are complex, it is helpful to summarize them on one piece of paper. Such a summary slide should state the:

- Mission, e.g., "incubate new growth businesses" or "advance corporate startups to scale-worthy and scale-ready."

- Playing Fields.

- Internal customers and stakeholders.

- Portfolio composition.

- Key performance indicators and success metrics.

- Budget (see below).

- Governance (see below).

A Funding Gap That Many Companies Are Not Aware Of

Many companies fail to address a funding gap in the context of new-business building. They focus on funding individual corporate startups/scaleups but fail to recognize the additional funding needs of those Core units that support Scaling-Up or absorb a scaled-up business.

From the perspective of these units, these situations are like performing open-heart surgery. They must run daily operations at full speed while providing additional resources. As a result, their performance metrics will inevitably suffer, and extra funding will be required to compensate for the loss in productivity.

In principle, the same issue appears when a scaled-up business should become a new business line within Core, In this case, it must establish itself within the corporate context of adjacent processes, such as procurement, financial control, and HR. This back-end integration also requires resources from corporate functions, which will also negatively impact their performance metrics and require additional funding to compensate.

Designing the Funding Apparatus

Typically, the funding apparatus that a company must build to support out-of-the-box innovation depends on five dimensions:

- Volume. This addresses the funding size and time horizon.

- Control. This refers to the balance between the autonomy of a corporate startup/scaleup and the level of control that NOW's stakeholders demand.

- Growth expectations. If the goal is to create so-called unicorns[143], a high funding level is necessary. During difficult periods, the company may opt to lower growth expectations and the corresponding funding.

- Acceptable risk levels. The level of risk a company is willing to take has a direct effect on the size of funding it provides. Sharing risks—but also rewards—with external investors might be an option in some cases.

- Team compensation. Generally, members of corporate startups receive monthly salaries as their compensation. Corporate scaleups, however, may require additional compensation elements, such as attractive bonuses or equity, to attract the right people (see chapter 16).

Adapt the Funding Logic

The case studies on Ørsted and Fujifilm illustrate the pivotal role of shifting funding from NOW to NEW. Fujifilm's CEO remarked that this decision was essential to break out of the existing business, operational, and mental models.

In my view, such a move also makes sense in the case when a company wants Core's operational units to create new, adjacent growth. Parts of the business units' budgets could then be allocated to fund individual initiatives.

Supporting out-of-the-box innovation and new-business building also requires a change in how to make funding decisions. Economic viability analyses in these spaces cannot match the level of detail of business cases related to Playing Field 1 and their payback expectations stretch out longer. If out-of-the-box innovation were to be measured with the same yardstick as Playing Field 1 innovations, they will inevitably be deprioritized.

---

[143] (Corporate) scaleups with a valuation over USD 1bn.

Three Levels of Funding

Funding is needed at three levels, within the guardrails mentioned above. From bottom to top, these three levels are as follows.

Level 3: the individual corporate startup/scaleup. With the Lean Scaleup's business graduation scheme in place, a company can fund the individual corporate startups/scaleups as follows:

- Business Foundation: a small, fixed budget that covers external market studies, some experiments, and some travel expenses.

- Business Strategy: a medium-sized, capped budget. In this stage, the Minimum Viable Product (MVP) and validating scale-worthiness needs to be paid for. Although it may be difficult to anticipate the number of MVP versions, the budget should nevertheless be capped to avoid over-engineering.

- Business Design: an individual budget. In this stage, the scale-ready validation and the development of the Minimum Marketable Product are the biggest cost blocks. The former might be estimated bottom-up, the latter must be estimated individually for every corporate startup.

- Transition to Scaling-Up: no significant budget needed.

- Scaling-Up: an individual budget. Scaling up the market footprint, the product's capabilities and the organization requires a sizable budget which depends on the individual scaleup.

Level 2: the portfolio. Funding at this level needs to pay for the Discovery stage and for managing the Pre-Scaling portfolio. The former includes all activities within the defined meaningful search fields such as hackathons, open innovation activities and ideation workshops. In the Discovery stage, it is not useful to budget for every idea. Therefore, the entire Discovery stage should be budgeted, not the single idea.

The latter includes dedicated individuals that work with the corporate startups to create the monthly progress scorecards and the costs for administrating and supporting them.

Level 1: the ambition. Funding at this level pays the office infrastructure and external costs related to, for example, licenses, collaboration with strategic partners, capability building and marketing.

Metered and Ringfenced Funding

Every corporate startup after the Discovery stage and every corporate scaleup competes for a fixed amount of funds. Due to the inherent uncertainty of out-of-the-box innovation, the funding apparatus must be based on defined deliverables. This approach is often referred to as metered funding and provides two benefits:

- Get a fast start. If the opportunity they are pursuing is well-defined and within a defined search field, metered funding gives corporate startups a small initial budget to get started fast, without the need to wait for stakeholder approval.

- Advance fast if the data suggests doing so. Every stage in the business graduation scheme represents a value inflection point. This means that the value of the emerging business opportunity has grown significantly. Once corporate startups/scaleups have achieved the deliverables for a certain stage, a significant jump in the size of funding is justified.

The company's business graduation scheme defines the deliverables that serve as the basis for metered funding. Companies that have adopted the Lean Scaleup utilize the deliverables outlined in Chapter 6 for their corporate startups and the Scaling-Up milestones, as shown in Chapter 8, for their corporate scaleups.

Of course, all funding for out-of-the-box innovation is part of the company's budgeting. But therein lies the danger: when a company has a string of bad quarters or cost-cutting programs are installed, the funding of out-of-the-box innovation is often questioned since they do not contribute to short-term results.

For this reason, I recommend that investments in out-of-the-box innovation be ringfenced. This is not easy, and a real test of senior management's commitment to create new growth. One way of achieving this goal is to ask Core's units to co-fund because when the funding is backed by many senior managers, such a ringfenced budget is practically untouchable.

Provide "Learning Buffers" in Funding

As emphasized frequently in this book, corporate scaleups work in an uncertain environment. While some tasks can be completed quickly and with less effort than anticipated, others may take significantly longer and require more resources than originally planned.

That reality should be reflected in funding by setting aside additional funding buffers. These are not on-top funds, nor a guarantee of infinite funding. They should be overseen by the relevant level-3 governance boards and only be released when there are singular setbacks. Gradually reducing the size of these buffers is a good practice. For example, a buffer of 20 percent in the first year and 10 percent in the following two years might be a practical solution.

Aligning Funding with Now's Annual Budgeting Cycle

Altering NOW's budgeting processes to ensure NEW's funding is not an option, as explained earlier. Apart from protecting NOW's mission it would be presumptuous to ask NOW, where 99 percent of staff works, to modify its established practices.

Therefore, funding new-business building needs to align with NOW. Fortunately, a practical and efficient solution can be found by combining the Lean Scaleup's business graduation scheme with the funding consider-ations mentioned earlier. To illustrate this point, let me provide a sanitized version of the portfolio of the business model incubator of one of my clients.

Via the Lean Scaleup Pre-Scaling provisions, an an efficient and effective mechanism to arrange funding for corporate startups can be established.

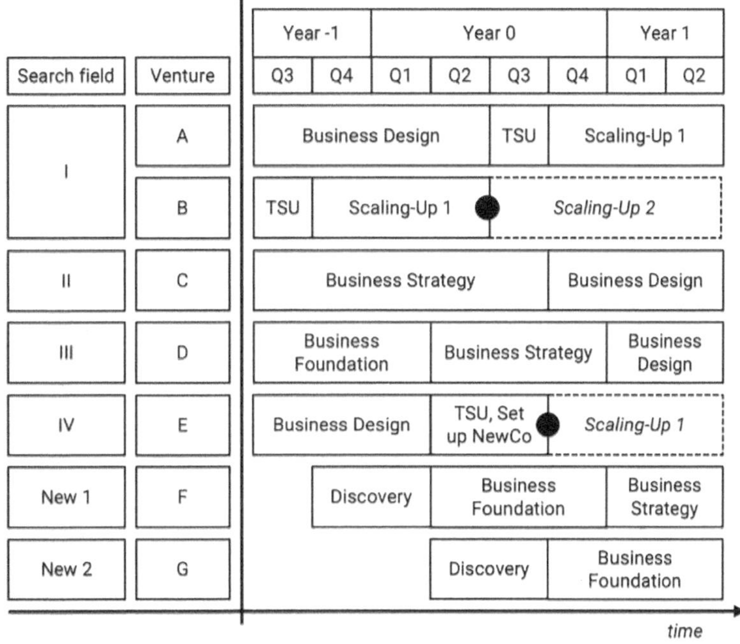

Exhibit 11–1: Aligning metered funding with annual budgeting cycles.

The exhibit illustrates the company's meaningful search fields and its corporate startups at their relevant stage of the business graduation scheme. The initial step is to sum up the level 3-funding requirements per quarter and then add funding for levels 2 and 1. The total budget that is agreed upon with NOW's stakeholders is then distributed top-down to level 2 and the individual corporate startups/scaleups at level 3.

Why an Effective Governance Is Crucial

Arranging the appropriate governance is a critical factor for success in out-of-the-box innovation since it ensures direction and cohesion. With inappropriate governance, chances are high that there is:

- Fragmentation. Without effective decision-making, smaller, short-term initiatives with calculable risks are likely prioritized over longer-running out-of-the-box innovations, as explained above.

- Ineffective allocation of resources. There is a risk that important initiatives do not get the funding they need.

- No critical mass. Egoism of Core's operative units may lead to a situation where resources are scattered and there are too few resources to launch a significant out-of-the-box initiative.

- Scaling-Up underfunding and failures: Early-stage initiatives may receive disproportionate funding compared to scaling of validated initiatives, as the latter is the most expensive part of the innovation journey.

How to Spot Ineffective Governance

Symptoms for ineffective governance are easy to spot. Among the ones that I often see are, for example:

- Many decisions require personal approval from senior managers.

- Unfocused meetings with long, irrelevant status updates that do not lead to making smart decisions.

- Confusion over decision rights.

- Resource and funding decisions tied to NOW's slow-moving processes.

- Competing priorities among members of the governance board.

- Rogue task forces and councils.

A Corporate Startup/Scaleup Is Not a Corporate Project

It is a serious mistake to view a corporate startup/scaleup as a corporate project with a large governance board that meets quarterly, requests decision-supporting documents two weeks in advance, and requires extensive reporting on every hour and dollar spent. I have seen that several times, predominantly in companies that operate in heavily regulated markets.

Members of these large governance boards understand the importance of out-of-the-box innovation in general but lack familiarity with the innovation domain and are hesitant[144] to break away from NOW. They do not want to put a lot of skin into the game and risk career-limiting moves, yet they want to see what is going on and raise concerns when they see their area of responsibility affected.

Such an approach is too bureaucratic and slow. It is even possible that discussions may be influenced by political considerations rather than by what is necessary to create new growth.

Lean Governance for an Individual Corporate Scaleup

I have seen four generic governance models for individual corporate startups/scaleups. However, only one is effective in my view. On-demand committees lack sufficient commitment and advisory committees do not guarantee the necessary NOW/NEW alignment. A single, high-ranking sponsor may be a viable option in the short term, but complications can arise when this individual changes position or leaves the company.

In my view, only a formal, standing committee with relevant senior managers is suitable for mastering the challenges of out-of-the-box innovation and new-business building. This governance board must be lean and

---

[144] For various reasons, as explained in chapter 13.

entrepreneurial. It must have a clear role in helping to navigate the uncertain waters. This role includes:

- Allocating resources.

- Staffing corporate startups/scaleups with the right mix of capabilities.

- Challenging the teams and asking the right fundamental questions.

- Holding the teams accountable for making good progress.

- Helping teams to mitigate the inevitable areas of tension between NOW and NEW.

- Supporting the teams when they run into other Playing Field 2 initiatives[145].

- Stopping the corporate startup/scaleup, if necessary.

Governance at Three Levels

To complement the funding apparatus described above, governance for out-of-the-box innovation must be established at the same three levels. Governance at level 1 should include:

- Synergies and interdependencies with corporate/digital transformation initiatives that go beyond increasing process efficiency, since these play out in Playing Field 2, where Scaling-Up takes place.

- How strongly ideas (in particular meaningful ideas) are connected to defined meaningful search fields.

- The fit of activities with the mandate of the NEW structure.

- Make/buy/partner preferences to drive individual ideas.

- Preferences for acquiring greenfield startups to de-risk and accelerate.

---

[145] The following chapter explains why Playing Field 2 is a resource bottleneck for corporate scaleups.

Level-2 governance should include monitoring the health of the portfolio, resource allocation, and decisions to stop individual corporate startups/scaleups.

Risk Management

During Scaling-Up, anticipated risks may become tangible and ad hoc risks may emerge. These relate to, for example, the corporate scaleup's business processes (especially those with touchpoints to Core's processes), cybersecurity, and corporate IT systems that are used by the corporate scaleup.

The governance scheme must address these risks and risk management. I found the following setup to be practical and effective:

- Level-1 governance defines guidelines and the interplay with Core's relevant functions such as corporate IT, corporate risk management, and corporate compliance.

- Level-2 governance defines the risk appetite and escalation mechanisms.

- Level-3 governance ensures that those risks are handled properly.

Stopping Corporate Startups/Scaleups

The Lean Scaleup takes a rational view on corporate startups/scaleups. If a corporate startup is not making progress, the level-2 governance board must stop it and select another meaningful idea. Similarly, if a corporate scaleup is not meeting milestones within the given time and budget, it is best to analyze whether the reason for this is the team and/or the view on the business opportunity and decide accordingly.

This view addresses a common challenge. In many companies, it is difficult to stop initiatives once they have been launched. There are many potential reasons for this, including:

- The idea is a pet project of a senior manager.

- The corporate startup/scaleup is not validated enough and so there is not a substantiated view on the impact, rather a vague hope that there will be a significant contribution.

- The corporate startup/scaleup team fell in love with their idea.

- The corporate startup/scaleup does not have rights to kill the initiative and senior managers are hesitant to decide.

- Corporate startups/scaleups hide bad news from their stakeholders.

- There is no defined process with clear metrics for deliberately stopping initiatives.

The resulting fuzziness inevitably clogs the out-of-the-box portfolio, resulting in productivity and quality problems, but also in increasing throughput times. However, any company operating in a VUCA environment cannot afford to waste resources and time on initiatives that are not on a solid path towards business impact. Therefore, any company with the ambition to generate new growth needs a process to stop running initiatives. The following four practices are essential to this process.

Practice 1: understand survival rates. Only 20-60 percent of ideas survive the Business Foundation stage. Survival rates are typically higher in subsequent stages. Once a level-2 governance board has access to these statistics, it can plan accordingly.

For instance, if the goal is to admit two corporate startups annually to Scaling-Up, the board can calculate how many corporate startups they need to launch. Additionally, they have a good reference point by asking: "Do we think that this corporate startup will be one of two that we want to scale?"

Practice 2: have the list of meaningful ideas handy. A level-2 governance board should maintain an up-to-date list of meaningful ideas. Utilizing this list during the regular review process simplifies the process of stopping a corporate startup. The issue is no longer simply to kill a questionable idea, but to free up resources to work on other promising ideas.

Practice 3: extract learnings and share them. When a corporate startup/scaleup is shut down, the goal should be to extract as many lessons as possible and share them widely. However, this can be challenging as some individuals tend to avoid acknowledging unsuccessful initiatives.

Practice 4: separate people from initiatives. A level-3 governance board should hold the corporate startup/scaleup team accountable for their results. But they should not associate a failure with the individuals who worked hard on it, as explained in the previous chapter.

Shifting the Mindset to "Growth Champion"

Senior managers who serve on governance boards often take on the role of gatekeepers. They believe it is their duty to protect and safeguard the company's limited resources. This is a limiting mindset. The level-1 governance board must ensure that each member of a governance board has a growth mindset[146] and is not a gatekeeper but a "growth champion" who relentlessly seeks opportunities to create new growth.

The role of a growth champion includes writing a check. But even more, it involves making sure that promising corporate startups/scaleups get the funding, talent, and management attention they need—as long as they are on a solid path to building new growth.

Connect Governance Groups

Once governance boards have been identified at all three levels, they must be linked together to ensure effective coordination. None of the governance boards make decisions in isolation, and there are dependencies between them.

---

[146] See chapter 17.

There are usually two links. The first is to establish meeting cadences to create a predictable rhythm. Level-3 governance boards will need to meet more frequently for shorter durations of time, while level-2 and level-1 boards should meet less often for longer durations of time.

The second link relates to information flow. Each board should have a predictable flow of information—for example, monthly scorecards of corporate startups—into their meetings, and defined decisions and conclusions coming out. These inputs and outputs contain critical information for other boards. Defining how information moves between the various boards will help ensure alignment between new-business builders and NOW.

Make Sure That Governance Boards Have Sufficient Expertise

Investing millions in a corporate scaleup that aims to conquer new markets with advanced technology is highly risky if none of the board members has experience in new-business building and a deep understanding of the underlying technology. Therefore, governance boards must make sure that they possess the necessary expertise to make informed decisions.

This is not a critique of the governance board members. They have a deep understanding of NOW. But NEW is, well it is new. To fill expertise gaps at the governance board, adding external experts in an advisory role is an elegant solution. Considering the amount of funding required to create a new business and the associated risks, I believe this is money well spent.

Chapter 12: Performance and Portfolio Management

Chapter 12
Performance and Portfolio Management

The Lean Scaleup framework comprises 12 modules, with 4 modules allocated to each of the Methodology, Leadership, and People/Culture dimensions.

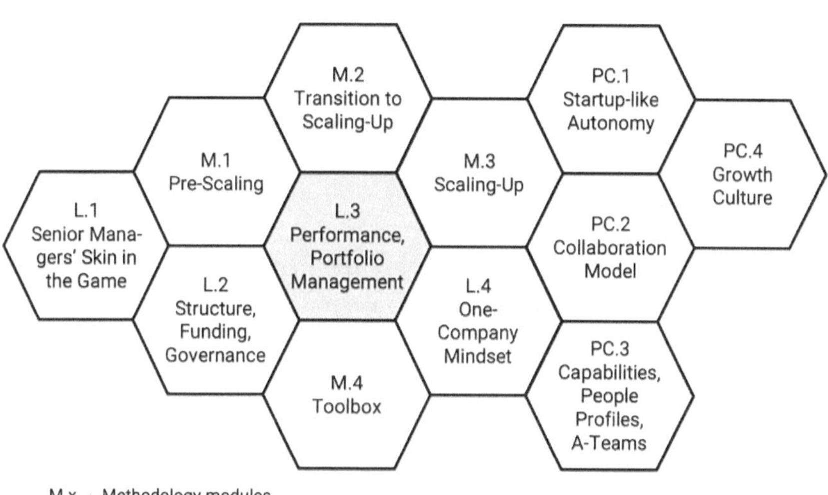

Key Points in This Chapter

1. Although every other European large company has new-business building as a top three priority, only few companies have quantified goals addressing the "win NOW while creating NEW" challenge.

2. Performance management in the out-of-the-box-innovation context needs to address two issues. The long-term ambition must be cut into 12-18-months pieces to fit NOW's time horizon and these pieces need to be aligned with other initiatives that "Reshape Core."

3. A so-called North Star metric that is relevant for both the corporate scaleup and NOW is a critical piece for making NOW/NEW performance management work.

4. Performance management should be installed at the same three levels as funding and governance.

5. One of the goals of managing a portfolio of emerging business opportunities is to ensure that there is a steady stream of scale-worthy and scale-ready corporate startups.

**

55 percent of large European companies acknowledge the importance of new-business building and have set it as one of their top three corporate goals[147]. This chapter outlines two essential provisions for companies seeking to succeed in this space.

First, the company needs to quantify the new-business building ambition and expand its corporate performance management system. Second, it needs to manage a portfolio of corporate startups.

Corporate Goals Do Not Include New-Business Building

Typically, companies have three categories of quantified corporate goals. First, goals related to financials and key business model aspects. Usually, goals in this category relate to:

- Growth at the levels of revenues and margins.

- Customer satisfaction.

- Operational efficiency.

- Strategic partnerships.

- Performance, security, and resilience of business processes.

---

[147] See https://mck.co/48Oc0vN.

Second, people and culture goals. Goals in this category typically relate to corporate culture, employee satisfaction, leadership development, and so on.

Third, ESG (environmental, social, and governance) goals. These typically relate to environmental goals, worker safety, gender diversity, ethical standards, and ensuring compliance standards across the company.

Such a set of quantified corporate goals does not include out-of-the-box-innovation. To win NOW while creating NOW, this aspect must be added. When adding those metrics to the corporate goal set and defining the associated incentives, it is important to keep in mind that out-of-the-box innovators are often not solely financially motivated[148].

What Performance Management Is Not

Senior managers who are responsible for new-business building or serve on the board of a corporate scaleup have typically built their careers in NOW. In NEW, their mindset is sometimes shaped by this cultural imprint. They often perceive emerging businesses as mature companies, as the two following vignettes from my advisory work illustrate.

The HIPPO Problem

I helped a large company to develop concepts for new businesses that should drive new growth and business transformation. Its business model incubation unit had assembled one of the most talented and multidisciplinary teams that I have ever worked with. We challenged ourselves

---

[148] See chapter 16.

with the famous Star Trek™ mission: "To boldly go where no man has gone before."

Each member of the team had been carefully selected for expertise, attitude, and team spirit. I coached the team on customer discovery, problem exploration and validation, value proposition design and experimentation. After six weeks of intensive work, the team presented their findings to a committee of high-ranked managers who would decide whether to fund the idea further.

The conversation took an unexpected turn. Instead of discussing the team's work, a senior manager brought up an idea that had already been on his mind. I could see that the team's energy dropped. They had listened to customers, explored potential solutions, and validated them in the field. They burned the midnight oil because they saw their ideas as a chance to make an impact. They found convincing proof points that there was a solid business foundation for a breakthrough idea.

After the meeting, almost the entire team felt dejected and demoralized. Only one team member agreed to work on the idea of the HIPPO (Highest-Paid Person's Opinion).

The P&L Problem

At a different company, I worked in a 12-week new-business sprint with teams nominated by the operative units. From my unbiased perspective, there was one promising idea that deserved to advance to the Business Strategy stage and receive more funding.

One team member presented the pitch deck that we had prepared together. Among other things, we came up with a back-of-the-envelope estimate of USD 30m revenues in year 5. During the presentation, a senior manager interrupted and challenged this figure. His questions and body language indicated that he was not satisfied with this figure. When we spoke a few days later, he asked me to look for more substantial ideas.

The team encountered the P&L (profit and loss) problem: the emerging business opportunity is inevitably small compared to the existing business. The senior manager's expectations were based on his experience running a billion-dollar business and the polished business cases presented to him for inside-the-box growth projects.

An Overarching Performance Management System

To succeed in NOW, the company has goals and senior managers who ensure execution, manage exceptions, and help teams cross the finish line. The same principles apply to create new growth from out-of-the-box innovation. **There must be goals that span across NOW and NEW and senior managers who insist on achieving those goals, establish a robust management process, resolve exceptions, and empower teams.**

A good starting point to achieve this is the Three Playing Fields model shown in chapter 3. Playing Field 1 is NOW, which is about operational excellence and small, incremental innovations within the existing business model. Goals for the former are typically expressed in the dimensions mentioned at the beginning of this chapter, while goals for the latter might be expressed in revenues from products that did not exist three years ago[149].

Playing Field 3, where NEW is created, also has a set of goals. Typically, these relate to:

– Funding volume.

– Health of the corporate startup portfolio (see below).

---

[149] For example, 3M Company claims that roughly one-third of its sales come from products introduced in the last five years, see https://bit.ly/49Y2M0n.

- Progress predictability for the corporate startup portfolio.

- Financial metrics for corporate scaleups (see below).

It is clear that such a two-component goal system is inadequate for addressing the challenge of "winning the NOW while creating NEW." Although both NOW and NEW have specific goals, there is no connection between them. The issue is that there is no bridge that connects NOW and NEW and consequently no goals for that space.

The bridge is Playing Field 2, the area where "Reshape Core" takes place. Hence, winning NOW while creating NEW requires expanding the company's performance management. As explained in chapter 3, Playing Field 2 consists of:

- The portfolio of corporate scaleups.

- Initiatives related to other transformational plays, for example, transformation from a product company to a service company and customer- and market-facing digital transformation initiatives.

- NOW initiatives that stretch the boundaries of the existing business and operating model, such as opening new sales channels.

The first point is directly relevant for out-of-the-box innovation and new-business building while the remaining are relevant for the context, as illustrated below.

A 3-Level Performance Management System

To effectively manage performance in that area, a performance management system must be established for each of the three levels of funding and governance described in the previous chapter. This is not a straightforward and short-term endeavor since senior management must align with the Board and ensure buy-in from the relevant middle managers.

Level 1: The Ambition

The first level addresses the entire out-of-the-box ambition. This level should have goals in the following dimensions:

- The magnitude of the ambition (for example, "build new businesses with USD 100-200m in annual revenues in the next five years").

- Make/buy/partner preferences for emerging business opportunities.

- Total funding and resourcing.

- Revenue and financial valuation projections.

- Preferences for acquiring greenfield startups to de-risk and accelerate.

Level 2: The Portfolio

In private, most people would not bet all their money on one number in roulette with a 2.8 percent chance of winning. However, in out-of-the-box and new-business building initiatives, this is not uncommon. It seems almost as if senior managers—without realizing it—believe they are playing a coin-flipping game, but in reality, they are playing roulette.

The goal should be to lose as little money as possible in the shortest possible time to find the right ideas. Investing small amounts in multiple promising ideas and testing them is the optimal approach. As soon as there is sufficient real-life evidence, the situation will change, and the likelihood of success will increase significantly. At that point, it is appropriate to allocate significant resources to design a scalable business concept, develop a Minimum Marketable Product, and prepare a successful market launch.

This means that the Return On Investment in Pre-Scaling cannot be measured at the level of the individual corporate startup. It must be measured at the portfolio level: the "Return On Portfolio" counts. Goals should include:

- The number and quality of emerging business opportunities for every meaningful search field.

- The number of emerging business opportunities at every stage of the business graduation scheme.

- Funding and resource allocation for late-stage corporate startups[150].

- Rolled-up statements about revenue and valuation projections.

Level 3: The Individual Corporate Startup/Scaleup

For a corporate startup, the scorecard described in chapter 6 can be used for managing progress and performance. Performance management for a corporate scaleup requires a different set of metrics. As already mentioned in chapter 8, the set of metrics should include:

- Financial metrics.

- Health of the customer base and how well it attracts new customers.

- Operational efficiency.

- Product metrics

- North Star Metrics that are relevant for NOW as well. These quantify the value that the corporate scaleup brings to NOW.

For financial metrics, I find a broad consensus among my clients that top-line growth should be prioritized in the early stages of Scaling-Up. That said, a corporate scaleup's financial metrics should include:

- Market growth, measured by, for example, growth in revenues or in the number of customers.

- Customer retention, measured by, for example, net dollar retention[151].

- Free cash flow.

- "Rule of 40," a rule of thumb stating that the sum of growth rate and margin of a corporate scaleup should exceed 40 percent.

---

[150] For the Discovery and Business Foundation stages, funding can be rolled up.

[151] Revenues from existing customers minus churn and downsell.

- Burn rate and financial runway.

- Revenue-burn multiple, i.e., how much cash is spent to generate an incremental dollar of revenue.

For asset-heavy corporate scaleups, these dimensions should be extended by capital expenditures, assets, and liabilities.

The Playing Field 2 Bottleneck, Maintaining Strategy-Fit

To succeed in out-of-the-box innovation, Core's resources such as sales professionals, procurement experts, and corporate IT specialists are essential. However, these resources are in short supply. **The challenge is compounded by the fact that these individuals are not only crucial for the day-to-day business and out-of-the-box innovation, but also for other Playing Field 2 initiatives,** as described above. Therefore, it is vital to manage these valuable assets carefully by:

- Applying rigor in admitting corporate startups to Scaling-Up.

- Outsourcing relevant pieces of work (for example, outsourcing the legal framework for a platform business model to an external law firm).

- Integrating external experts on an interim basis.

- Establishing an effective resource management.

This is the deeper reason why the level-2 governance board must be involved in discussions surrounding "Reshape Core" and the various initiatives from different angles. Some of the Lean Scaleup's co-creators have established a strategic portfolio team for that purpose. The team is comprised of senior corporate, business unit and strategy managers. It is responsible for identifying, monitoring, and adjusting the mix of projects in Playing Field 2. Their objective is to ensure that the most valuable initiatives receive the necessary resources and move quickly.

But even after carefully selecting and prioritizing projects, the strategic portfolio team may find that there are more Playing Field 2 initiatives that the company can reasonably support. In those cases, they set further limits, either by establishing a maximum number of initiatives in the portfolio or a maximum budget for them.

Make the Ambition Digestible for Performance Management

Success in out-of-the-box innovation takes time. New businesses in adjacent spaces may not generate significant revenue for three to five years, and those that are further out may take five to ten years. This time span exceeds the typical three-year strategy horizon and often surpasses the tenure of senior managers. As a result, the time horizons of new-business building and NOW do not align.

To illustrate this point, let us consider an example from one of my automotive clients. The company aims to transform itself from a product-centric to a service-centric company: the share of service revenues should grow from 20 percent to 50 percent within eight years. But this eight-year period is **too long for NOW to feel compelled to act and too long for a meaningful performance management**.

There are three good reasons to break down the multi-year ambition into smaller pieces. These smaller steps can be:

- A part of the NOW/NEW performance management system.

- Integrated into NOW's planning system to support the operational alignment with the corporate scaleup.

- An effective way to win NOW for the ambitions. As one of my corporate scaleup clients stated: "I initially assumed we could move much quicker, but I had to adapt to what the company could handle. Surprisingly, I found this approach to be helpful. It provided success stories for Core and stakeholders before we took more ambitious steps."

Roadmapping is a useful tool in this context. To align the ambition with NOW's planning and execution engines, interlinked deliverables must be defined. These steps are typically specified in dimensions such as:

- Resources and capabilities.

- Technology.

- Components and sub-systems.

- Products and systems.

- Services.

- Business and Operating Models.

- Markets.

The Crucial Role of the North Star Metric

A corporate scaleup of a global beverage company scales a direct-to-consumer business model innovation. Their primary metric is "number of points-of-sale." Another corporate scaleup had developed a breakthrough technology that allows customers to "see and hear" into underground assets, thus increasing production volume. This corporate scaleup's key metric is "customer value generated."

These two examples demonstrate how some corporate scaleups define their primary metric so that it:

- Is relevant for the corporate scaleup and NOW at the same time.

- Can easily be understood and is free of jargon.

- Expresses why the corporate scaleup's product matters to customers.

- Is measurable but not a "vanity metric."

- Represents a leading indicator of success, allowing the corporate scaleup to focus its energy on controllable inputs.

Such a North Star metric is crucial for the Playing Field 2 discussions mentioned above because it states the value that the corporate scaleup generates. Additionally, such a metric is an anchor point for the corporate scaleup to solve the alignment/autonomy challenge[152] and a strong pillar for the one-company mindset described in the next chapter.

The Incentives Issue

Incentivizing the right behaviors that support out-of-the-box innovation is a major lever to achieve success. Incentives must be tied to transparent outcomes and performance metrics. They are relevant for Core's functions that support corporate scaleups and for the corporate scaleup.

Identifying suitable, transparent incentives for the former group should be straightforward, when the roadmapped Scaling-Up milestones are incorporated into the goal system of those functions that support Scaling-Up.

For the latter group, determining monetary incentives should be rather straightforward by linking them to Scaling-Up milestones, as mentioned above. The size of the incentives, however, depends on the company. I have seen incentives for corporate scaleup CEOs that range from a year's salary to several millions. Similar to greenfield startups, the monetary incentives might also include equity or a share in the profits.

But it is important to note that for corporate scaleup team members, particularly those from Gen-Z and Millennial age groups, financial compensation is a significant factor, but not the sole motivator. Additional incentives could be:

- Providing opportunities to acquire new skills or enhance existing ones.

- Clear pathways for career advancement within the company.

- Visibility with senior managers.

- Autonomy and entrepreneurship.

---

[152] For example, via Objectives and Key Results (OKRs), see chapter 8.

Managing the Portfolio of Corporate Startups

Effective management of a portfolio of corporate startups must achieve two goals. First, it must provide decision support for key issues that relate to the progress and the needs of the individual corporate startup. Second, it must ensure the health of the portfolio so that there is a good chance that at least one idea comes out which is scale-worthy and scale-ready. In this context, my client discussions often center on three key questions:

– Are we doing the right things? This refers to, for example, how well the individual corporate startups fit the meaningful search fields and how effectively they are targeting the most valuable positions.

– Do we do too much, too little, or the right amount of the right things?

– Have we allocated the appropriate resources for each individual corporate startup?

Healthy Corporate Startup Portfolios

Healthy portfolios ensure a steady flow of corporate startups through the Pre-Scaling phase. The exhibit below shows a healthy portfolio and five suboptimal portfolios.

To assess the health of the corporate startup portfolio, count the number of corporate startups in the pre-Scaling stages of the business graduation scheme.

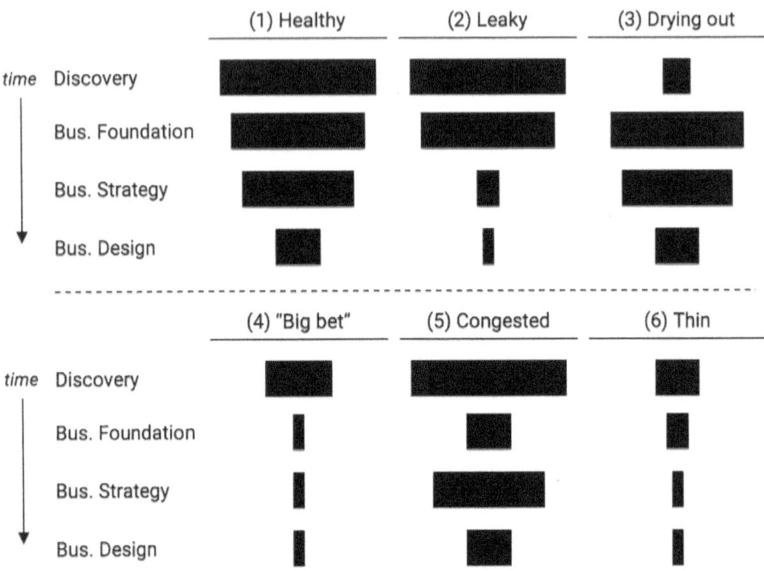

Exhibit 12–1: Corporate startup portfolio health (various situations).

Good Practices in Portfolio Management

The co-creators of Lean Scaleup have identified three best practices in managing a portfolio of early stage out-of-the-box and new-business building initiatives:

- Portfolio review meetings should be held quarterly and as needed in case of significant events.

- The goal of these meetings is to optimize portfolio value and reallocate resources if necessary.

- During review meetings, other initiatives in Playing Field 2 should be considered because they impact new-business building.

Chapter 13: One-Company Mindset

Chapter 13
One-Company Mindset

The Lean Scaleup framework comprises 12 modules, with 4 modules allocated to each of the Methodology, Leadership, and People/Culture dimensions.

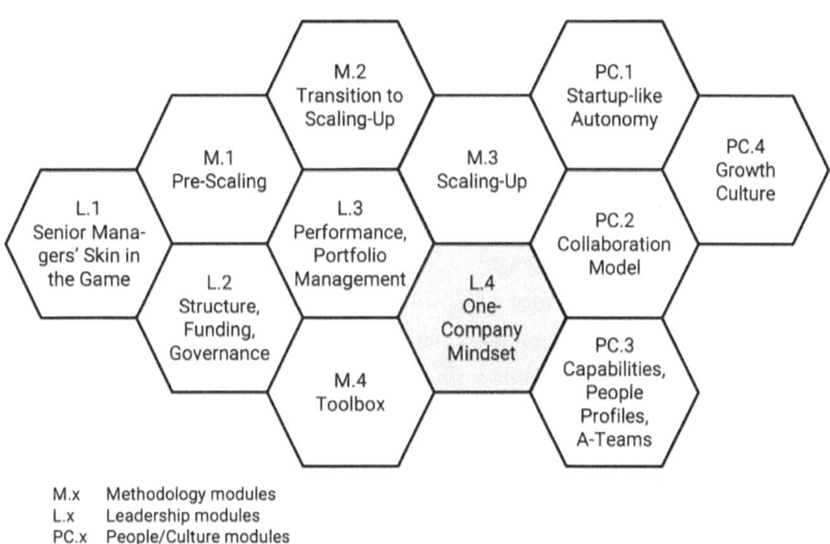

Key Points in This Chapter

1. When senior managers promote out-of-the-box innovation, they also send a second message: yesterday's success recipe will not count tomorrow. This might be hard to swallow for Core's managers and staff since they often define themselves by their expertise in NOW.

2. Even at the senior management level there might be individuals who do not embrace out-of-the-box innovation and creating NEW. In practice, one finds eight reasons.

3. When there is no imminent urge to act—when the company is not yet on a "burning platform"—private data can help to make the case.

4. Intensive and persistent communication is a prerequisite for success.

**

The case studies about Fujifilm and Ørsted in chapters 4 and 10 portray two companies that succeeded in out-of-the-box innovation. They share several common traits. They:

- Started with meaningful search fields (Surface Chemistry and Green Energy, respectively).

- Discovered meaningful ideas for sizable new businesses in these fields, and then validated and scaled these ideas.

- Demoted or dismantled their legacy businesses.

- Acquired other companies to seize pivotal positions in the new businesses and to accelerate the transition.

However, there is a more profound similarity between the two companies. Their senior managers successfully integrated NOW and NEW into a new corporate identity. They gained the support of both sides by emphasizing that there is only one company future-proofing itself, rather than a NOW company and some out-of-the-box initiatives.

When senior management creates a new corporate identity by integrating NOW and NEW, they touch the soul of the company. Many members of staff joined an organization that monetarized the historic, proven business model. They worked for years in a corporate environment where defined processes and existing culture were crucial to both corporate and individual successes.

But when senior management emphasizes venturing beyond NOW, it sends a clear message: "Tomorrow's recipe for success will not be the same as today's." Senior management must help middle managers and staff to overcome the organizational and cultural inertia that comes from decades of repeating a proven success recipe. They must ensure that staff and middle managers understand the rationale behind the change and embrace a spirit of determined optimism. If these three goals are not achieved, resistance may emerge.

This resistance can be observed in a tangible way. Staff members with a fixed mindset[153] may state: "We have always done it this way," "we have never done it that way," or "this is far too risky." Resistance can also manifest in more sophisticated ways, such as in strategic discussions. In Ørsted's case, there were discussions about the company's lack of capabilities to succeed in creating NEW.

While this question needs to be thoroughly discussed, there is one crucial aspect that must not be overlooked. If a company restricts its exploration to fit existing capabilities, it will not be able to break free from the constraints of the old business model. **The Kodak case study in chapter 4 serves as a reminder that today's capabilities could be tomorrow's legacy**.

Senior management must proactively address the one-company mindset issue, or the discussion will not stop and slow down progress. This chapter offers guidance on how to navigate common challenges.

The One-Company Mindset at the Top

When working with senior management teams to foster a one-company mindset, I often encounter conflicts and reservations. These may be expressed openly or remain hidden beneath the surface. Although the specific mix differs from company to company, they will inevitably arise.

First, the gravitational pull of past success. Senior managers made their careers in NOW. They learned the rules to succeed in the company's culture and processes and acquired in-depth knowledge to analyze weak, fluffy, or even wrong arguments in proposals to optimize NOW. They also developed the appropriate leadership style for the parts of the company that they are responsible for.

---

[153] See chapter 17.

One could say that they found the recipe for their individual success. However, when asked to move in uncharted territory, these individuals may feel that this recipe is no longer fully relevant and hence it might be safer for them to stick to the status quo.

Some senior managers may not fully embrace new-business building to future-proof the company. There are eight frequent reasons.

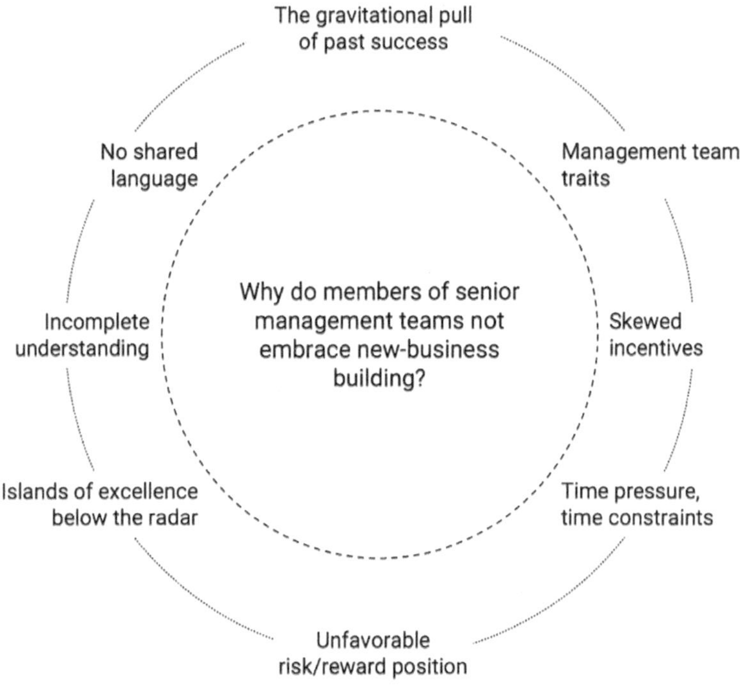

Exhibit 13–1: Why senior managers might not foster new-business building.

Second, management team traits. Some senior management teams have found ways to work with individual weaknesses of their members, but they struggle with open conflicts. New-business building, however, creates many conflicts, such as conflicts over resources, budgets, or priorities between NOW and NEW. Therefore, some senior management teams may choose to avoid those conflicts.

Third, skewed incentives. Most companies' top goals prioritize short-term results over future revenue streams and corporate transformation, as described in the previous chapter. Consequently, senior managers may focus on what matters most, which is winning the NOW.

Fourth, time pressure and time constraints. A senior manager's schedule is typically consumed by day-to-day business operations and aligning with other parts of the company. As a result, there is often little time left for deep thinking about out-of-the-box threats and opportunities.

Fifth, protecting the career. Why should senior managers make decisions with an inherent risk when the potential reward is far in the future—perhaps even so far that they will no longer be with the company then? Some senior managers may oppose NEW for this very personal reason.

Sixth, islands of excellence below the radar. Out-of-the-box innovation is driven by individuals, not companies. Within every organization, there are intrinsically motivated individuals who think beyond the day. These individuals collaborate with others from different parts of the company to solve specific challenges.

However, they often prefer to remain under the radar because they do not strive to transform the company. Their senior managers may also choose not to create visibility for these individuals because they are afraid of losing experts for their own business function.

Seventh, incomplete understanding of NEW. It has been said that while technology develops exponentially, human learning grows linearly. For instance, in the last generation, the internet, social media, the internet of things, blockchain, cryptocurrencies, genetic engineering (CRISPR), and AI have become mainstream. For some senior managers, understanding a rapidly changing technology landscape can be challenging.

Eighth, no common language. Senior management teams often lack a common language to discuss out-of-the-box innovation, and new-business building. That lack naturally hinders alignment on what is NEW and how to get there[154].

Building the One-Company Mindset

One should not expect that senior and middle managers are aligned on company goals and priorities. Only 28 percent of senior managers can list the top three strategic priorities of their company[155]. In other words, senior managers must create and maintain alignment on the why, what, and how of new-business building across all management levels. This involves both rational and psychological aspects. The rational part can be broken down into two key questions.

First, what business are we in? Chapter 4 illustrates how Amazon and Fujifilm redefined their businesses beyond the historic business models. Amazon defined itself not as an e-commerce retailer, but as a media company. Fujifilm did not define itself as a silver-film company, but as a surface-chemistry company.

Some senior managers may suggest answers to this question that are adjacent to NOW, while others may propose definitions that are farther away. There is no one-size-fits-all answer to how far the future identity should go beyond Core. Valuable pieces for the answer may be found by analyzing the gaps between NOW and the company's VUCA environment.

Second, how high is the need to act? Three years after Apple introduced the iPhone and two years after his company's global mobile phone market share peaked, Nokia's then-CEO described the company's situation as

---

[154] See chapter 3 for a language and chapter 9 for a toolbox addressing this issue.
[155] See https://bit.ly/47v7LEO.

being on a burning platform[156]. He described an imminent life-threatening situation with only unpleasant options to choose from in order to survive. Fujifilm faced a similar situation when the market for silver film collapsed in less than a decade. And when Amazon decided to enter the digital media space, its platform was not yet on fire, but the flames were clearly visible.

Fortunately, for most companies the platform is not burning yet. They are not in the same situation as Nokia and Fujifilm. However, nearly every industry has its own VUCA challenges. Therefore, opportunities should be seized, and disruption be fended off before the platform burns. Senior management must align on the urgency to act.

One method to achieve this is to analyze current revenue drivers and future assumptions critically. When senior managers articulate their assumptions about the future business environment and the relevance of today's revenue drivers in the future, these can be scrutinized and discussed.

In most cases, the discussion will not immediately eliminate diverging views, but rather bring different points of view to the forefront. This approach helps to counteract the so-called ambiguity effect[157], which is the tendency for people to select options with known probabilities of favorable outcomes over options with unknown probabilities.

What to Do When the Platform Is Not Burning Yet

Despite the similarities between Fujifilm and Ørsted, there is one fundamental difference. The former operated in a market that collapsed within a decade while the latter recognized a long-term threat to its business model and acted in due time.

---

[156] See https://bit.ly/3R6ZBw3.
[157] See https://en.wikipedia.org/wiki/Ambiguity_effect.

Winston Churchill famously said: "Never let a good crisis go to waste." In other words, senior managers may find it easier to justify new-business building when the financial outlook is doom and gloom. However, creating a sizeable new business takes time, and by the time the new business reaches scale, it may be too late.

But how should the case for out-of-the-box innovation be made when the platform is not burning yet? How should senior managers motivate middle management and staff to leave the comfort zone and embark on creating NEW? Creating a false sense of urgency might not be the answer since "transformation theater" might lead to transformation fatigue.

Senior management teams must base their decisions on reliable data. The challenge in new-business building is that by the time when publicly available data indicates that the company is already in a precarious position, it may be too late. On the other hand, basing substantial decisions on 10-year market estimates from market research agencies and consultants who have no skin in the game has its challenges as well.

In my practice, I use publicly available data and long-term market estimates only as backup. They can be debated and discussions about whether a certain technology is a little bit more to the left or to the right on the "technology hype cycle" typically do not generate value. Instead, I use private data, such as:

- Interviews with customers of the company's customers.

- Strategy dialogues between the company's out-of-the-box innovators and corporate venture capital (CVC) units and operative units.

The former avoids confirmation bias, and it removes a blind spot: current customers seldom advocate opportunities that come from disrupting their own role. Some of my clients use the latter approach, where the mentioned units convene for a one-day workshop every six months.

In the first part of the dialogue, the operative units share signals related to out-of-the-box innovation. In the second part, CVC units and out-of-the-box innovators share insights gained from observing where VC money is flowing and what is happening in innovation ecosystems.

As a result, there is shared view on where out-of-the-box innovation and new-business building could add tangible value and help to future-proof the operative units. Since these insights are private data with high relevance, senior managers typically consider them as a valuable input.

Communicate, Communicate, And Communicate Again

To gain support from middle managers and staff, senior management must have skin in the game and put their standing and reputation on the line. Serial new-business builders like Fujifilm view the one-company mindset as being of equal importance to the identification, validation, and scaling of emerging business opportunities.

In his book[158], Fujifilm's former CEO Shigetaka Komori provides valuable insights into how to instill and amplify the one-company mindset. "With Fujifilm's core photographic film market crumbling, it was my job to determine our future direction, the type of company Fujifilm should be, and a practical program for achieving those ends—and finally to communicate all this to the company's employees, whose motivation was essential to make the plan work."

He made the case for new-business building personal by holding "ask me anything" lunch meetings with small groups of managers and requested that Fujifilm's top 1,000 employees each write a two-page memo identifying the necessary steps to generate new growth and potential obstacles to progress. With this feedback, he improved his impact in speeches and

---

[158] Shigetaka Komori, Innovating Out of Crisis, Stone Bridge Press, 2015.

in-person meetings and became aware of issues that the senior management team had initially not considered.

Senior managers should not underestimate the effort necessary to take NOW out from the gravitational pull of the past. They must be prepared to communicate, communicate, and then to communicate again. The following communication pieces might be helpful:

- Show the cost of non-acting.

- Limit new-business building priorities to a handful (fewer are better).

- Explain concisely what a priority means, why it matters, and how it will be accomplished.

- Provide spaces for questions and discussions. Communication is a two-way street, rather than a one-way megaphone.

- Require upper and middle managers to provide a detailed explanation of the obstacles preventing the company from creating NEW.

- Illustrate what good looks like in a small, critical number of personal behaviors. Statements such as "we are entrepreneurial" will not change behavior since they are too general.

- Develop leadership communication plans to leverage the individual engagements of the members of the senior management team.

- Ensure that middle managers have sufficient insight into the what and how of new-business building.

- Find, educate, and empower communication catalysts within the corporate functions and operative units.

Chapter 14: Startup-like Autonomy

Chapter 14
Startup-like Autonomy

The Lean Scaleup framework comprises 12 modules, with 4 modules allocated to each of the Methodology, Leadership, and People/Culture dimensions.

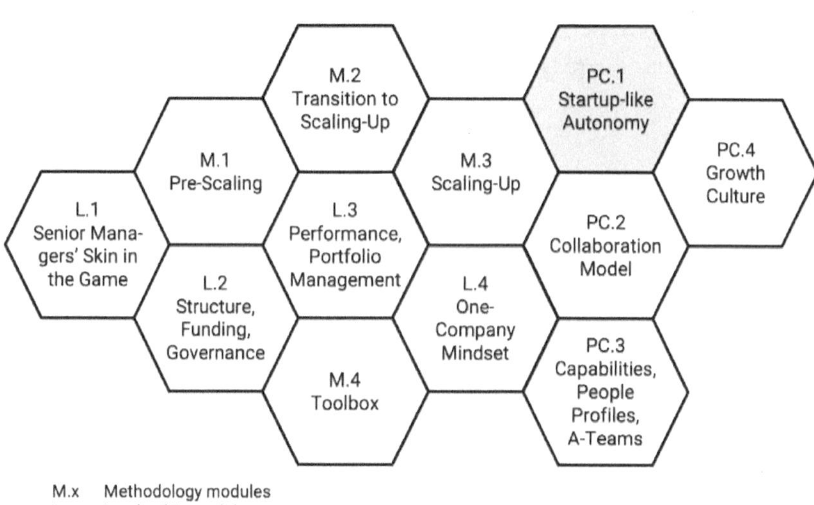

Key Points in This Chapter

1. Corporate scaleups need some entrepreneurial freedom to scale out-of-the-box innovations at pace. Tying them to corporate bureaucracy limits the chances for success significantly.

2. Since a corporate scaleup is operating in a corporate context, their freedom cannot be the entrepreneurial freedom that greenfield startups have. They need to have a so-called startup-like autonomy.

3. This startup-like autonomy has five elements and should be negotiated in the transitional phase between validating and scaling.

4. NOW should make two adjustments to support the startup-like autonomy: installing empowered "functional tags" in the interfaces and enabling accelerated growth.

**

As described in chapter 2, NOW is designed to flawlessly execute a proven business model. Established processes and a stringent governance ensure that activities are performed as specified and workflows are managed as defined.

Such a rigid and process-driven approach is not suitable for greenfield startups. These operate in a fundamentally different business environment which has many unknowns and requires quick adaptation. To succeed, they use their autonomy to establish a high degree of entrepreneurial freedom.

When it comes to the operating model, corporate scaleups sit somewhere in the middle between NOW and greenfield startups. To achieve success, they must have entrepreneurial freedom to win in the market. But they also must collaborate with Core to leverage corporate assets and capabilities that provide them with a competitive edge.

The challenge, then, is how to provide corporate scaleups with the support they need, while at the same time creating a startup-like autonomy within a corporate context based on processes and rules? This chapter explains how to achieve it.

Leveraging Corporate Assets and Corporate Rules

"We counted them all," said one of my clients, the head of a corporate Scaling-Up factory of a large German engineering company. "Our company operates on 800 rules. Some of them, such as those relating to procurement and finance, are hardwired in our IT systems. Others, such as recruitment rules, are codified in corporate policies. Then there are policies that apply to individual business units and functions. And finally, there are procedures on the intranet, such as those governing when and how to use the corporate brand."

Create and scaling a new business while complying with 800 rules is not feasible. **Since these corporate rules also govern access to corporate experts and assets, the bureaucratic strings attached to potential sources of "unfair advantages" generate significant delays and inefficiencies**. But when bureaucracy restricts entrepreneurial freedom, corporate scaleups face a two-front war: on the one hand, they compete in the marketplace against greenfield startups, incumbents, and their corporate startups; on the other hand, they battle corporate bureaucracy.

My client said: "We need to identify 20 essential rules that are consistent with the underlying intent of the corporate rules. Then we negotiate with Core's senior management to create the mandatory startup-like autonomy within the corporate context."

Entrepreneurial Freedom inside the Corporate Context

Due to its mission, NOW cannot operate with a startup mindset. Trying to scale an emerging business opportunity with NOW's operating model and its process-driven, risk-averse mindset will not work either. Therefore, to build a new business using corporate assets and capabilities, **a corporate scaleup must have a defined bridge to NOW where relevant and entrepreneurial freedom everywhere else.**

The required size of the bridge and the level of entrepreneurial freedom depends on how the new business is related to Core. If the goal is to create adjacent new businesses and to "Reshape Core," a larger bridge is required.

If the goal is to create a new business that is distant from Core, the bridge can be smaller.

My client was tasked with creating businesses that were distant from Core. He said: "To succeed, we need to be strictly separate. We need to be a separate legal entity with separate processes, a different culture, working contracts, and so on. We need a different tech stack, our own ERP system, and our own legal and HR processes. Only with such a setup, we can move quickly and attract a different kind of talent."

There Is Little Entrepreneurial Freedom to Be Found

Some companies have found a way to create startup-like autonomy within the corporate context. For example, in a German technology company, new-business building is one of its four business units and has a seat at the leadership table. This unit's targets are to:

- Reshape Core.

- Build adjacencies to existing digital products and services.

- Launch two corporate scaleups per year.

- Create new, AI-based revenue streams.

However, most companies struggle to arrange[159] startup-like autonomy for their corporate scaleups:

- Less than 10 percent have entrepreneurial freedom.

- 90 percent of all decisions must be approved by stakeholders.

- 25 percent were denied even one of Core's assets and capabilities.

---

[159] See https://mck.co/46WhzGB.

How to Negotiate the Startup-like Autonomy

Corporate scaleups should negotiate their startup-like autonomy during the Transition-to-Scaling-Up phase. This way, they avoid creating an endless stream of exception requests that take time and energy to resolve.

The negotiation[160] involves three steps and a defined escalation mechanism. The first step is to specify the rules that the corporate scaleup would like to have in place. The second step is to identify the corporate rules that need modification and provide a rationale for the exception:

— Why is the corporate scaleup's rule needed?

— What are the consequences if it is not implemented?

— Are there limitations to the rule such as a maximum limit to the number of customers contacted, or a maximum spend?

— What impact will this scaleup rule have on existing corporate rules?

— What are the risks for NOW, and how will these risks be mitigated?

The third step is to negotiate with Core's relevant functions. If the request is not accepted, a senior manager will then make the final decision.

Elements of the Startup-like Autonomy

A startup-like autonomy in the corporate context has five major elements. These are the areas where a corporate scaleup should negotiate with NOW, using the process described above.

---

[160] Adapted from Steve Blank's "Getting to Yes" (See https://bit.ly/3RqhK7p).

A corporate scaleup needs to negotiate a startup-like autonomy in five dimensions with NOW to avoid a "two-front war."

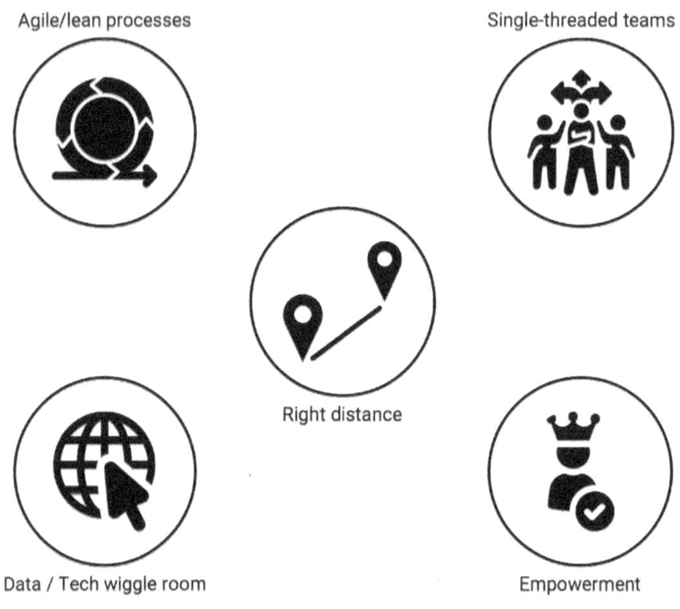

Exhibit 14–1: Five dimensions of a startup-like autonomy in the corporate context.

The Right Distance

In astrobiology, the study of life in the universe and the search for extra-terrestrial life, the so-called habitable zone is a key concept. This zone refers to the area around a star where conditions are suitable for liquid water to exist on a planet's surface. For a planet to support life, it must be at the right distance from its star—not too close and not too far.

The same principle applies to the right distance between a corporate scaleup and NOW. If the distance is too close, the corporate scaleup will inevitably be subject to the gravitational pull of NOW's processes and compliance requests. Conversely, if the distance is too far, NOW's senior managers may not view the emerging business as an integral part of the company. In this situation, creating the one-company mindset[161] may be challenging. The right distance refers to two issues:

- Physical location. For example, one of my SME clients located their corporate scaleup's offices in a former production building. This allowed Core's staff to easily interact with the corporate scaleup team.

- Financial autonomy. Once the metered funding scheme for the corporate scaleup has been set up as described in chapter 11, it should have financial autonomy to spend the allocated budget.

Single-Threaded Teams

Jeff Bezos, the founder of Amazon, once said: "The best way to fail at innovation is to make it someone's part-time job[162]." To achieve success in Scaling-Up, it is essential to have a dedicated team of full-time professionals. When key individuals are burdened with multiple responsibilities, including Scaling-Up, and work with other individuals handling other projects, everything becomes a priority, and in the end, nothing is a priority.

The Amazon case study in chapter 4 demonstrates that for organizing teams, incorporating all necessary capabilities and aligning them towards an external or internal customer is an effective strategy. This approach provides a corporate scaleup with empowered teams that are fully focused and not distracted.

I recommend going one step further: Core's experts should also work full-time for a suitable timebox within the corporate scaleup. It is much easier for them to work on, for instance, the market entry in Southeast Asia continuously for four weeks than to spend four hours per week over a six-month period. Additionally, the corporate scaleup saves precious time.

---

[161] See chapter 13.
[162] See https://bit.ly/4acXm17.

Empowerment for Two-Way-Door Decisions

In his 1997 letter to shareholders, Amazon's founder Jeff Bezos described his decision-making model:

- "One-way-door decisions" refer to significant and irreversible decisions that must be made in a methodical and thorough manner.

- "Two-way-door decisions" are changeable and reversible. These decisions can and should be made quickly.

In my experience, a corporate scaleup with a proper startup-like autonomy can make 90 percent of all decisions independently because they are two-way-door decisions. These include hiring new employees, making product design choices, or allocating marketing budgets. 9 percent of decisions are made jointly with the governance board, and only 1 percent are true one-way-door decisions which require alignment with senior management. These include, for instance, acquiring other startups to accelerate the journey or changing the corporate scaleup's mission.

Empowering the corporate scaleup to make the by far biggest parts of decisions autonomously is vital for success. **Such an autonomy often goes beyond the decision-making authority of Core's upper managers. Senior managers and CEOs of corporate scaleups need to keep this point in mind when they want to establish the one-company mindset.**

Access to Data and a Tech Stack Wiggle Room

Core's transactional data can be a valuable asset for a corporate scaleup when it is building, for example, AI-powered solutions. In this case, they must have rapid access to relevant data sets and negotiate how these data sets are accessed and used, including the boundaries of their usage.

To move rapidly, corporate scaleups also must have degrees of freedom to decide on their tech stack. This term refers to the set of technologies to develop applications, including programming languages, frameworks, databases, front-end and back-end tools, APIs (application programming interfaces), and a defined integration with relevant Core systems. The front-end part of the tech stack, which includes the user interface and basic customer interactions, must be owned by the corporate scaleup because it is a differentiating factor in the market.

The tech stack also comprises the systems the corporate scaleup needs to conduct its operations, including the seemingly trivial tasks such as invoicing customers. Since the business context of the corporate scaleup is different—for example, with respect to types of customers, the nature of products or the revenue model—it is often not feasible to use Core's heavy-weight and highly specialized operational systems.

However, the situation is different in the back-end. For instance, one of my corporate startup clients built its Minimum Marketable Product on Amazon Web Services because this allowed them to save time and effort. In the Transition-to-Scaling-Up phase, it was decided that they would migrate its back-end to Core's Microsoft Azure infrastructure. This migration was included in the Scaling-Up plan and NOW's stakeholders allocated additional resources to ensure a smooth transition without overburdening the corporate scaleup.

Agile and Lean Processes

To streamline the collaboration between corporate scaleup and Core and free it from the shackles of corporate bureaucracy, pre-defined waivers and agile, lean processes should be installed at the interface. For example, during the negotiation process mentioned above, the corporate scaleup could:

- Negotiate to make payments up to a pre-defined threshold without requiring lengthy corporate approval workflows.

- Streamline collaboration with the corporate procurement function. The processes must reflect essential principles such as traceability and compliance, but do not have to be full-blown corporate processes.

To facilitate these agile and lean processes, senior management must implement two adjustments to Core's interfaces with corporate scaleups.

The first adjustment is to enable accelerated growth, as described in chapter 10. The second is to arrange empowered functional experts as the interface between Core and NEW, as described below.

Functional Tags in Corporate Functions

A startup-like autonomy requires suitable collaborators in Core's functions and units. These individuals must be educated about out-of-the-box innovation, especially about the importance of using Core's assets and capabilities, and they must be empowered to implement the lean and agile processes within their respective units.

For example, one of my corporate clients installed these so-called functional tags in each function. When one of its corporate scaleups, which developed low-cost, small sensors that challenged industry orthodoxies, started Scaling-Up, a lean procurement process with a defined functional tag in corporate procurement allowed for rapid global sourcing of sensor components. This turned out to be a sustainable competitive advantage.

In my experience, the appropriate individuals for the role of a functional tag appear when the message goes out. Often, they have terms like innovation, digitalization, excellence, automation, or optimization in their job titles or their job descriptions. They share similar character traits. They:

- Understand the potential of testing not-yet-industrialized solutions.

- Have a growth mindset (see chapter 17).

- Are impact-driven, tenacious, and resilient.

- Know how far they can push the processes, systems, and structures inside their respective corporate function.

These individuals must also be empowered; otherwise, they risk flaming out in their process-driven, risk-averse context. Senior management must engage in four activities to empower them:

- Advocating for the functional tags.

- Protecting their time.

- Checking in regularly to understand impediments and blockers.

- Harnessing their business creativity.

A Defined Bridge

Even with the best preparation, establishing a startup-like autonomy within a corporate context may give rise to issues and conflicts. So, there should be a defined bridge between NOW and the corporate scaleup (or the new-business building unit) to discuss and resolve these issues. This bridge is made up from four elements:

- A senior manager with new-business building goals.

- The corporate scaleup's CEO.

- The governance board for the individual scaleup.

- A collaboration model that outlines how Core and the scaleup should work together, as described in the next chapter.

Chapter 15: Collaboration Model

Chapter 15
Collaboration model

The Lean Scaleup framework comprises 12 modules, with 4 modules allocated to each of the Methodology, Leadership, and People/Culture dimensions.

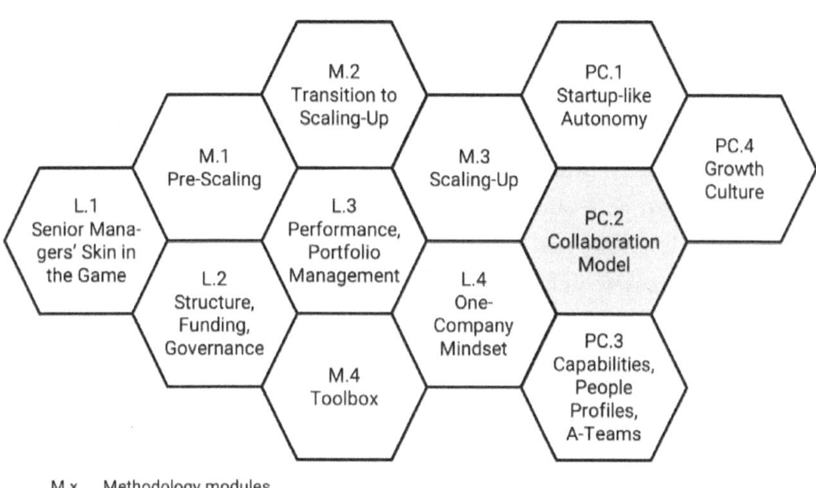

Key Points in This Chapter

1. Since NOW and NEW are inherently incompatible and corporate assets and capabilities are managed by NOW, leveraging these to create an "unfair advantage" must be done via a collaboration agreement.

2. There are three generic collaboration models. In many cases, a win/win agreement is suitable which plays out on three levels.

3. These three levels are the formal alignment, the partnership equation, and the working level.

4. "What is in for the customers?" is a powerful question to align the corporate scaleup and Core's functions.

5. The collaboration agreements could serve as a basis for a Scaling-Up kick-off workshop.

* *

Situated on the picturesque shores of Lake Constance in Germany is the headquarter of a USD 500m global manufacturer of paint spraying equipment. The company has a long history of producing sprayers for DIY enthusiasts, professional craftsmen, and industrial applications. It is now determined to enter the skincare market.

One of its corporate scaleups has developed a skin care sprayer that applies sunscreen, self-tanner, or body lotion precisely and evenly to all areas of the skin, including hard-to-reach areas. Entering the skin care market helps the company to achieve two goals. It:

– Contributes to the company's goal of becoming a technology leader in wet paint spraying.

– Creates new growth[163].

Six of Core's engineers provided technical expertise in the development of the skin care sprayer. They remained on Core's payroll and reported to the Chief Technology Officer but were managed by the corporate scaleup. Core also provided funding, engineering capabilities, the IT infrastructure and support in secondary processes, such as accounting and HR.

This is an illustrative example of how incumbents can leverage corporate assets and capabilities to expand beyond their historical business model. But there is a second point to this story. Finding an effective collaboration model between Core and corporate startups/scaleups is a key success factor in new business building.

---

[163] Skin care experts estimate that the Serviceable Addressable Market for this disruptive innovation, not including the marketing of skin care data, is worth billions.

Design Principles

Every corporate scaleup should maintain good relationships with Core's relevant middle managers since these control access to corporate assets and capabilities. However, good relationships alone are not enough to establish an effective and productive collaboration with Core's functional experts.

People might be collaborative, but systems are not. These experts operate in NOW's process-driven, short-term-focused business environment where every dollar and every hour counts. Hence, when they need to prioritize, they will inevitably focus on what matters most: NOW. Alternatively, building the collaboration solely on a formal, transactional model will not be effective either. This approach will not create the alignment and trust necessary to win together in uncharted territory.

The Lean Scaleup provides a solution to the challenge of establishing a solid, productive collaboration between NOW and NEW. The solution has two parts. First, creating the right environment[164], which includes:

- Senior managers' skin in the game.

- Establishing a suitable performance and portfolio management.

- Fostering a one-company mindset.

Second, incorporating the success factors of collaboration between large and small companies[165] which state that two things are critical for success:

- Embracing the diversity of mental models, operating styles, and other potential areas of disagreement.

- Prioritizing the quality of the work relationship over a pre-established plan.

---

[164] See chapters 10, 12 and 13, respectively.
[165] See https://bit.ly/3Ny2qnY.

Three Types of Collaboration Models

I have observed three types of collaboration in practice. The first model is the joint development agreement. In this model, Core and the corporate scaleup develop a software product such as a software platform or an enterprise API that allows NOW to connect its back-end IT systems to third parties. This approach is suitable when NOW can reuse the product for its own purposes. Essentially, the corporate scaleup is the first user.

In the second model, the corporate scaleup pays for the time of Core's experts who remain within their functions. This may seem like an obvious solution, but it is not so easy in practice. On the one hand, Core's resources are typically right-sized to meet NOW's needs and there is little wiggle room for non-Core activities. On the other hand, making innovation someone's part-time job is often a recipe for failure, as Amazon's founder Jeff Bezos once remarked.

The third model aims at establishing a win/win collaboration; it is described below.

When to Set up the Collaboration Model

Setting up the collaboration model is one of the work streams in the transitional phase between validation and scaling, as described in chapter 7. It involves two steps. The first step is to determine where collaboration is needed.

To identify these areas, the scaleup's support needs are plotted against Core's functions. The exhibit below displays Core's functions and operative units on the x-axis and the key processes and challenges of the corporate scaleup on the y-axis.

To identify the areas that require a collaboration model, work through the latter step by step. At each step, mark the corporate functions that can support. If a corporate function has not yet been discussed, add a new column.

Identifying the "docking points to Core" shows where a collaboration agreement between a corporate scaleup and Core is needed.

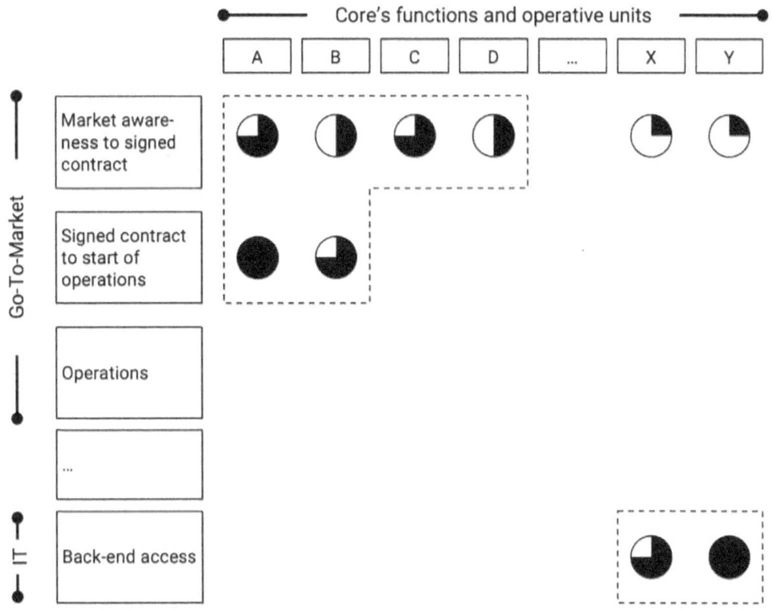

Exhibit 15–1: Identifying areas where collaboration agreements are needed.

Typically, there are a few hot spots. In the exhibit above, there are four functions in the top left and two functions in the bottom right that stand out. Collaboration for other functions in the exhibit can be arranged on a case-by-case basis as their expertise is of secondary importance.

A 3-Level Collaboration Model

The second step is to define the collaboration. I found that discussing three levels is helpful. At the first level, the corporate scaleup and Core's relevant senior manager discuss integrating Scaling-Up milestones into the function's goal planning and performance tracking systems, as described in chapters 7 and 12. The corporate scaleup must be included in these systems so that it becomes visible for the function's middle managers.

An effective collaboration agreement plays out on three levels: formal alignment, the partnership equation and the working level.

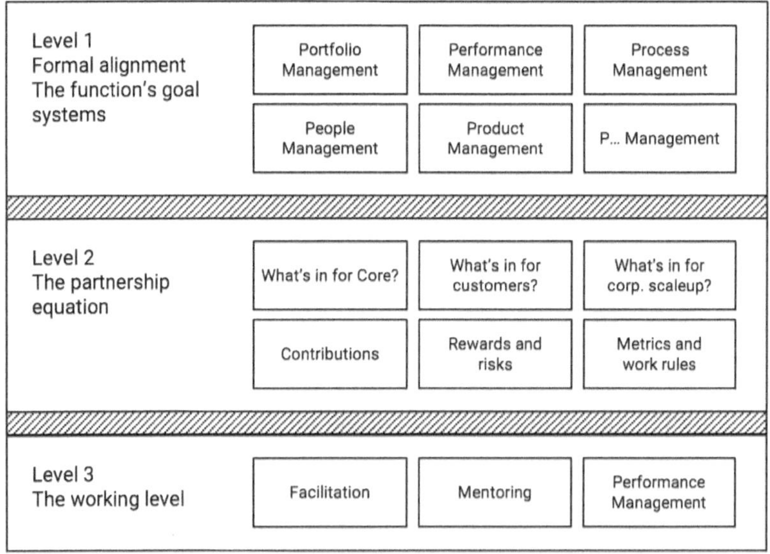

Exhibit 15–2: Elements of a collaboration model.

At the second level, the corporate scaleup and the responsible middle manager detail the collaboration agreement as described in the next section. Finally, at level 3, both parties discuss the infrastructure required for an effective collaboration, which may include office space and facilitators that support an agile work style.

Elements of a Collaboration Model

Here is an example of a collaboration model that relates to a corporate scaleup which was tasked with creating a new adjacent, service-centric business. The new business should augment the company's products and third-party products with remote monitoring and predictive maintenance capabilities and integrate all these products into the company's IT cloud.

Any collaboration model must answer the key question: "What is in for me?" for each party involved. The answer to this question, of course, depends on the point of view. The corporate scaleup measured the benefits of collaboration in dimensions such as:

– Revenues.

– Market credibility.

– Market access via the operative unit's salesforce.

– De-risking and accelerating Scaling-Up.

– Expert resources to fill define talent gaps.

– Benefits in talent acquisition ("startup with a safety net").

Core's functions used dimensions such as:

– Growth, measured initially in number of new customers.

– Solution to the Innovator's Dilemma[166].

– Improved image and reputation.

– Re-use of capabilities and assets.

---

[166] See https://en.wikipedia.org/wiki/The_Innovator%27s_Dilemma.

Making these dimensions as detailed and measurable as possible is essential to focusing joint efforts[167]. In addition, the two parties had discussed the critical question: "What is in for customers?"

Once the benefits to all parties were clear, each party's contributions were discussed. The corporate scaleup committed to provide advanced technical, engineering, and consulting capabilities, while the corporate function committed to support industrialization.

It is also mandatory to discuss risks and how to mitigate them. The corporate scaleup identified the greatest risk as the operational support to diminish rapidly while Core's sales units identified market confusion, cannibalization, and the Osborne effect[168] as the most significant risks. After the list of major risks was completed, both sides defined mitigation activities and incorporated these into the common game plan.

Get Everybody on the Same Page

After the collaboration agreements have been made, a corporate scaleup should arrange a half-day workshop with its collaboration partners which could be positioned as the Scaling-Up kick-off. A typical agenda includes:

- Explaining background and the vision of the business model innovation.

- Demonstrating of the Minimum Marketable Product.

- Explaining the validation results with a focus on customer insights.

- Outlining the growth strategy and the 100-day plan.

- Aligning on work rules and how to measure collaboration quality.

- Discussing contingency plans and mitigation activities.

---

[167] The FAST Goals™ Methodology, see https://bit.ly/3Pv4IFI, yields a common visual expression of joint interests and respective accountabilities, with success measures.

[168] See https://en.wikipedia.org/wiki/Osborne_effect.

Corporate Scaleup, Stay Humble

At times, I sense that corporate scaleups are being carried away by their enthusiasm. Key people may see the opportunity to "make a dent in the universe," as Apple's founder Steve Jobs said. They are motivated by the mandate and the opportunity to generate new growth for the company.

However, this is only an opportunity. The opportunity will likely materialize only through an effective partnership with NOW. The corporate scaleup's leadership team may view their entity as a unique company. However, it is not unique because it is distinct from NOW. It is unique because it has the opportunity to leverage decades of hard work that created NOW to build a piece of the company's future.

I remind my corporate scaleup clients to remain humble. Areas of tension will be felt on both sides. Core may be reluctant to see expert resources redirected to what initially is just a distraction. Core's functions may be resentful about the fact that they must tightly manage their budgets, while the corporate scaleup spends money with only a distant promise of a profit.

NOW's senior and upper managers may be worried that the corporate scaleup will, out of inexperience, damage brands and customer relationships that have been nurtured for decades. They may feel envy about the management attention that the corporate scaleup gets and feel they deserve more respect. After all, they are the foundation of the company's current profitability, and the architects of the company's success to date.

Despite these barriers to collaboration, it is possible to establish a solid win/win between NOW and the corporate scaleup. It takes humbleness, empathy, and some thinking about common interests that both sides share.

Chapter 16: Capabilities, People Profiles, A-Teams

Chapter 16
Capabilities, People Profiles and A-Teams

The Lean Scaleup framework comprises 12 modules, with 4 modules allocated to each of the Methodology, Leadership, and People/Culture dimensions.

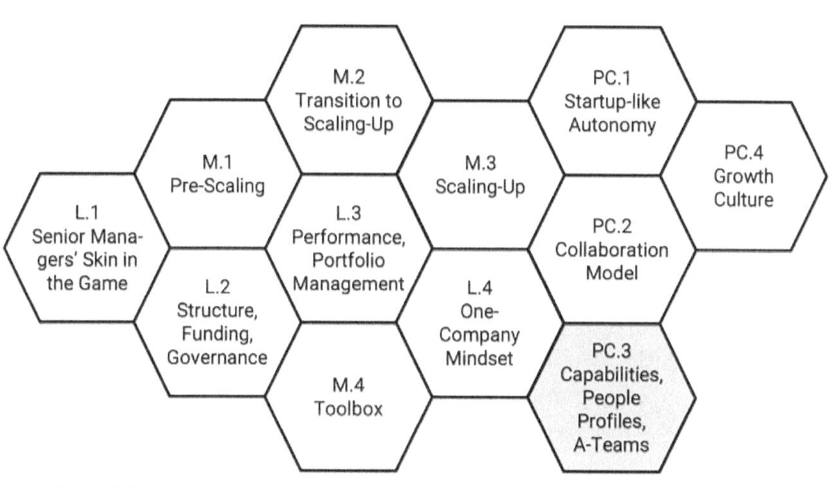

Key Points in This Chapter

1. Having individuals with domain expertise and capabilities that relate to the target market is crucial for validation and scaling. Interim resources should be built in if such individuals are not available.

2. Generative AI is a powerful tool in the hands of out-of-the-box innovators. Evidence seems to indicate that it could be helpful in the early stages. There is no evidence that this tool could help in aligning NOW and NEW.

3. Five different people profiles are needed to succeed in out-of-the-box innovation: creative strategic thinkers, ethnographic researchers, validators, builders, and scalers.

4. Apart from certain qualities, the CEO of a corporate scaleup must be effective in the corporate context. This individual must adapt to the challenges at different levels of growth.

5. Selecting one of NOW's senior managers as a CEO of a corporate scaleup has drawbacks. The life of a corporate senior manager is fundamentally different from the life of a corporate scaleup's CEO.

* *

The head of a business model incubator at a large software company asked me to assess their existing setup. I typically conduct such assessments by evaluating individual corporate startups/scaleups, the new-business building process, and the level of maturity in the 12 modules of the Lean Scaleup framework.

I presented my findings and a lean upgrade program that would improve the situation without boiling the ocean. Such an upgrade program can be developed by applying the "theory of constraints" and focusing on those issues that are the tightest bottlenecks for the new-business building engine. We discussed six areas for improvement[169]:

- Moving from a product-centric approach to a business-centric approach with rigorous progress management.

- Integrating the corporate context.

- Getting the Minimum Viable Product right.

- Assessing scale-ready by using leading indicators.

- Establishing a three-layered governance scheme.

- Arranging a Transition-to-Scaling-Up phase.

After we had discussed these points, I said: "And then there is the people issue. I found lots of canvases, but they have not been updated in the last six months. It appears that your teams prioritize filling out thinking tools and

---

[169] See chapters 5 and 6; chapters 2 and 6; chapter 19; chapter 6; chapter 11; chapter 7.

the process over the desire to deeply understand customers and the emerging business opportunities."

I made sure that I had my client's attention and continued: "Your teams conduct many experiments, but they are not working on the biggest assumptions. They lack a sense of urgency and entrepreneurial drive. The quality of your teams should increase the likelihood of generating new growth. However, I doubt that this is the case."

A Gen-AI-Powered People Business

As of early 2024, Generative AI (Gen AI) is a topic of great interest to businesses worldwide. There is a growing body of evidence suggesting that it could enhance the early stages of out-of-the-box innovation in:

- Problem finding.

- Suggesting target customer profiles, including an indication of their jobs-to-be-done.

- Problem-understanding and market-sizing.

- Outlining customer solution objectives and attributes of ideal solutions.

- Creating initial solution ideas.

- Suggesting appropriate experiments to validate assumptions.

Furthermore, several corporate scaleups already use Gen AI to support its market-facing activities and customer interactions, for example in:

- Pricing.

- Supporting customers to find the right products.

- Creating content for social media.

Gen AI is a powerful tool. But I am convinced that people will continue to be the driving force behind innovation. It takes human capabilities to:

- Understand the specific needs of individual customers.

- Empathize with them.

- Grasp how they perceive the innovation.

- Identify the specific obstacles to switching from established practices to the innovation.

- Build trust so that an individual customer takes the risks and the efforts and invests into making the switch.

One needs to keep in mind that all the functions mentioned above relate to the content of the out-of-the-box and the innovation process. **I have not yet observed much in the field of Gen AI that addresses the NOW/ NEW challenge**.

What Makes up Excellent Teams?

I have had the privilege of working with many corporate startups/scale-ups in a variety of industries. In my view, superior teams share a number of characteristics. Some of these qualities can be observed from the outside, while others relate to mindset and character. The latter can be identified by how the team approaches its challenges.

Easy-to-Spot Characteristics

Superior teams are small in size since small teams are more effective at communication, coordination, and decision-making than large teams. Small teams are also fundamental to an agile way of working, where team members agree on the most significant assumptions, design and run experiments, learn from the results of the experiments, and adjust priorities.

Superior teams demonstrate a high degree of accountability for results. They have full-time resources and all the necessary capabilities to deliver these results to an external or internal customer[170].

Customer Obsession

Superior corporate startups/scaleups aim to gain a deeper understanding of the problems they want to solve for customers than the customers themselves. They recognize that it is not just about the problem itself, but also about the problem context and the corresponding decision-making processes. They engage with customers before, during, and after building the Minimum Viable Product and the Minimum Marketable Product.

Outstanding corporate startups/scaleups are customer-obsessed, even in technical roles. It is invigorating to hear a member of their leadership team speak with passion about customers, their problems, and how the corporate startup/scaleup plans to succeed. There is nothing more gratifying than the feeling when everything clicks.

Data-Driven

Average corporate startups/scaleup teams work behind the desk and run some experiments. Superior teams are data-driven. They view relentless, experiment-based validation as the primary tool for cutting through the jungle of assumptions, opinions, and options. A leader of a corporate startup said to me: "I am not the master decision maker. We run experiments. Lots of experiments, cheap ones, and fast ones. And then we let the data speak."

This data-driven mindset delivers the hard facts that the corporate startup/scaleup needs to lead internal discussions—especially if the data tells a story that contradicts stakeholders' expectations.

---

[170] See the Amazon case study in chapter 4.

In my view, corporate stakeholders should insist more on experimentation and data. It is not only about the individual corporate startup/scaleup; it is also about Core. The insights collected could also be relevant for Core's sales, marketing, business development, and strategy departments. **In my view, this backchannel into NOW is a significant untapped potential in many companies.**

A Sense of Urgency and Focus

Corporate startups/scaleups are in a constant race against time. They race to outperform their competitors in the market, and they must succeed before they run out of corporate funding and support. In superior corporate startups/scaleups, I observe a high sense of urgency. I sense the desire of all team members to make every single day count.

These teams also do their best to avoid distractions. Not all distractions can be avoided. For example, if the corporate environment is not supportive, the team must constantly fight for funding and manage corporate politics. A CEO of a corporate scaleup told me that she spends 25 percent of her time on these activities. Another example is when the corporate startup/scaleup has to devote significant time serving as an innovation showcase.

Insight-Driven, Not Process-Driven

Validation processes are essential because they help corporate startups/scaleups to operate effectively and efficiently. They help to deliver a solid business foundation, a winning strategy, a scalable business design, the first version of the product that is launched into the initial market and a rapidly growing market footprint.

But if one is not watchful, the process can become the main thing. Some teams pay more attention to ticking the boxes that take them to the next funding round than to validation rigor and the innovation content.

Working on the Affordable Loss Principle

In their race against time, superior corporate startups/scaleups continually trade speed against what they can afford to lose for a crucial learning. This is the so-called affordable loss principle.

Superior corporate startups/scaleups continually ask themselves what they can lose on a decision or by taking an action and is that affordable to them? If it is an affordable loss and the potential gains are large, they act.

Curiosity

Superior startups/scaleups are curious by nature. They go far beyond what is required and constantly explore what is possible. And perhaps the best methodology for deeply understanding customers is not a methodology at all, but curiosity.

I advise my corporate startup/scaleup clients to stay curious. I recommend that, if possible, they should work at the customer's premises. They should read the blogs their customers read, be active in the relevant online communities, listen to the webinars their customers attend, join their customers' trade associations and professional networks, and so on. By their example, the most curious team members tend to inspire the whole team to immerse themselves in the customer context.

Learning at Pace

Superior corporate startups/scaleups learn quicker and more deliberately than others. "Learning at pace" refers to:

- The context of the innovation, for instance, the underlying technology.

- What has been learned from things that did not work out as planned.

- Effective thinking models, experiences from other companies, and behaviors and processes that improve teamwork.

Learning at pace is based on two pillars: absorbing impulses from other people and rapid double feedback loops. For the former, lunch-and-learn sessions with free food and an inspiring talk on the side, or evening sessions with a few pretzels and beers might be options. Some of these sessions could even be an "open house" within the company, helping the team to promote their work.

Rapid double feedback loops involve experts from within the company or from a pool of trusted advisors. These experts help the corporate startup/scaleup understand what they need to learn. They identify the root causes of difficulties—and often uncover unknowns in time to prevent them from becoming future challenges.

Courage and Perseverance

Most great ideas are controversial before they are popular. Typically, ideas that change the order of things are not universally welcomed. They are met with skepticism and sometimes even sarcasm.

Superior corporate startups/scaleups have the courage to accept being misunderstood for a long time without becoming stubborn. They are prepared to defend a big idea for an extended period, even if it ultimately proves to be less impactful than anticipated. It takes perseverance and storytelling skills to keep winning the debate over and over again.

Ensuring That the Right Capabilities Are in the Team

I advised a large medical device company that wanted to implement a service-centric business model. Instead of selling expensive machines to hospitals, they wanted to establish a service-centric business model. Hospitals would pay a monthly fee that covered the rental of the machines and the use of a proprietary AI-powered software. The software was designed to evaluate medical images, identify irregularities, cross-reference its findings with medical literature, and recommend a patient-specific therapy.

The company asked me to investigate why their corporate startups were not scaling despite excellent connections with leading experts at the best hospitals in the world. One of the root causes I identified was that the teams lacked members with deep experience in the customers' jobs-to-be-done. None of the team members had a therapy career at lower-tier hospitals, which correspond to the mainstream customers mentioned in chapter 6.

This example shows why corporate explorers and corporate startups/scaleups need to have the right capabilities on their team. Domain expertise is crucial:

- In the Discovery, Business Foundation, and Business Strategy stages for generating meaningful ideas and validating scale-worthiness.

- In the Business Design stage for designing a repeatable sales process and a scalable organization that is capable of delivering rapid growth while keeping customer acquisition costs low.

- In the Scaling-Up phase to scale the market footprint rapidly and to influence product design.

These domain experts do not need to be on the payroll of the company or the corporate startup/scaleup. They could also be contracted on an interim basis.

In my view, the money spent on using their expertise for a few months is well worth it compared to the investments that would go into a corporate scaleup that is built on shaky assumptions.

Five Different People Profiles Are Needed

The term "people profiles" refers to the mindset and strengths of team members, excluding the capability issue mentioned above. Many companies struggle with determining the optimal people profiles. They either have teams that do everything, or they lack clarity about the profiles.

Based on my experience, there is no single optimal profile for building a new business; I believe there are five different profiles. The first two profiles are needed to find meaningful ideas in the Discovery stage: the "creative business strategist" who thinks strategically about potential disruptions and emerging value pools, and the "ethnographic researcher" who identifies high-priority/high-value customer problems and needs.

The first profile requires a deep understanding of business model patterns and the ability to identify risks and flaws in a potential new business model early on. The second profile refers to individuals with an educational background in behavioral science and design thinking who see the world through the eyes of potential customers and understand where they struggle, even if these are not fully aware of it.

The third profile is the "validator" who works in the Business Foundation, Business Strategy, and Business Design stages. Outstanding validators are assumption hunters who identify and prioritize assumptions related to the validation items mentioned in chapter 6. They approach their work with an unbiased, scientific mindset, developing hypotheses, designing optimal experiments, and then drawing conclusions from the experiment results.

The fourth profile is the "builder." This individual works to a lesser degree in the Business Strategy stage to co-create the Minimum Viable Product, more in the Business Design stage to build the Minimum Marketable Product and predominantly in the Scaling-Up phase. Great builders are not driven by technology, they are customer-obsessed. They burn for creating the best solution to the problem that the other roles have unearthed.

Finally, the fifth profile is the "scaler" who works in the Scaling-Up phase. These individuals are highly action-oriented, purpose-driven, and passionate about their mission. They thrive in fast-paced, ambiguous environments where there is often no blueprint for their daily decisions.

Scalers understand the technical and non-technical challenges of industrializing validated concepts and have a long-term perspective. They are adept at working cross-functionally, with Core's functional experts and stakeholders, and with external partners who are essential to create and deliver the value proposition.

Validator, Meet the Scaler; Scaler, Meet the Validator

In many companies, validation is based on a product-centric Lean Startup approach. **There is often an excessive focus on validating scale-worthiness and a lack of attention to validating scale-readiness and the corporate context.** When there is no dedicated Transition-to-Scaling-Up phase, it becomes evident why the transition from validation to scaling is so challenging for these companies.

Due to the different people profiles, there is sometimes a gap between the individuals that "do exciting stuff in the innovation center" and the ones that "implement what has been found and tested." To bridge this gap, job rotation is an option, with scalers placed in validation teams and vice versa.

The Scaleup Leadership Team

Occasionally, my clients ask me for an unbiased, outside perspective on who should be on the leadership team of a corporate scaleup. Since these people are tasked with turning transforming company investments into revenue streams, the decision is critical.

In my view, a scaler profile (as described above) and domain expertise in their respective areas are basic factors. However, since this is a leadership team and not just a gathering of intelligent individuals, additional factors must be considered. The assessment criteria used in this context should also include personal qualities such as:

- Grit and tenacity.

- A sense of urgency.

- "Paranoid optimism[171]".

- Endless curiosity to learn more about the emerging business, its customers, and its ecosystem.

- Integrity and trustworthiness.

- Leadership qualities to attract top talent.

- Business and organizational creativity.

- Team-player qualities.

The question of which proxies are useful in assessing these qualities is an interesting one. Previous experience, such as a track record as a serial founder or being a senior team member of high-growth startups, an "immigrant mentality" (i.e., fighting step-by-step for opportunities) and strong referrals are significant predictors of future success.

The Scaleup's CEO

CEOs of corporate scaleups must possess all the qualities listed above, and one more: knowing how to be effective in a corporate context. They should treat their governance board and their corporate stakeholders with the same level of attention as CEOs of greenfield startups would treat their lead investors.

Serving as the CEO of a corporate scaleup also entails navigating the leadership challenges inherent to a rapidly growing company. Based on my experience working with these individuals, there are five challenges.

---

[171] Being deeply convinced about the corporate scaleup's success yet being aware that others might be quicker or better.

From Leading by Example to Leading through Others

The leadership approach of a CEO transitioning from a few clients and small revenues to a USD 10m business differs significantly from that required to take it to a USD 30m business and then again to a USD 50m business. The adage: "What got you here will not get you there" is particularly relevant in this context. A corporate scaleup's CEO needs to adopt a new leadership approach for each level of revenue.

In the initial Scaling-Up stages, the CEO can lead a small organization by example. But as the company grows, the CEO must lead through other leaders. This may be the underlying reason why Amazon is so committed to its leadership principles[172]: the first 12 principles were published when the company had only 160 employees.

Widen the Aperture

The second challenge is to widen the aperture and to think long-term. During the early stages of Scaling-Up, the CEO is likely pondering questions such as: "How are we acquiring next months' customers?" and "Which points should I raise in next week's governance board?" Most of the questions that keep the CEO awake at night are probably short-term concerns.

But as the corporate scaleup grows, the CEO will likely shift the focus to quarterly and annual planning, including the annual governance board plan and multi-year business plans. If the CEO fails to plant the right seeds this year, the corporate scaleup will not be where it needs to be in two years.

Find an Effective Communication Rhythm

Scaling-Up requires orchestrating dozens or even hundreds of people to work together toward the right set of goals. The CEO of a corporate scaleup

---

[172] See https://bit.ly/3U0ein8.

must establish the appropriate communication rhythm to achieve this. It is not realistic to expect staff and middle managers to make the right operational decisions without them having a clear understanding of the long-term view and the quarterly milestones.

To achieve this goal without excessive time or effort, I recommend scheduling monthly all-hands meetings to keep everyone informed about the progress and interdependencies of major projects. Additionally, two more strategic events are required.

At the beginning of each year, an event should establish priorities and initiatives for the upcoming year. Each initiative must have defined owners, goals, and metrics. The plan should have more details for the first quarter and bullet points for the subsequent quarters, as described in chapter 8. A similar meeting should be held in the middle of the year to provide progress updates for each of the defined initiatives, reassess the mix of initiatives, and revise the initiative portfolio if necessary.

Maintain Speed in Decision-Making

Challenge number four is to maintain the speed of decision-making in the face of growing interdependencies. As the corporate scaleup grows, the days of quick decisions made by a few people around a whiteboard are over. The CEO needs to prevent bureaucracy and slow decision-making from taking hold.

Speed is not predetermined; it is a choice. The CEO of a corporate scaleup must make a deliberate decision for speed and create a culture of urgency in which people are empowered to make two-way-door decisions and act on the affordable loss principle.

To maintain speed in decision-making, middle managers and staff should have an escalation option. For example, one corporate scaleup established a rule for cross-functional decisions: if they could not align within three days on who should be involved and on the decision-making process, they could escalate to the CEO. It was understood that involving the CEO should only be considered as a last resort, not as a regular practice.

Bake Culture into Every Stage of the Employee Lifecycle

For a corporate scaleup, a lot of things can change over the course of two quarters. However, one of the few constants, if the CEO makes a conscious choice and gets it right, is culture. In my opinion, it is impossible to scale an emerging business with annual growth rates of more than 100 percent without scaling culture as well.

If CEOs of corporate scaleups leave their company culture to chance, they will quickly lose control. For example, when the company plans to hire 100 new employees over the next year, more than 50 percent of all interactions will involve new hires. Every time someone deviates from the culture without being called out, the CEO gives tacit approval to that behavior. It is easy to imagine how quickly a corporate scaleup's culture can morph if the CEO does not lead through others, based on shared principles.

For the reasons mentioned above, establishing a growth culture is a key success factor in new-business building and hence one of the 12 modules that make up the Lean Scaleup framework. More detail is provided in the following chapter.

Core's Senior Managers as CEOs of Corporate Scaleups

When discussing staffing for the CEO position of the corporate scaleup, appointing a seasoned NOW manager is often considered an option. While this is generally not my primary recommendation, I have worked with exceptional senior managers who made a significant impact, mainly because they fully embraced the corporate context.

Before selecting a senior manager from Core to take the CEO position of a corporate scaleup, there should be an open discussion about the differences between corporate life and the life of a corporate scaleup's CEO with the candidate. In my opinion, there are six differences.

First, a corporate scaleup's CEO must have a strong sense of ownership, taking responsibility for both successes and failures without the opportunity to blame other parts of the organization—which is sometimes an aspect of corporate life.

The second difference concerns the level of uncertainty. CEOs of corporate scaleups are entrepreneurs in uncharted waters. They must determine the goal, how to get there and who should be on the team. They must also lead the team to create products that have never been created before, selling these to new customer groups, and race against the clock to win in the marketplace while maintaining corporate support.

Working with people is also different. In a corporate environment, senior managers typically work with a stable group of people. In a corporate scaleup, however, there is a constant stream of new hires. The corporate scaleup's CEO must learn to trust these individuals, even without a shared history of experience.

A fourth difference relates to hierarchies. NOW's tried-and-true structures, such as titles and hierarchies, do not work in corporate scaleups. Informal leaders will emerge in different parts of the organization who may not have big titles but a big impact. The CEO of a corporate scaleup must be able to recognize these individuals and protect and empower them.

The pace of operations is another major difference. In contrast to NOW's slow decision-making, corporate scaleups operate at pace. As one corporate scaleup CEO clients puts it: "Scaling-Up is as easy as riding a bicycle. Except that the bicycle is on fire and everything else is on fire, too."

A sixth difference is how to deal with the corporate context. A senior manager who is part of Core will adjust to it and gradually nudge the organization towards change. However, when a corporate manager is on the other side of the fence, this individual must challenge Core and its orthodoxies in a very direct way in order to achieve the Scaling-Up goals.

For these reasons, I believe that most corporate senior managers would not be great CEOs of corporate scaleups. It rarely works because they often prefer to continue developing the skills that made them a good corporate manager. However, it is possible—and an entirely new challenge for those who take on the role.

Chapter 17:
Growth Culture

Chapter 17
Growth Culture

The Lean Scaleup framework comprises 12 modules, with 4 modules allocated to each of the Methodology, Leadership, and People/Culture dimensions.

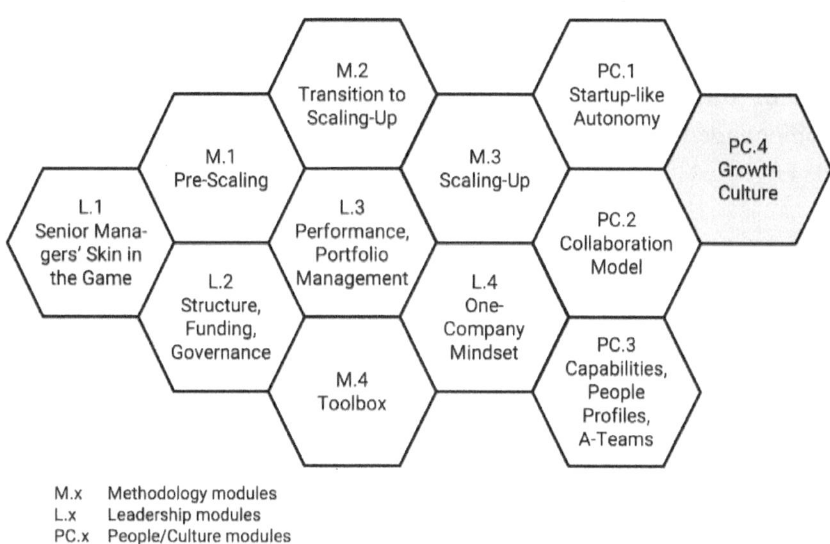

Key Points in This Chapter

1. Successful corporate scaleups have a compounded annual growth rate of 150 percent or more. To sustain such a growth over several years, it is vital to cultivate a special culture, a so-called growth culture.

2. This growth culture builds on people with a growth mindset. This is about win/win and appreciating diversity, collaboration, and growth.

3. Eight elements make up a growth culture. Two of them are psychological safety, widely recognized to be a key enabler for innovation, and intellectual honesty. Many people prioritize the former – but they belong together.

4. Activating or cultivating the growth culture should start with the right behaviors that are linked to leading (as opposed to lagging) business metrics.

**

At the outset of Scaling-Up, a corporate scaleup has a few initial customers who use the Minimum Marketable Product. Let us do the math. Suppose the initial annual revenues are USD 500k. To achieve revenues of USD 10m after three years, the corporate scaleup needs to grow with a Compounded Annual Growth Rate (CAGR) of more than 170 percent. If the target is USD 30m after five years, the CAGR is over 150 percent.

Building an organization that supports a CAGR of 170 percent and sustains that rate for three or five years is not easy. But all corporate scale-ups that are growing at that rate share one common trait. It is not easy to describe, but it can be felt in their offices. It is a distinctive culture.

This culture is not a one-time event, it is pervasive. It is not a one-time event but a year-round phenomenon. This so-called growth culture is vital for success. Around 85 percent of startup and scaleup leaders, both in greenfield and corporate settings, agree on three key statements about the proper culture[173]. It:

- Contributes to organizational growth.

- Is important in attracting new talent.

- Can play a role in its ability to secure further investment.

This chapter summarizes my observations on what constitutes such a growth culture and how it can be cultivated.

---

[173] See https://bit.ly/4b7TDTm.

The Lean Scaleup and Growth Culture

A corporate scaleup with the revenue growth mentioned above must manage a significant growth in staff. Hence, building organizational growth and a supportive culture is as important as market growth and advancing the product. The Lean Scaleup addresses important issues in this context[174]:

- Selecting the CEO and the leadership team.

- Adding structure without killing the startup spirit.

- Identifying people with a growth mentality.

- Finding and onboarding the right hires.

- Cultivating a growth culture.

It Is Not Only about Customers and Product

Many corporate scaleups believe that their technological expertise sets them apart. However, technology can be a tempting lure because it offers a multitude of potential applications. But when a corporate scaleup loses sight of its customers and does not have the passion to solve their problems better than anyone else, they will never create a compelling solution with a superior value proposition and a sustainable competitive advantage.

In fact, I would go a step further. If the goal is rapid revenue growth, **a corporate scaleup must have a strong Employer Value Proposition**. This is imperative because top talent has choices. For example, 80 percent of technology professionals who were laid off in 2022 found another job within just three months[175].

---

[174] See the previous chapter, chapter 8 and below.
[175] See https://bit.ly/47a5pdy.

Many studies show that having a fulfilling and meaningful work experience is more crucial than ever. Top talent such as leading scientists, rockstar business developers, and digital-native Millennials seek an inspiring and creative work environment to deliver their best work. They prioritize personal development and collaboration with other exceptional individuals and choose companies that offer these opportunities.

If a corporate scaleup fails to provide such a work environment, it will struggle to attract and retain top talent. This leads to a loss of momentum, losses in the market, and ultimately, losing the corporate investor's support.

The Growth Mindset

Every culture starts with the individual. For the purpose of this book, a "mindset" should be seen as the sum of thoughts and beliefs that determine how individuals make sense of their world and which behaviors they choose.

There are two types of mindsets. The first is a fixed mindset which has a zero-sum game view and the basic belief that one's intelligence and talent are limited. People with such a mindset think that:

- Efforts are fruitless.

- Challenges should be avoided.

- Criticism, even when useful, is a bad thing.

On the other side of the spectrum are people with **a growth mindset which is about win/win and appreciating diversity, collaboration, and growth**. People with a growth mindset think that:

- Efforts are the path to mastery.

- Challenges should be embraced because they support learning.

- Criticism can be a valuable source for personal development.

Growth Culture

Culture is one of the most overused, yet often least understood, concepts in business. For the purpose of this book, I define **culture as the set of shared beliefs that define "us and them", emotional safety, and success:**

- What do I need to do to be "in" (and not "out")?

- What are the behaviors so that I can feel emotionally safe?

- What do I need to do so that others see me as a winner?

On the surface, the cultures of corporate scaleups with 170 percent annual growth rates share many similarities. I like to think of them as the manifestations of a growth culture. These corporate scaleups:

- Have the ambition to make a positive impact on the world.

- Show an extreme determination to reach growth targets.

- Have a competitive stance towards other companies that aim at solving the customers' problems.

- Embrace diversity in people's expertise, backgrounds, perspectives, and ways of thinking.

- Take manageable risks to introduce new approaches or processes.

- Show cohesion, togetherness, and a company spirit.

- Are resilient in responding to crises and keep the soul of the corporate scaleup alive in challenging times.

Growth Culture vs. Performance and Learning Cultures

When CEOs of corporate scaleups want to nurture a growth culture, they must first understand how a growth culture differs from other cultures and then, as described in the next section, identify its key elements.

Growth cultures are closely related to performance cultures and learning cultures. The former rewards high performance and motivates people by creating a zero-sum game in which individuals either succeed or lose and "losers" are pushed out. The latter prioritizes building and sharing knowledge over producing tangible, measurable results.

A growth culture integrates aspects of both of these cultures. Like the performance culture, it is result-oriented because otherwise the corporate scaleup could not achieve its growth goals. Like a learning culture, it emphasizes building and sharing knowledge. However, there are two aspects that distinguishes a growth culture from the other two. In a growth culture:

– Building and sharing knowledge is linked to business results.

– How people feel, and how they make others feel, is as important as the results they create or how much they know.

Elements of a Growth Culture

When working with corporate scaleups, I notice eight visible elements that make up a growth culture. First, a delicate balance between challenging and nurturing. Too much challenge over a 3-5-year horizon without sufficient reassurance can overwhelm individuals and break the organization. Insufficient challenge or excessive comfort in steady but slow growth can result in a culture that is unable to build a substantial business within the timeframe expected by the corporate investor.

Second, attracting individuals with a growth mindset. These individuals stimulate the growth mindset of others and foster a virtuous circle. In a growth culture, there are plenty of "what if?" and "why not?" discussions.

Third, a psychologically safe environment where individuals can focus on creating value instead of constantly demonstrating or defending their individual worth.

A growth culture is mandatory to achieve a 170% CAGR.
This growth culture has eight elements.

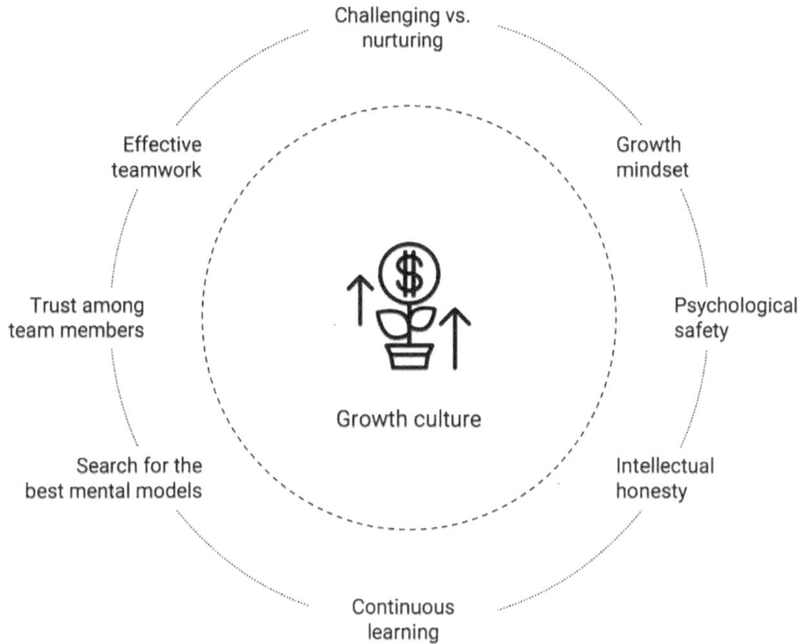

Exhibit 17–1: Elements of a growth culture.

Fourth, intellectual honesty. This element is closely related to the preceding one. Superior corporate scaleups have intense discussions about ideas and the options on the table. But these discussions take place in a psychologically safe environment. The debates are focused on the challenges; they are not about individuals or relationships. In a growth culture, team members feel comfortable expressing ideas and opinions, and they encourage one another to excel in pursuit of shared goals.

Fifth, continuous learning. Learning impulses can come from experts, peers, partners, competitors, customers, or from quantitative analysis. Corporate scaleups with a growth culture are data-driven; they rely heavily on objective data to support continuous learning. They also provide a wide range of learning styles so that the individual can select what is needed to support continuous learning.

Sixth, relentlessly pursuing the search for the best mental models. Corporate scaleups with a growth culture strive to always have the best explanations for what happened, what works, and what does not work. Their mental models are concise and easy to understand because if they are too complex, they will not help people to learn quickly.

Seventh, trust among the team members. When team members trust each other, they are more likely to collaborate effectively, communicate openly, and take risks together since trust is positively correlated with team effectiveness and productivity[176].

Eighth, effective teamwork. The optimal size for a business team should start with five to seven people and it should not exceed the two-pizza-size[177], i.e., 10-14 people. This allows for effective teamwork, ensures a diversity of perspectives and skills, and prevents the group from splintering, which would increase the risk of miscommunication.

A culture built around these eight elements empowers people. For example, when the CEO of one of my corporate scaleup clients asked employees to submit ideas for improving a customer-facing process, three of the top ten ideas came from the receptionist.

Psychological Safety and Intellectual Honesty

Psychological safety has become a widely accepted concept to foster innovation. Thought leaders in that space see four levels of psychological safety[178].

---

[176] See https://bit.ly/3H2c4LX.

[177] See the Amazon case study in chapter 4.

[178] Adapted from Timothy Clark: The 4 Stages of Psychological Safety, Berrett-Koehler Publishers, 2020.

Psychological safety is a key concept for effective innovation work. It has four levels.

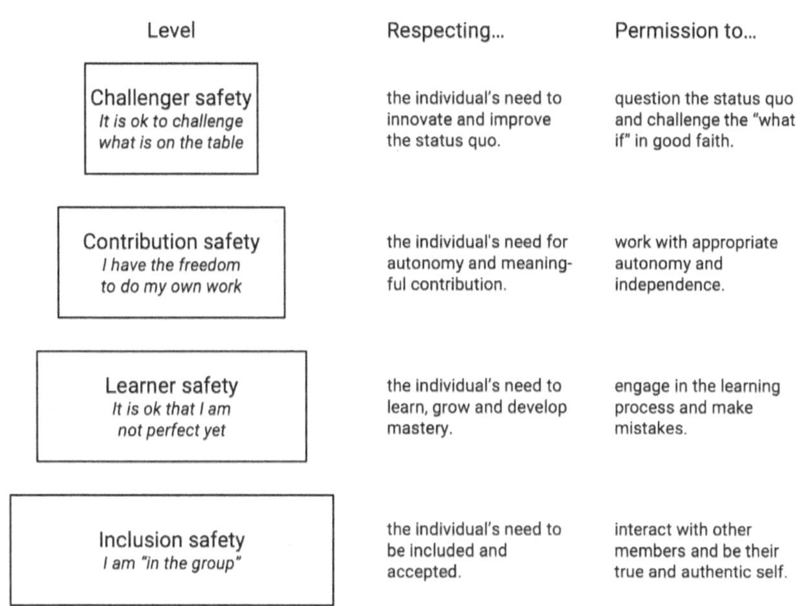

Exhibit 17–2: Four levels of psychological safety.

But feeling psychologically safe is not the only factor for finding the best solutions. A culture in which team members proactively speak out their ideas and disagreements in a rational and constructive way is another key factor[179]. A corporate scaleup's leadership team that can balance psychological safety and intellectual honesty will facilitate great debates that offer a wealth of insights and opportunities for growth.

There is a story that relates to the Amazon case study in chapter 4[180]. Jeff Wilke, then CEO of Amazon's retail business, was one of the senior managers who opposed the idea of creating an e-book reader. He viewed

---

[179] Amy Edmondson, The Fearless Organization, Wiley, 2019.
[180] See https://bit.ly/3QTyjcA.

the company as a software company with no experience in the hardware business. His arguments led to a more thorough discussion of the pros and cons of the decision, during which Jeff Bezos conceded to these points but still argued that Amazon would be better served by developing a new set of capabilities.

In retrospective, Jeff Wilke says that that the courage to speak up came from one of Amazon's leadership principles: the company's leaders are obliged to "have a backbone" and "disagree, even when it is uncomfortable or exhausting," and then to unite behind whatever decision the team has made, without negative repercussions.

Cultivating the Growth Culture

"I understand all these points," said the CEO of one of my corporate scaleup clients. "I also understand that selecting the right people and properly onboarding new hires are key to maintaining culture. The question is: How do I activate and cultivate the growth culture?"

Of course, there is no one-size-fits-all answer to such a fundamental question. Typical corporate approaches to culture change, such as having leadership define the target culture and cascade it throughout the organization, are not compatible with the elements of a growth culture described above and will not work within a rapidly growing corporate scaleup.

In my view, cultural change starts by establishing new behaviors. "Acting your way into new thinking," i.e., changing culture by installing new behaviors, is more effective than "thinking your way into new acting," i.e., defining a new culture and implementing it. When working with corporate scaleups on growth culture, I typically recommend a three-step approach.

First, link behaviors to business metrics. Culture is a broad term, and it is too vague for the fast-paced environment of a corporate scaleup when there is no link to business metrics. These metrics need to be specific and leading (as opposed to lagging) so that they can be influenced by the teams and individuals. This has two benefits. It is easier to:

- Identify the behaviors that will help to achieve business outcomes.

- Establish objectives and key results for teams and individuals.

Second, encourage the right behaviors rather than impose them. If the corporate scaleup's leadership team sees its role as shaping and reinforcing better behaviors, those behaviors could become the predominant culture.

Third, make improved behaviors visible. Providing early examples of how changed behaviors have led to improved business results is essential for widespread adoption. They are the building blocks for telling the story that the company has a greater chance of fulfilling its mission.

Chapter 18:
New-Business Building
with Greenfield Startups

Chapter 18
New-Business Building with Greenfield Startups

Key Points in This Chapter

1. On the surface, the collaboration between a company and suitable greenfield startups seems to be a win/win. However, statistics say that both sides are not satisfied with the results of their collaborations.

2. By their mindset and operating model, greenfield startups have many similarities to NEW. Hence, six of the 12 modules of the Lean Scaleup can be adapted.

3. Successful collaborations start with pinpointing a problem in NOW that the collaboration with greenfield startups should solve. Solving that problem requires to arrange a proper corporate context.

4. Scaling-Up in the context of greenfield startups could be a technical scaling or scaling the relationship. The latter provides a number of challenges.

**

The previous chapters focused on corporate startups and corporate scaleups, which are initiatives created within the company to create new growth via out-of-the-box innovations, especially new businesses. At least as important for creating new growth are initiatives in which the company collaborates with greenfield startups.

The mindset and operating model of greenfield startups is similar to that of NEW. Since the Lean Scaleup was designed to address the NOW/NEW problem, it also addresses essential aspects of working with greenfield startups[181]:

– Pre-Scaling validation.

– Transition to Scaling-Up.

---

[181] Addressed in chapters 6, 7, 8, 10, 14, and 15 respectively.

- Scaling-Up.

- Senior managers' skin in the game.

- Startup-like autonomy.

- Collaboration model.

One example for how well the Lean Scaleup supports corporate startups/scaleups and greenfield startups at the same time is bp Launchpad, the "Scaling-Up factory" of bp. It was designed in accordance with Lean Scaleup principles and hosted at the end of the initial build-up phase seven scaleups. Five of these were corporate ventures (greenfield startups with a minority investment from bp) and two were corporate scaleups.

This chapter focuses on the specific challenges of collaborating with greenfield startups. These challenges stem from the fundamentally different natures of the partners.

What This Book Does Not Cover

Co-innovating with greenfield startups is a discipline in itself. To limit the scope of this book, I have chosen to focus on the collaboration aspect, being aware that this implies leaving out key aspects such as:

- Selecting suitable greenfield startup ecosystems and working with them.

- Identifying suitable startups.

- Selecting the best startups.

- Investing into greenfield startups, including topics like startup valuation, due diligence, and so on.

- Legal aspects, especially Intellectual Property arrangements, around the issues mentioned above.

It Seems Like a Match Made in Heaven

A collaboration between a company and a suitable greenfield startup appears to be a mutually beneficial arrangement at first glance. The company benefits from gaining access to the startup's innovative ways of working and expertise with new technologies. In return, the greenfield startup gains:

- A potential customer.

- Access to the company's expertise in industrialization.

- Its proficiency with running operations at scale.

- Enhanced reputation.

- Tailwind for their go-to-market.

- An improved negotiation position in subsequent funding rounds.

On the surface, it appears that companies that succeed in transforming the theoretical win/win into a tangible reality could unlock significant synergies and take quantum leaps.

Neither Companies nor Greenfield Startups Are Satisfied

However, neither companies nor greenfield startups are satisfied with their respective relationships[182]. The exhibit below shows that companies are satisfied (measured by "at least 50 percent") with only one of their top seven goals and greenfield startups with only one of their top three priorities. These areas of tension are similar to the differences between NEW and NOW outlined in chapter 3.

---

[182] See https://on.bcg.com/3VMIlPM.

Neither companies nor greenfield startups are satisfied with what they get from their respective relationships.

Expected benefits	Importance	Satisfaction
Company view		
Piloting new technologies	43%	49%
New revenues / new businesses	39%	45%
Cultural shift	28%	47%
Access to talent via acquisition or hiring	27%	35%
Access to products / tech / IP / data	24%	52%
Employer branding	23%	44%
Tech and market scouting	23%	58%
Startup view		
Winning new customer	73%	44%
Getting access to customer's customers	60%	42%
Reputation gain	50%	59%

Exhibit 18–1: Satisfaction of companies and startups with their relationships.

Provide a Scalable Setup

In my experience, pinpointing the exact problem that should be solved through collaboration with greenfield startups is mission-critical. If the search field is too fuzzy, there is a significant risk that related activities will be no more than "greenfield startup innovation theater."

Love the Problem, Not the Solution

Core's units which are responsible for greenfield startup co-innovation must align with Core's functions to define the focal point for collaboration.

This helps to increase effectiveness in identifying greenfield startups and to measure the value of their solutions. It also ensures that stakeholders are engaged and invested in the process. Questions in this context include:

- Which is the most significant pain point today and in the future?

- Why is it important to solve that problem?

- Which solution could be envisioned?

- What are the key features that a solution needs to deliver?

- What are the key evaluation criteria to select a solution?

Typically, there are a number of problems that could justify working with greenfield startups. Prioritizing the problem landscape requires a wide lens that goes beyond immediate commercial benefits. Often-used factors to rank problem statements that should be solved via collaboration with greenfield startups include:

- Commercial benefit, both locally and for an envisioned roll-out.

- Complexity of integration.

- Fit with business, technology, and IT strategies.

- Competing in-house activities.

Elements of a Scalable Setup

To ensure the quality, speed, effectiveness, and efficiency of greenfield startup collaboration, it is essential to define a consistent and scalable setup. This setup should include at least six elements:

- Legal framework, for example a standardized NDA.

- A template for a collaboration charter that foresees specification of the area of collaboration, scope and non-scope, resources, responsibilities, timelines, and quantitative success criteria.

- A standard IT compliance, comprising for example light-weight tech due diligences and IT security checks.

– Guidance on how to assemble a core team, comprising typically representatives from Core's functions, IT, and cybersecurity.

– Guidance on how to set up an effective governance, including on how to select the senior sponsor and how to align on the two next steps. The senior sponsor should approve the above-mentioned collaboration charter and the success criteria.

– A package that describes how to handle corporate bureaucracy, including how to set up the greenfield startup in the vendor management and accounts payable system, the provisions about data transfer and so on. The designated contact persons in the relevant corporate functions and units should have a role as a functional tag, as described in chapter 14.

Collaboration Models

The collaboration between a company and greenfield startups can involve one or more of six collaboration models:
– Informal collaboration.

– Corporate incubation programs.

– Corporate accelerator programs.

– Corporate venture capital (CVC).

– A defined technical proof-of-concept.

– "Venture clienting" and scaling of greenfield startups.

The initial option does not require complex formal arrangements, but it is does not involve substantial collaboration. The second option is to learn more about an external startup, its technology, and its key people, and to explore the value of a more substantial collaboration. This may involve admitting the greenfield startup into corporate acceleration programs, which could result in a minority investment or even acquisition.

The last two options refer to testing the greenfield startup's solution in real life inside the company.

Venture Clienting

In the last ten years, venture clienting[183] has emerged as an innovative way for companies to collaborate with greenfield startups. In this approach, a company purchases a product developed by a greenfield startup.

The company accepts the corresponding risks and does not make an investment. The point about this approach is that it makes the company more attractive for greenfield startups because from their perspective, time and revenue are crucial for scalability. When a greenfield startup sells its solution to one company, which then rolls it out to dozens of manufacturing plants, and this reference helps to win new customers, they are on a good path. Additionally, they can test, refine, and implement its product in a real-world environment, gaining critical feedback and validation.

Venture clienting is initially deliberately not about corporate investments. This can complicate matters for both sides. From the company's perspective, negotiations with a portfolio of individual greenfield startups is challenging when they are in different stages of maturity. For the greenfield startup, having an additional party on its cap table increases the risk of added complexity in future funding rounds.

Aligning NOW and NEW in Venture Clienting/Partnering

A growing number of companies systematizes collaboration with greenfield startups, especially venture clienting, to ensure a steady inflow of greenfield startup solutions that support their innovation agenda. For these companies, it is essential that they extend their NOW/NEW alignment,

---

[183] See https://en.wikipedia.org/wiki/Venture_client.

the structural setup, and the governance model for innovation, as described in chapters 10 and 11. In particular, they need to:

- Align functional strategies and the innovation strategy to ensure a steady stream of pain points that should be addressed.

- Detail level-1 governance with respect to make/buy/partner decisions, as shown in exhibit 18–2.

- Augment their innovation structure with venture clienting teams.

When a company decides to ramp up greenfield startup collaboration via venture clienting, it should systematize the make/buy/build decision-making.

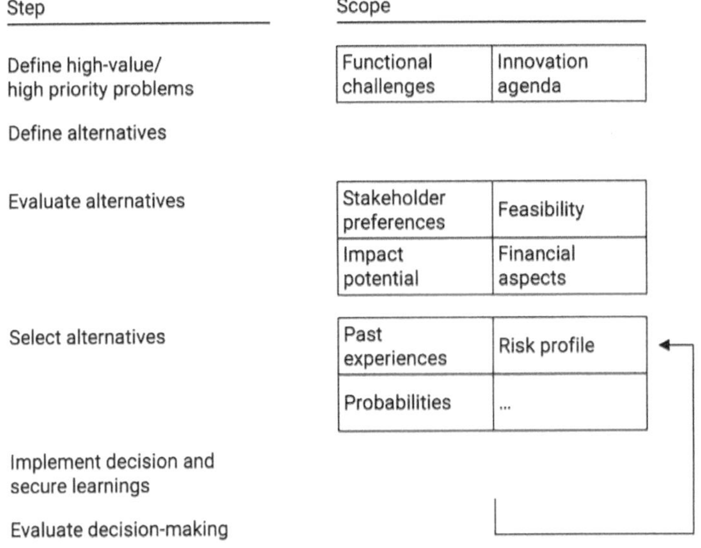

Exhibit 18–2: Make/buy/partner process.

In these companies it is good practice to establish regular update meetings between Core's functional stakeholders and the units that are responsible for greenfield startup innovation. Typically, the standard agenda of such meetings includes:

- Understand existing and emerging pain points that should be solved via collaboration with greenfield startups.

- Startup pipeline in the defined and emerging areas.

- Status of current venture clients.

Scaling Greenfield Startup Solutions / Greenfield Startups

When a collaboration with a greenfield startup has been set up properly and the initial collaboration was successful, the technical scaling of the solution is on a solid ground because it has:

- Demonstrated that the solution works.

- Delivered convincing quantitative results for a high-value/high-priority problem.

- Assessed the technical scalability of that solution.

- Provided a set of data points for the business case.

- Secured senior manager sponsorship.

Nevertheless, technical scaling will face some challenges. In designing the roll-out plan, it is good practice to think along the lines of technology adoption[184] and put internal pioneers at the top of the list.

Scaling a greenfield startup is an interesting option with a financial rationale since the company can benefit from increasing the value of its original investment. However, this is a different game, fundamentally different from running an isolated test[185].

---

[184] See chapters 8 and 19.
[185] Adapted from https://bit.ly/3PTAvA9.

Scaling up a greenfield startup by leveraging corporate assets and capabilities is a multi-year journey, adding additional layers of complexity.

Dimension	Venture Clienting	Venture Scaling
Strategic alignment	Low, pain point focus	High, vision and goals
Depth of engagement	Purchase and test	Deep, joint development
Product	Out-of-the-box	Joint solution
Risk profile	Diversified	Concentrated
Resource commitment	Minimal	Significant
Relationship dynamics	Transactional	Strategic partnership
Intellectual Property	Typically: startup	Typically: Jointly owned
Knowledge Transfer	Technology	Mutual learning
Cultural integration	Minimal	Significant
Exit strategy	Easy termination	Complex

Exhibit 18–3: Key differences between venture clienting and venture scaling.

Chapter 19: Avoiding Pitfalls

Chapter 19
Avoiding Pitfalls

Key Points in This Chapter

1. Successful out-of-the-box innovations are built on a robust foundation of validated assumptions. A comprehensive understanding of customers is vital. However, few companies invest in the excellence of their innovation interviews.

2. Problem/solution-fit is not just about the fit. It involves working on the right problem and ensuring this is a "good problem."

3. A Minimum Viable Product (MVP) is a tool for learning what product the corporate startup should build. Any work beyond what the team needs to learn is waste. The individual MVP versions are used only in fully controlled environments. Every MVP version must be technically reliable, should be designed to test functionality and usability and have one "delight feature."

4. A corporate startup has achieved product/pioneer-fit with the first customer, but not product/market-fit. It is now relevant for 2.5 percent of the market. Good product/market-fit can be shown via traction metrics and relevance for mainstream customers.

5. Core's sales functions are not prepared for selling out-of-the-box innovations since the sales engine is not designed for that. When the corporate scaleup wants to collaborate, they need to determine where it makes sense to collaborate and then define how to collaborate.

**

Chapters 6-8 provide an in-depth explanation of the Lean Scaleup methodology, outlining the end-to-end process that covers Pre-Scaling, the transitional phase between validation and scaling and the Scaling-Up phase.

This chapter complements these chapters by highlighting nine common mistakes and shortcomings. The purpose of this chapter is to help corporate startups/scaleups to become even smarter by avoiding key pitfalls and running ahead where others stumble.

Innovation Interviews

A prerequisite for building a new business is a deep understanding of the customer. This understanding requires conducting meaningful innovation interviews with carefully selected interview partners since responses from a Generative AI solution or surveys alone are not sufficient for a strong foundation. In my experience, in the Discovery and Business Foundation stages, the number of interviews should be planned as follows:

- At least eight interviews are needed, if the corporate startup uses the brand of a large company.

- If the corporate startup is not using the corporate brand, more than 30 interviews should be scheduled.

- If the company is mid-sized, at least 20 interviews should be planned.

Upgrading Interview Skills

Most companies do not invest sufficiently in the quality of their innovation interviews. They leave it to untrained corporate explorers and members of corporate startup teams to select the interviewees and to conduct and evaluate the interviews. This presents a significant risk to the reliability of the foundation for a new business, ultimately jeopardizing the success of the ambition.

Effective innovation interviews are more than question-and-answer sessions with predetermined queries. They are conversations aimed at uncovering valuable insights:

- In the Discovery and Business Foundation stages, these insights relate to the problem space surrounding an envisioned solution.

- In the Business Strategy stage, interviewers aim to elicit the value points of the Minimum Viable Product and the sources of a sustainable competitive advantage.

- In the Business Design stage, the insights relate to the quality of the product/market-fit (see below).

Interview Scripts Must Be Customer-Centric

Effective innovation interviews are based on clearly defined learning objectives. These objectives include the insights to be gained and the assumptions to be tested. Interviewers should always seek a second opinion on the interview script. This helps to prevent the interviewer from confirmation bias and ensures that the interviewer speaks the language of the interviewee.

The latter point ensures that the interview maintains a customer-centric perspective. Corporate startups often use jargon that outsiders may not understand. Interviewers should therefore not assume that interviewees know this language. Otherwise, there is a risk of confusion and misunderstanding.

Ask Effective Questions

Open-ended questions encourage detailed responses and prevent simple yes-or-no answers. For instance, instead of asking: "Would you recommend our product?", the interviewer should ask: "What are the main reasons you chose our product?" to gain more insights.

Interviewers should also avoid leading questions that suggest a particular answer and refrain from nudging potential customers to make "future promises[186]". Instead of asking: "How much would you pay for this product when it is ready?", the interviewer should ask: "How much do you think it costs your company to solve this problem today?" or use the van-Westendorp-method[187] to elicit an acceptable price range.

Great Questions in the Scaling-Up Stage

Below is a list of questions that have proven their worth in innovation interviews after the launch of the Minimum Marketable Product:

– Can you walk me through the process of how you use our product?

– What is the biggest problem that our product has helped you solve?

– How do you measure the value of our product?

– How does our product fit into your bigger picture?

– What alternatives have you used or considered?

– Which features make you keep using our product?

– Which product feature would you sorely miss if it were not available anymore? Why?

– Can you recall a specific moment when our product provided significant value to you?

– Are there specific tasks that you would like our product to assist with?

– What concerns do you have about our product?

– Have you recommended our product to others? If not, why?

---

[186] Rob Fitzpatrick, The Mom Test, Independently published, ISBN 1492180742.
[187] See https://bit.ly/46kq6nc

For Solution-Discovery, Have an Artifact with You

Using a rapid and cheap solution artifact during innovation interviews improves the quality and quantity of insights generated by enhancing the conversation and prevents misunderstandings.

During the Discovery and Business Foundation stages, the artifact should not be a polished piece of art (e.g., a professionally designed website), as this would create a psychological barrier for the interview partners. They may be hesitant to criticize something that appears to have required significant effort. Instead, the artifact should be rough and unfinished, a so-called pretotype (see chapter 6).

How to Challenge the Interviewers

Challenging the interviewers is a good practice since many activities depend on getting the interviews right and drawing the right conclusions. Here are four questions that can be used to challenge interviewers during debriefing sessions:

- What assumptions were tested and how were they incorporated into the interview script? Which control questions were used?

- What did we learn about the assumptions? What other insights were gained? What are the customer's pressing issues, if any?

- What have we discovered about customer stakeholders who influence decision-making?

- What is the evidence that the issues that the interviewee raised are not just specific but a more general issue for the target market?

Problem/Solution-Fit

Problem/solution-fit is one of the deliverables of the Business Foundation stage. When there is also a solution/company-fit, the problem is

worth solving, and the solution allows for building a sustainable superior value proposition around it, the seed of a sizable new business may have been planted.

What Problem/Solution-Fit Is (Not)

"Reasons to believe" that are not validated via direct customer contact do not constitute problem/solution-fit. I have witnessed numerous situations where an idea that looked promising on paper was called problem/solution-fit. Frequently, these ideas came from statistics, a hunch, or from ideation sessions. At times, even technical prototypes or lab samples were called problem/solution-fit because they "provide customer benefits."

Far too many corporate explorers and corporate startups fail to understand **two fundamental points: first, value is defined by the customer, not the corporate startup; second, an innovation only succeeds if it is adopted.**

There may be a dozen great reasons why the customer should care about what the corporate startup is creating. But it is the customer who defines the priority of the problem, quantifies the value of the product, and decides whether it is a wise decision to switch from existing practice to the innovation, including the risks and costs associated with the transition.

Nevertheless, "reasons to believe" can serve as useful starting points. Field research helps to understand what the real problem is and what needs to be done to achieve problem/solution-fit.

Are You Working on the Right Problem?

How should the gas station of the future be designed, knowing that petrol- and diesel-powered cars will remain the dominant vehicle type for the near future, even as electric vehicles become more prevalent? I have asked this question to hundreds of senior managers. Usually, they recommend adding a coffee shop, making the station an Amazon drop-off point, or having robots pump the gas.

The key point for innovation is to address a real-life, high-priority/high-value customer problem. Are the ideas above addressing one of the most pressing problems that customers want to be solved? I am not sure. Most people consider refueling their vehicles an unavoidable inconvenience. If people need to refill their vehicles but dislike the process, how do you solve the problem? Not by putting coffee shops in gas stations. But what if we could bring petrol to the cars?

The responses above also highlight another issue. **Although many companies claim to be customer-centric, they tend to be product-centric.** They think in terms of existing offerings (by adding services to gas stations) rather than empathizing with their customers and addressing their needs (by helping them avoid the gas station altogether). Building a new business is not about creating products that the innovator thinks are important to customers. It is about creating products that really matter to customers.

Let me make the point clear by comparing two banks in the mortgage business. Bank A believes that home buyers will appreciate a mobile app that simplifies the application process, speeds up processing via AI-based algorithms, and offers live chat support.

Bank B's approach goes beyond the mortgage product. The bank's corporate explorers investigated what could help customers find their dream home. They developed a mobile app that allows customers to search neighborhoods and view recent transaction prices. When customers see a home on the market, a mortgage calculator helps to determine if they can afford it, and then the app guides them through the mortgage process.

A product-centric approach, like the one from bank A, carries the risk that the corporate startup is working on the wrong problem. A customer-centric approach is essential to avoid this risk. It is not the customer's responsibility to identify their problems and needs. Customers often have difficulty articulating the problem they are trying to solve or identifying its root causes. Therefore, the hard thinking work must be done by the innovators—as I like to say: "Innovators innovate, customers validate."

Love the Problem, Not the Solution

It is of the utmost importance for corporate explorers to prioritize identifying the right problem before anything else. By gaining a deep understanding of the problem and all of its related aspects, such as customers' barriers to switching and a value proposition that is superior to all other approaches to solve the customers' problem, they can create a meaningful solution and a solid business foundation.

Jumping to solutions without fully understanding the problem is a common mistake. **It is easy to jump to solutions when the facts are weak and there are only opinions.** Hard facts come from observation and well-crafted interviews. They do not come from surveys because survey respondents:

- May understand the question differently than intended.

- Struggle to express their imagination in the answers provided.

- Imagine a completely different solution.

- Have no skin in the game when they submit a survey response.

There is a tell-tale symptom that innovators are more attached to their solution than the problem: they state the problem in a way that suggests that there is only one meaningful solution—which happens to be the solution they already have in mind. When I encounter such a situation, I challenge the team to rethink their problem statement. Instead of jumping to a solution, the team should review how they got to this point[188] to broaden the perspective.

Jumping to solutions too quickly may be an individual mistake but it may also be rooted in the company's culture:
- Presentations that appear to offer brilliant solutions are valued more than results that emerge from untangling problems and evidence-based research.

---

[188] Using https://bit.ly/3Vjb0eJ and https://bit.ly/3wU60nB.

– Demonstrating progress is important. However, falsely checking the problem/solution-fit box is not progress; it is a step in the wrong direction.

Ideal Problems

Identifying a "high-value/high-priority problem to be solved" is one of the foundations of a potentially sizable and profitable new business. However, as explained in chapter 6, substantial validation is necessary to provide the necessary proof points. A quick litmus test shows corporate startups working in the Discovery or Business Foundation stages if an individual problem justifies this validation work:

– Size. Many customers have this problem or, alternatively, few customers have a high-value problem.

– First to remove market orthodoxies. When the corporate startup is the first to solve commonly accepted trade-offs[189], it can create a new market and be the initial market leader.

– Growth. A growing number of customers will have the problem in the future.

– Frequent. A large customer group stumbles upon this problem often.

– Urgent. A problem that needs to be solved as soon as possible.

– Cost-efficient. Good problems have an interesting payback period for the customers.

– High willingness-to-pay. Innovation interviews show that customers are willing to pay for getting the problem solved.

– Mandatory. A problem that is enforced, for example, by regulation or by technological shifts.

---

[189] See the examples of Nespresso and Hilti Fleet Management in chapter 2.

When Have You Achieved Problem/Solution-Fit?

Even when a corporate startup has validated a problem as worth to be solved and field research has confirmed that potential customers view an envisioned solution as convincing, it can be challenging to determine if problem/solution-fit has been achieved. This might happen when, for instance, there are too many unknowns in the context of the problem.

In these situations, I recommend using the skin-in-the-game test. The test is to determine whether potential customers are willing to make a commitment at this early stage of the innovation journey. For example, a commitment to co-create the Minimum Viable Product (MVP) by investing time and resources would be a meaningful commitment.

If none of the potential customers interviewed are willing to put their skins in the game, the level of market interest may not be significant enough to proceed with confidence. These individuals cannot be considered as potential future customers. They are merely spectators since they do not commit and have nothing to lose. They may even enjoy watching the corporate startup and the idea fail.

Getting the Technical Pilot Right

Provided the use case makes sense, corporate startups should use their corporate context to test a pre-version of the Minimum Marketable Product (MMP) in a real-life situation within the company. This test is commonly referred to as a technical pilot.

However, many companies do not pilot the technology developed by their own corporate startups. There may be technical reasons, for example, if the technical performance is not convincing. However, I also observed instances where the technical performance showed promise, yet the company did not test—let alone adopt—the technology. The Lean Scaleup's co-creators identified six elements that enhance the likelihood of adoption.

First, senior management's skin in the game. A carefully chosen technical pilot project can create significant commercial benefits for Core and also increased confidence that the corporate startup deserves further company support. For these reasons, at least one senior management sponsor should put skin in the game.

Second, align with KPI improvements. To gain this senior management sponsorship, the goals of the technical pilot must be expressed in terms of the KPIs that matter to the operational business of that sponsor.

Third, avoid the pilot trap. A common corporate attitude is to wait and see, and therefore the scope of a technical pilot tends not to go beyond the technical pilot itself. To avoid this trap, the corporate startup and its sponsor should agree before the start of the technical pilot on the next two steps if the test is successful.

Fourth, avoid creating an "us and them" dynamic. Technical pilots often require collaboration between Core's experienced process engineers and "digital natives." The pilot should be designed so that both sides benefit: process engineers can enhance their industrial processes using an innovative approach, while the corporate startup gains a robust reference.

Fifth, de-risk it. The technical pilot must not produce harm. Operational data must be protected, and there should be minimal interference with ongoing systems and processes. Technical pilots must be quick and easy to shut down, and they must not create new vulnerabilities.

Sixth, less is more. When discussing the scope and details of a technical pilot, corporate startups often try to pack several tests into one. I strongly urge the team to focus on the single most important insight to be gained. This approach helps to align with busy engineers and senior management sponsors, reduces setup time, and typically increases the quality of learning from the technical pilot.

Minimum Viable Product

The term "Minimum Viable Product" was coined by Frank Robinson in 2001 and became mainstream with the Lean Startup movement in the 2010s[190]. In my opinion, a better term would have been Minimum Valuable Product: a precursor to the first product that hits the market, with a minimum set of features that provides value to the customer. But since so many practitioners use this term, the Lean Scaleup uses it as well.

A Learning Tool

An MVP is a tool for learning step-by-step what product the corporate startup should build. Any work beyond what the team needs to learn is waste, regardless of its perceived importance at the time. The individual MVP versions are used in fully controlled environments, such as demos or pre-arranged co-creation sessions. They are not intended for use by customers in their own environments, which is one of the key differences between an MVP and an MMP.

The MVP versions are optimized for learning, not for generating revenues. The concept of "building for learning" can be challenging:

- Engineers are not used to build something that will be discarded once the team has learned what it needs to learn.

- Senior managers may also find it difficult to understand the team's desire to start from scratch and "do it right now."

- Some team members may struggle to accept that customers who co-create the MVP define Viable while the team's responsibility is to define Minimum.

---

[190] Eric Ries, The Lean Startup, Redline, 2014

However, MVP versions cannot be something ugly, glued and soldered together with some functionality. In today's market, customers have numerous options, and when they encounter a half-baked product, they do not become co-creators of the prototype; instead, they walk away.

I typically use a three-step ladder to organize the discussion about what should go into the next MVP version:

- Functionality (core and housekeeping).

- Usability.

- Delight.

We then cut across these three levels and identify the elements that should be included in the next iteration, based on the assumptions that should be tested. On the functional level, it is beneficial to distinguish between core and housekeeping functionality. The former relates to a few features or benefits that should be validated. The latter comprises a basic set of features that customers would expect from any comparable product.

The Traps in Over-Engineering the MVP

Corporate startups sometimes prioritize engineering work over co-creating MVP versions with potential customers. But there are two psychological traps in over-engineering MVP versions:

- The more time a corporate startup invests in something, the more valuable it becomes to the team—though not necessarily to the customer.

- Customers may be reluctant to give honest feedback to avoid hurting the feelings of those who worked hard on a product that "looks quite good."

These psychological traps can lead to poor decision-making. Spending too much time on engineering reduces the time for learning. Therefore, MVP versions should be timeboxed. When there are strict time constraints, the corporate startup needs to focus relentlessly on what matters most.

Minimum Marketable Product and Product/Pioneer-Fit

Once the corporate startup has understood what product it should build, it should work with customers to co-create the initial version of the product that will be launched in the market. **This different environment is one of the key differences between an MVP and an MMP.**

Across industries, these co-creating customers share common characteristics. They are visionary and open to innovation, and they are often:

– Actively looking for next-generation technology.

– Open to discuss ahead-of-the-curve concepts, even though these may not be perfect yet.

– Prepared to realize the technology vision together with a (corporate or greenfield) startup.

– Innovation or technology leaders in their industry (although they may not be the biggest company).

– Pursuing a first-to-market strategy.

Studies that have examined how successful technologies have been adapted by their respective markets[191] refer to these customers as so-called pioneers or innovators. They represent the first market segment to purchase new technologies, followed by so-called early adopters who get on board once they see the new technology working in real life.

These studies show that these two market segments buy new technology differently than mainstream customers. The latter expect a complete solution that includes the product, integration with their existing infrastructure, and meaningful services that ensure they capture the value proposed by the corporate startup.

---

[191] Geoffrey Moore, Crossing the Chasm, Collins, 2014.

Here is one of my personal experiences. A corporate scaleup was tasked with building a business by marketing an innovative software to a specific industry. After signing its first customers, the corporate scaleup's leadership team assumed it had achieved product/market-fit and hired a sales team, anticipating a surge in customers and revenue. However, they failed to make significant progress.

I recommended to reassess the market segments. Among other things, we analyzed attendee lists from recent events. We found that the initial customers of the corporate startup were primarily attending technology-focused events. We also identified mainstream customers from general industry conferences and scheduled innovation interviews with them.

These interviews revealed that mainstream customers prioritized practical support over technological sophistication. They wanted clear decision support, practical help in identifying relevant sensor data, guidance on organizing trials, support in adopting and rolling out the technology, and help in integrating the technology into their existing IT landscape.

Product/Pioneer-Fit, Not Product/Market-Fit

The key takeaway from the story above is that, once the first customers have been signed, the corporate startup has not yet achieved product/market-fit. Instead, it has only achieved product/pioneer-fit. This means that it is relevant to 2.5 percent of the market.[192]

Securing a first customer is a significant achievement for a corporate startup, as it provides a reference and a foundation for future growth. However, **the needs of pioneer customers are not representative for the entire market. Their needs may be years ahead of the needs of mainstream customers or they may even be so sophisticated that they never become an issue for this market segment.**

---

[192] Geoffrey Moore, Crossing the Chasm, Collins, 2014.

Scaling-Up after acquiring the first customer is often premature and is one of the most common mistakes made by corporate startups. Therefore, the Lean Scaleup methodology strongly recommends that corporate startups explore how to acquire mainstream customers during the Business Design stage. To achieve this, they need to:

- Validate the value proposition for this market segment.

- Understand the product features and the service elements they request.

- Collect proof points that this market segment can be won within a reasonable time and with adequate customer acquisition costs.

Product/Market-Fit

According to Silicon Valley venture capitalist Marc Andreessen, a successful startup's life can be divided into two phases: pre-product/market-fit and post-product/market-fit. All steps before are prologue, providing increasing reassurance that further funding is justified. All steps beyond this point are about capturing as much of the discovered value as possible. In other words, product/market-fit is essential for the Scaling-Up decision.

A Quality Indicator, Not a One-Time Event

The Lean Scaleup has a different view. For corporate startups, product/market-fit is not a one-time event that is achieved on a particular day. Instead, it has a quality, ranging from very poor to excellent. The quality of the product/market-fit is influenced by two forces: the restraining force and the driving force, as explained in chapter 6.

Corporate startups tend to overestimate the quality of their product/market-fit. I use three litmus tests to start discussions in this context:

- What makes us sure that we are beyond product/pioneer-fit?

- In terms of the product aspect of product/market-fit: what makes us sure that we understand the extended competition, i.e., all the companies that offer solutions to customers' problems?

- As for the market aspect: what makes us sure that we have understood the market well enough? Are we talking about a market or a broader competitive arena in which we are only working in a small segment?

Traction Metrics

The quality of the product/market-fit can be indirectly measured by examining leading indicators for future revenues, so-called traction metrics. Examples of traction metrics include:

- Success rate in customer acquisition (continuously improving).

- Costs of acquiring a new customer (decreasing).

- Speed of customer's purchase decision (increasing).

- Customers' views on the superiority of value proposition (increasing).

- Churn rate, measuring customer loyalty (decreasing).

- Proportion of new customers who use the product (increasing).

- Net Promoter Score, i.e., the proportion of customers who recommend the product to others (growing).

- Sean Ellis test[193] (increasing).

Traction metrics are crucial in convincing a corporate investor that the corporate startup is scale-ready. Starting Scaling-Up without significant traction, and therefore with a low product/market-fit, is likely to result in failure due to premature scaling.

---

[193] When trial users are asked: "How would you feel if you could no longer use the product?" an increasing number of respondents answer "very disappointed".

But what if there is not enough proof for traction? When the leader of a corporate startup asked me: "What if we do not find trial users?" I replied, "Then you probably have not even achieved problem/solution-fit."

Working with Core's Sales Functions

On the surface, it appears that expanding a corporate scaleup's market presence and accelerating time-to-revenue by using Core's sales functions is a straightforward move. However, in practice, it is a challenging task. This section will explain why and provide guidance on identifying the right areas for collaboration and for designing a meaningful partnership.

The Salesperson's Persona

Corporate salespersons are typically rational individuals with a clear understanding of what is required to achieve their quarterly and annual targets. They possess in-depth knowledge of the company's products and the customers' buying centers with whom they negotiate.

Experienced sales professionals excel at managing the sales process, handling objections, and negotiating commercial agreements. They are well-versed in the back-office processes required to prepare a commercial proposal, log an order, and plan sales activities to achieve next quarter's goals.

For a corporate salesperson, being effective and efficient is paramount in meeting their sales goals. They avoid risks and ambiguities in their sales activities as these can lead to prioritization problems, delays, and missed opportunities. Corporate salespeople frequently define themselves as trusted advisors to their customers, effectively "owning" the relationship with their clients.

The Missing Innovation/Salesperson-Fit

But here is the problem: a new business model and its products are not "sellable" for those corporate salespersons and the well-oiled, fine-tuned sales engine. For instance:

- The new business model and the products are hard to understand for the salesperson.

- The product is hard to explain to potential customers.

- The necessary sales activities are not streamlined.

- The buying center is different.

- The buying center asks new questions and puts up new objections.

- It may not be clear how to price the innovation.

- It can be unclear how to calculate a legally binding commercial proposal.

Rational corporate salespersons will inevitably view these inefficiencies and frictions as a risk to achieving personal sales goals. They may also perceive the risk of losing their status as an expert and trusted advisor to their clients. Therefore, when they are given the choice to sell established products or the innovation, they will prefer the former.

Consequently, more thoughts are needed regarding how a corporate scaleup should collaborate with Core's sales functions. I usually address this challenge in two steps: first, identifying where collaboration is needed, and then deciding how to collaborate.

Define Where It Makes Sense to Collaborate

To illustrate the first step, here is an example from my advisory work. A global industry leader launched a corporate startup to create and scale a platform business model innovation. The platform should provide the entire ecosystem with the opportunity to digitize their commercial activities, such as planning, tendering, contracting, and conducting transactions.

In discussing the "Strategy, market, and revenues" track of Scaling-Up, as described in chapter 8, we created the bowling alley. Each bowling pin was defined by a unique combination of a customer group, geographic region, and platform capabilities at different points in time. We then analyzed each pin based on its proximity to existing business and the digital maturity of Core's sales functions.

As a result, we discovered pins close to the existing business with strong sales organizations and opportunities to cross-sell. Therefore, we decided that the corporate scaleup should aim for collaboration with the relevant sales functions in these cases. However, we also found pins targeting new customer groups and geographic regions where the sales organizations were not so strong. We concluded that in these situations, the corporate scaleup should build its own sales functions.

Define How to Collaborate

Once suitable areas for collaboration have been defined, there are two generic options. The first option is a joint go-to-market initiative, in which the corporate scaleup's sales team works closely with Core's sales functions. The second option arranges incentives for the salespersons to sell the business model innovation.

In the first option, alignment on common goals, activities, and boundary conditions between the head of the relevant sales functions and the corporate scaleup is mandatory. For instance, one of my corporate scaleup clients aligned on four boundary conditions:

- Core's existing sales process should be changed as little as possible to maintain the salesforce's productivity in selling established products.

- For defined customer segments and defined salespersons, there should be a direct and intense collaboration.

- The existing customer relationship management system (CRM) should be used.

- Core's salespersons generate prospects, but it is up to the corporate scaleup to close deals.

Using the same CRM system was a wise decision. On the one hand, Core's salespeople could easily enter sales leads into a system they were already using. On the other hand, the corporate scaleup could benefit not only from those sales leads, but also from a wealth of corporate data, such as information from contact forms on the corporate web site.

The sales team of the corporate scaleup then identified "champions" within Core's sales unit, with whom they worked directly. The motivation of the champions was twofold: they were interested in the corporate scaleup's mission, and they wanted to offer something truly new to their customers.

The champions were evaluated based on the number of customers they engaged, not on revenues, because it was initially unclear how much revenue a new customer would generate and how quickly those customers could be moved to larger contracts.

One incentive for these champions was increased visibility within the sales organization. The head of the sales unit created a new award for the annual sales meeting called "Selling Innovation." Being on stage next to the corporate sales stars proved to be a significant motivator for the champions.

For some companies, arranging a joint initiative between the scaleup's sales team and Core's sales functions as described above can be challenging. In these cases, arranging incentives for selling the business model innovation might be an option. To make this approach effective, the right basis for incentivization needs to be picked. Basing incentives on revenues is unlikely to work, as explained above. It is more effective to base incentives on other dimensions such as the number of presentations, the number of doors opened, or the number of new customers.

International Expansion

Geographical expansion is a crucial aspect of almost every Scaling-Up plan. However, many corporate scaleups struggle because they undervalue thorough validation of their bowling alley. Corporate scaleups should be deliberate about the scope, timing, and speed of international expansion.

Five Challenges

Below are five challenges that I frequently encounter when working with corporate scaleup clients.

First, international expansion is inherently complicated. Many mundane issues such as employment contracts, compensation packages, legal frameworks, and taxation will be different. To succeed, a corporate scaleup must be committed to following through and avoiding getting bogged down by those mandatory, but not mission-critical issues.

International expansion also brings in an additional layer of organizational complexity, including time zone differences, cultural challenges, and the need to rethink the structure without killing the startup spirit[194].

Second, expanding internationally requires resources. Localizing products, understanding the needs of international customers, and investing in culturally appropriate marketing activities cannot be accomplished quickly. There are no shortcuts, especially when the corporate scaleup is competing against local companies that have a deep customer understanding and whose survival depends on success in their home market.

Third, each investment in international businesses will be compared to the already successful domestic business. It may seem ironic, but the corporate scaleup may find itself in the same situation as Core when it decided to create a new business.

Fourth, key assumptions already validated for the original market must be re-validated. One common error in scaling via geographical expansion is to pursue unvalidated expansion routes. The unvalidated set of assumptions

---

[194] See chapter 8.

often includes the maturity of the new region, the willingness of customers to pay, the Serviceable Obtainable Market, and the availability of ecosystem partners to create and deliver the value proposition.

This often results in overestimated potential and underestimated difficulties. From a cost perspective, the corporate scaleup should not underestimate expenses associated with international expansion. One element is product localization, which may involve adapting the product to function in right-to-left languages or incorporating different colors[195].

Fifth, internal challenges. If the corporate scaleup aims to expand into regions where Core has a strong presence, it may encounter internal challenges. Core's regional managers may consider their local business to be unique and may see innovations coming from other parts of the company as problematic.

Furthermore, since Core's regional organizations are often managed on tight budgets and with headcount constraints, the corporate scaleup may not receive the necessary management attention for its ambitions.

When Is the Right Time for Geographical Expansion?

There are two strong indicators that a corporate scaleup should consider geographic expansion: traction signals and market signals. Traction signals relate to various levels of purchasing intent. There are lighter signals such as an increase in the number of visitors to the corporate scaleup's website from that region. On the other end, there are stronger signals such as an increase in the number of self-service online purchases.

However, these traction signals should be taken with a grain of salt for two reasons. First, these signals relate to the pioneer segment of this market and constitute rather a product/pioneer-fit rather than a product/market-fit, as described above. Second, these signals may not always be

---

[195] In Chinese stock markets, red signifies an increase while green signifies a decrease.

coming from the target segment of the corporate scaleup and lure it away from a validated growth path.

On the other hand, market signals relate to competitive activities that demonstrate the commercial potential of the corporate scaleup's product. These signals include activities from competitors with a comparable product in the intended geography or increasing online search related to the problem that the corporate scaleup addresses and the solution it provides. When these signals intensify, it may be the right time to enter that market.

Alignment with the Governance Board Is Mandatory

Since international expansion provides the opportunity for accelerating growth but also significant challenges, the corporate scaleup's CEO must align with the governance board on the game plan:

- When/Where. The timeline and set of milestones for international expansion. It should be clear to everyone why certain regions are prioritized above others.

- How. A playbook outlining how the company will reach its milestones in the new region. This playbook should start with small tests to confirm the expansion hypotheses and include a set of predictable and repeatable levers it can use to drive sustainable growth in a new region.

- What. A set of clear milestones and success criteria can help the governance board determine if the corporate scaleup is on track with its expansion. Each milestone should be tied to specific success criteria so that the governance board can clearly evaluate a particular milestone has been achieved and the corporate scaleup can safely move on to the next.

Chapter 20:
Upgrading
Out-of-the-Box Innovation

Chapter 20
Upgrading New-Business Building

Key Points in This Chapter

1. Upgrading a company's setup for out-of-the-box innovation and new-business building can be done at three levels: cherry-picking, using corporate startups/scaleups as change catalysts, and upgrading the system.

2. Due to the NOW/NEW system problem, the first two options will have only limited impact.

3. In challenging business environments, senior managers will inevitably prefer NOW over NEW. There are three strategies to protect the new-business building ambition: (1) the mandate for explorative units should be "beyond Core;" (2) multi-year initiatives must be roadmapped to make them digestible for Core; (3) explorative units must establish a strategy dialogue with the operative units.

**

In my advisory work, I have observed that companies utilize the Lean Scaleup framework to enhance their new-business building efforts at three distinct levels.

Applying the Lean Scaleup: Three Levels

Level 1: cherry-picking. Some of my clients decided to adopt a few select elements while leaving the rest of their approach untouched. For instance, one company incorporated select scale-worthy validations into their framework, while another company enhanced its approach by validating scale-readiness elements and a third company incorporated the Transition-to-Scaling-Up module. These activities are implemented quickly, but since they do not address the fundamental NOW/NEW system problem, the impact of these improvements will be limited.

Level 2: using corporate startups/scaleups as change catalysts. At this level, a company assigns a dual mission to a corporate startup/scaleup. The first mission is to create or scale an emerging business opportunity. The second is to identify areas for improvement, which will then be addressed with the support of senior management. Typically, these areas for improvement show up in eight of the twelve Lean Scaleup's modules[196]:

- Pre-Scaling.

- Transition to Scaling-Up.

- Scaling-Up.

- Senior managers' skin in the game.

- Startup-like autonomy.

- Collaboration model.

- Capabilities, people profiles, A-teams.

- Growth culture.

This level addresses the NOW/NEW system problem at some distinct points and should be moving the needle a little bit.

Level 3: upgrading the system. A smart way to improve the performance of the out-of-the-box innovation engine is to apply the theory of constraints[197]: the company identifies which of the Lean Scaleup's 12 modules creates the biggest bottleneck and resolves it before turning to the next important constraint. Such an approach solves the NOW/NEW system problem. It moves the needle—but it is a multi-year journey.

---

[196] See chapters 6, 7, 8, 10, 14, 15, 16 and 17.

[197] The theory of constraints is a methodology for identifying the most limiting factor (i.e., the constraint) that stands in the way of increasing the throughput of a system. Systematically improving that constraint will lead to an increase in the system's performance.

Two Fundamental Considerations about Level 3 Ambitions

To achieve success at level 3, senior managers must consider two key factors. First, outsourcing is not a feasible solution at this level because it fails to address crucial issues. For instance, relying on external corporate venture builders is inadequate for effectively leveraging the base of corporate assets and capabilities[198] It is also inadequate for re-integrating a scaled-up business and for designing the NOW/NEW interplay.

Second, **new-business building is a legacy, not an initiative.** In many companies, senior management support for out-of-the-box innovation revolves around a single individual, typically the CEO or the CTO. However, when that person leaves the company, the momentum can falter, and the pendulum swings back to a narrow focus on NOW.

Change Management at Level 3

To successfully manage the change that comes with prioritizing NEW and upgrading out-of-the-box innovation, seven essential elements must be in place[199].

If any one of these elements is missing, the change effort will fail, with varying degrees of negative consequences:

- As described in chapters 10 and 13, senior management's ambition, determination and resilience is a vital component.

---

[198] As an example, 3M Company lists 54 technology platforms, that are the basis for out-of-the-box innovations, see https://bit.ly/4ab0GdH.

[199] Adapted from https://bit.ly/3PIjgBJ.

Change management in upgrading corporate new-business building requires seven components.

Top Management ambition, determination, resilience	Vision	Consensus	Skills	Incentives	Resources	Action Plan	= Success
		Consensus	+ Skills	+ Incentives	+ Resources	+ Action Plan	= Confusion
	Vision +		Skills	+ Incentives	+ Resources	+ Action Plan	= Sabotage
	Vision +	Consensus +		Incentives	+ Resources	+ Action Plan	= Anxiety
	Vision +	Consensus +	Skills +		Resources	+ Action Plan	= Resistance
	Vision +	Consensus +	Skills +	Incentives +		Action Plan	= Frustration
	Vision +	Consensus +	Skills +	Incentives +	Resources		= False Starts

Exhibit 20–1: Key elements in upgrading new-business building.

– Building new-businesses that might even change the corporate identity requires a "reason why" and a vision about the future state. Without a clear vision, there may be confusion.

– Senior management cannot assume that they can push through a change that touches the soul of the company without consensus. Buy-in from upper and middle managers is critical. Without consensus, some managers may be deliberately or unintentionally sabotaging the efforts.

– Skills empower people. In the new-business building context, four learnable skills are decisive, as explained in chapter 5. If middle managers or staff feel they lack skills or necessary training, they may experience change anxiety.

– Employees typically also need incentives to embrace new-business building. Incentives can be monetary or "soft" such as internal visibility or the opportunity to work on the "next big thing."

– Resources are another key success factor. When middle managers or Core's functional experts say things like, "They want us to do more with less" or "Senior management does not support me," it shows that they lack physical or emotional resources, which may lead to frustration.

– The final element is an action plan. Without a plan, progress monitoring is not possible, and people may get the feeling that they are not progressing at all. By the nature of the topic, the action plan must be agile. The planning approach shown in chapter 8 is a good solution to provide direction and agility at the same time.

Protecting the New-Business Building Ambition

In-between mid-2023 and mid-2024, when this book was written, a number of companies closed their explorative units, for example:

– General Motors closed its Arizona-based IT innovation center.

– Walmart shut down its business innovation unit, Store No. 8.

– Unilever closed its direct-to-consumer incubator, The Uncovery.

– Alphabet closed Google's innovation lab, called X, as it adopted a new structure.

– Migros, the USD 35bn Swiss retail giant, shut down its future lab, Sparrow Ventures.

– SAP closed its startup accelerator SAP.io Foundries and dissolved its business model innovation unit.

Although the reasons for closing these units may vary, they provide insight on how to protect NEW. In my view, the examples mentioned above provide three learnings for senior managers who want to generate new growth by striving for excellence in out-of-the-box innovation:

- **The mandate for explorative units should be "beyond Core,"** rather than Playing Field 3. This allows strategic flexibility for NEW units. Their scope could swing closer to NOW or farther away, depending on company-specific preferences and external factors.

- **Multi-year initiatives must be roadmapped** to make them digestible for Core, as explained in chapter 10, and to ensure a consistent flow of short-term successes.

- **NEW must establish a strategy dialogue** (as described in chapter 13) with the operative units to continuously demonstrate its value for these units and to have their skin in the game. However, the explorative unit should not just become an extended innovation workbench for the operative units. To avoid this situation, the funding apparatus must ensure two things: (1) cross-business-unit and corporate initiatives must receive the necessary funding; (2) an "innovation adoption fund" should incentivize operative units to integrate scaled-up businesses.

Index